PERSPECTIVES IN SCOTTISH SOCIAL HISTORY

essays in honour of
ROSALIND MITCHISON

edited by Leah Leneman

ABERDEEN UNIVERSITY PRESS

First published 1988
Aberdeen University Press
A member of the Pergamon Group

© The Contributors 1988

British Library Cataloguing in Publication Data

Perspectives in Scottish social history:
  essays in honour of Rosalind Mitchison.
  1. Scotland. Social conditions—history
  I. Leneman, Leah
  941.1

ISBN 0 08 036574 4

PRINTED IN GREAT BRITAIN
THE UNIVERSITY PRESS
ABERDEEN

PERSPECTIVES IN SCOTTISH SOCIAL HISTORY

AUP titles of related interest

ABERDEEN AND THE ENLIGHTENMENT
edited by Jennifer J Carter and Joan H Pittock

PATRONAGE AND PRINCIPLE
A political History of Modern Scotland
Michael Fry

WILLIAM ELPHINSTONE AND THE KINGDOM OF SCOTLAND 1435–1514
Leslie J Macfarlane

THE SCOTTISH SALT INDUSTRY, 1570–1850
an economic and social history
Christopher A Whatley

THE SCOTTISH HISTORICAL REVIEW

Contents

Acknowledgments

The Editor would like to thank Roger Davidson, Head of the Department of Economic & Social History, University of Edinburgh, whose idea this volume was, and who provided support and assistance throughout.

The Contributors

GEOFFREY PARKER is Professor of History, University of Illinois at Urbana-Champaign.

T C SMOUT is Professor of Scottish History, University of St Andrews. A Gibson is his Research Assistant.

LORNA EWAN is a postgraduate student in Geography, University of Edinburgh, and a freelance researcher.

ROBERT A DODGSHON is Reader in Geography, University College of Wales, Aberystwyth.

IAN D WHYTE is Lecturer in Geography, University of Lancaster. Kathleen A Whyte is his wife and Research Associate.

LEAH LENEMAN is a Research Fellow in Scottish History, University of St Andrews.

MALCOLM GRAY was Reader in Economic History, University of Aberdeen, and is now retired.

T M DEVINE is Professor of Scottish History, University of Strathclyde.

R H CAMPBELL is Emeritus Professor of Economic History, University of Stirling.

Rosalind Mitchison's Publications

*1	1945	'Some voluntary organisations for the Welfare of Children', in A F C Bourdillon (ed), *Voluntary Social Services*, under the auspices of the Nuffield College Social Reconstruction Survey, pp 31–56
*2	1959	'The Old Board of Agriculture, 1793–1888', *English Historical Review*, vol 74, pp 41–69
*3	1962	*Agricultural Sir John* (Bles), 292 pp.
4		'Pluralities and the poorer benefices in eighteenth-century England', *Historical Journal*, vol 5, No 2, pp 188–90
5	1963	'Two Northern Ports', *Scottish Studies*, vol 7, pp 75–82
*6	1965	'The movements of Scottish corn prices in the seventeenth and eighteenth centuries', *Economic History Review*, 2nd series, vol 18, pp 278–91
7		Review of E R Cregeen, *Argyll Estate Instructions, 1771–1805* (Scottish History Society) and *Inhabitants of the Argyll Estate, 1779* (Scottish Record Society) in *Scottish Historical Review*, vol 44, pp 177–80
*8	1970	*A History of Scotland* (Methuen), 468 pp.
*9		'The Government and the Highlands, 1707–45', in N T Phillipson and Rosalind Mitchison (eds), *Scotland in the Age of Improvement*, pp 24–46
10		'The Forty Five', in *History of the English Speaking Peoples*, pp 240–5
11	1971	Review of J F D Shrewsbury, *A History of Bubonic Plague in the British Isles* (1970), in *Scottish Historical Review*, vol 50, pp 75–8
12	1972	'Scotland since 1850' in Alastair Dunnett (ed), *Alastair Maclean introduces Scotland*, pp 92–107
13		'Restoration and revolution' in Gordon Menzies (ed), *The Scottish Nation*, pp 136–46
14		'Attitudes to Social Welfare' in *Scottish International* (October), pp 17–19
15	1973	60 entries in G H D Howat (ed), *Dictionary of World History* (Nelson)
*16	1974	'The making of the Old Scottish Poor Law', *Past and Present*, No 63, pp 58–93
17		'The recurring face of Malthus', *Theoria to Theory*, vol 8, pp 241–7
18		'Sources for Scottish Local History, No 2, Kirk Session Registers', *The Local Historian*, vol 11, No 4, pp 229–33
19	1975	'Religion and Glencoe', *Scottish Historical Review*, vol 54, pp 114–6
20		'A Parish and its Poor: Yester in the second half of the seventeenth century', *Transactions of the East Lothian Antiquarian and Field Naturalists' Society*, vol 14, pp 15–28
21		'A rejoinder' in 'Debate, the Making of the Old Scottish Poor Law, *Past and Present*, No 69 (November), pp 119–21

*Major publications

Introduction

It could never have been predicted that the young woman who took First Class Honours degrees in Mathematics and Modern History at Lady Margaret College, Oxford in 1940 and 1942 would go on to become one of the most important Scottish historians of the twentieth century. Perhaps because her career in Scottish history did not begin until relatively late in her life, Rosalind Mitchison's retirement in 1986 caught many people by surprise. There was another reason for that surprise too. By the time most professors reach retirement age, if they are still producing books at all then they will normally have established a time-worn groove of their own and have stuck to it. Rosalind Mitchison has never been content to remain thus confined, and it is the constantly new and unexpected areas of study which she has continued to explore—up to and since her retirement—that makes her outlook perennially young and dynamic.

Rosalind Mitchison began her career in Scottish history in the same place where she retired: in the Economic History (now Economic & Social History) Department at Edinburgh University. (She also spent several years in the 1960s lecturing in the Scottish History Department of Glasgow University.) She began as an Assistant, progressed to becoming a Lecturer, then (in 1976) a Reader, and in 1981 was awarded a Personal Chair in Social History.

Her first book was a biography of Sir John Sinclair, notable Improver and editor of the first *Statistical Account*, that invaluable source for Scottish historians of the late eighteenth century. After *Agricultural Sir John* (3) in 1962 her next major publication was an article in *Economic History Review* in 1965, 'The movements of Scottish corn prices in the seventeenth and eighteenth centuries' (6), an innovatory paper which has remained an important source for students of Scottish economic history to this day. After biography and economic history, she then turned to politics in the broadest sense with *A History of Scotland* (8), first published in 1970 and revised in 1982. Since the day it appeared this elegantly lucid book has been *the* one-volume history which everyone interested in Scotland's past has had to read. That book alone would have earned Rosalind Mitchison an enduring place in the pantheon of twentieth-century Scottish historians, but there was much more to come.

That same year of 1970 saw the publication of a volume of essays edited by N T Phillipson and Rosalind Mitchison, entitled *Scotland in the Age of Improvement*, to which the co-editor also contributed an important piece, 'The Government and the Highlands' (9). At that time the very idea of publishing a complete volume of essays on a subject so specialised must have seemed a terrific gamble (and indeed it was to be nearly a decade before the market for such books was convincing enough for publishers to risk commissioning them in any numbers). Because of the high quality of the contributions, this pioneering work is still very widely read.

Another seminal paper appeared in *Past and Present* in 1974: 'The making of the Old Scottish Poor Law' (16). In that essay Rosalind Mitchison traced the changes over time which culminated in the very different nineteenth-century systems of poor relief in Scotland and England (in Scotland the able-bodied poor were not eligible for relief and funds were mainly raised voluntarily and not through assessment). The main thrust of her paper was to reveal that the Scottish law was not actually finalised until the end of the eighteenth century and that nineteenth-century writers then falsified history to make it seem that it had always been so. If there is one subject that Rosalind Mitchison has made her own it is that one. She has written on the topic several times, with the most important subsequent paper being 'The Creation of the Disablement Rule in the Scottish Poor Law' in T C Smout's book of essays, *The Search for Wealth and Stability* (31) in 1979. This area of study has continued to occupy her attention, and a book on the Old Scottish Poor Law is in the pipeline.

Next, after seminal works on economic, political and social history, came demography, with *British Population Change since 1860* (23) and Part 4 of M W Flinn's *Scottish Population History from the Seventeenth Century to the 1930s* (24), in 1977. Another departure was 'Patriotism and national identity in eighteenth-century Scotland' in *Historical Studies* Volume 11 (20) in 1978, and *The Roots of Nationalism: Studies in Northern Europe* (33), which she both edited and contributed to.

When Edward Arnold decided to publish a multi-volume history of Scotland, it was obvious who the author of the seventeenth-century volume should be. *Lordship to Patronage: Scotland 1603–1745* (41), which appeared in 1983, gave Rosalind Mitchison the scope to demonstrate the inter-relationship between political, social and economic history. Indeed, the whole trend of the 1980s has been the breaking down of these artificial barriers—not only between different aspects of history, but between history and other disciplines as well. Clear proof of this is the high proportion of geographers amongst the contributors to this volume.

One might well ask, then, why a volume of essays in honour of Rosalind Mitchison should confine itself to social history. Social history hardly existed as a subject when Rosalind Mitchison's career began, yet her own view of the past always encompassed so much more than the narrowly political that when it emerged as a fashionable area of study in the late 1970s she was already a leading exponent. She is, in fact, the doyenne of Scottish social historians. The subjects of her immediate post-retirement research—poor relief and illegitimacy in early modern Scotland—have a strong social history focus. Then too, as anyone who reads this book will find, social history takes in such a richly varied field of study that it could hardly be termed a limitation at all.

The main sources for Rosalind Mitchison's latest research interests—poor relief and illegitimacy in early modern Scotland—are registers of kirk sessions (the parish level church courts), so it seems very fitting that the first essay in this volume, by Geoffrey Parker, should reveal how kirk sessions 'tamed' Scotland after the reformation. His paper focuses particularly on St Andrews kirk session in the late sixteenth century, thereby providing a sort of 'prequel' to Rosalind Mitchison's own work, which begins in the seventeenth century.

Gibson and Smout's paper also begins in the mid sixteenth century, but it covers a hundred-year span to the mid seventeenth century. In line with Rosalind Michison's propensity for asking unusual questions about seemingly straightforward subjects, they have looked at a fairly obvious topic for any social historian—food—from a new and different angle, the relationship between food and status. The viewpoint is not what could be afforded but rather what was considered suitable and fitting for those on different rungs of the social ladder. At the same time they have been able to reveal much more than has been known before about what Scots actually ate in earlier centuries.

Lorna Ewan (who, along with A Gibson, represents the younger generation of scholars) has looked at debt and debtors in Scotland, a subject which, rather like Scottish poor relief before Rosalind Mitchison got to work on it, seems so straightforward that most historians have never thought to look below the surface. As little has hitherto been known about the history, customs and laws relating to debt as was once known about the actual workings of the Old Scottish Poor Law, and this paper therefore breaks new ground in outlining the legal and social developments in relation to debtors.

We move to the countryside with the next paper, by Robert A Dodgshon, which suggests that many farming customs in early modern Scotland commonly assumed to have been based on pragmatic reasoning may well have had a very different basis, dating back to Pictish times, when certain patterns and rituals of work were assumed because of men's conception of their place in the universe. It is a fascinating idea which lifts rural history onto a different plane altogether.

The Whytes' essay may be planted more firmly in statistics and factual evidence but it is equally important. Only in recent years has it been discovered just how mobile early modern Scots really were, and no one up to now has thought to look specifically at female mobility. Much (in fact most) of Rosalind Mitchison's recent work in Scottish poor relief and illegitimacy also relates to women, who have long been neglected in Scottish history. The balance is finally beginning to be redressed with papers such as this one.

Leah Leneman's paper taps into another subject mentioned earlier to which Rosalind Mitchison has addressed herself; the subject of national identity. The changing attitudes of Lowlanders toward the Jacobite movement, and the identification of Highlanders with that movement, are part of the phenomenon whereby in the course of the eighteenth century Gaels ceased to be objects of distrust and antipathy but instead became imbued with romantic associations, allowing Lowlanders to include the population of the Highlands in their conception of what it meant to be Scottish.

The last three papers all deal with rural Scotland in the nineteenth century. It is notable that there are no papers in this volume on urban history, but this is perfectly logical, because until quite recently the bulk of Scotland's population dwelt in the country rather than in towns. The other factor which the three papers have in common is that they each concentrate on a particular geographical area. Scottish historians in the past wrote about 'the Lowlands' and 'the Highlands' as though they were complete entities. Rosalind Michison's work on kirk session registers, as revealed in the paper written with Leah Leneman, 'Scottish illegitimacy ratios in early modern Scotland' (47), shows just how much variation there was between Scottish regions, and now that social historians are studying particular areas important differences are emerging.

Malcolm Gray concentrates on the North-East, where agricultural improvements came relatively late, and shows how the timing of the change made it easier to learn from the mistakes of others. He also demonstrates that the popular conception of Improvements as imposed from above by landlords does not hold true for this region where credit for change has to go largely to the tenants.

T M Devine writes about landowners in the north and west Highlands, the area where the potato famine hit the populace in the mid nineteenth century. The potato famine, an important and hitherto neglected subject, has at last been tackled in depth, and this paper looks at one topic which has arisen out of recent research. The stereotyped Highland landlord makes no appearance in this paper; instead it asks serious questions about the landowning class during this period of crisis (for example, at a time when tenants ended up years in arrears with their rent, how did so many of these landowners survive?) and comes up with some unexpected answers.

The final paper, by R H Campbell, also studies a particular region—in this case the South-West—and also looks at landlord/tenant relations. Once again, we move away from stereotypes and examine what actually occurred as revealed by the primary source material. The picture which emerges is a far cry from the traditional idea of landowners as oppressors of the tenantry, for Campbell shows how in Galloway landowners actually made possible the survival of many tenants, and hastened their own demise as a class by so doing.

The diversity of subjects and the new ways of looking at familiar themes make this volume a fitting tribute to Rosalind Mitchison, who, over the years, has been an inspiration not only to all the contributors but to scores of others.

The 'Kirk By Law Established' and the Origins of 'The Taming of Scotland': St Andrews 1559–1600

Geoffrey Parker

In August 1590 Mr James Melville, minister of the Church of Scotland, delivered a stirring exhortation to the General Assembly calling for major improvements in the condition of the Kirk. One of his principal arguments was

> that discipline was maist necessar in the Kirk, seing without the saming, Chrysts Kingdome could nocht stand. For unles the Word and Sacraments war kiepit in sinceritie, and rightlie usit and practesit be direction of the discipline, they wald soone be corrupted. And therfor certean it was, that without sum discipline na kirk; without trew discipline, na rightlie reformed kirk; and without the right and perfyt discipline, na right and perfyt kirk.

At the end of the session, the Assembly endorsed Melville's stand and resolved that

> euerie minister sould haiff a copie of the Book of Discipline and peruse it; and euerie presbyterie sould cause thair haill members subscryve the sam; and the refusars to be excomunicat.

Melville's autobiography, which includes the text of his speech, makes it clear that at the forefront of his mind lay the troubles that he had witnessed for more than a decade in planting Godly Discipline in the town of St Andrews in Fife.[1]

St Andrews in the age of the Reformation was the seat of both a university and the metropolitan see of Scotland; it was also a lively burgh, with considerable sea-borne trade and jurisdiction over a number of outlying villages.[2] Although in the absence of contemporary registers of births and deaths, or a census, it is hazardous to offer an estimate of the parish's population, it seems likely that it consisted of some 4,000 people in the early seventeenth century, of whom perhaps 2,500–3,000 lived in the town.[3] But there are two

1

reasons for thinking that the population in the previous half-century is likely to have been lower than this. On the one hand, the disruption caused by the Reformation caused both some Catholic clergy and many students to pack their bags; on the other, the plague of 1585–6 'raget till almaist utter vastation' and the principal towns of Scotland, including St Andrews, were left 'almost desolat'.[4] But despite these losses, and perhaps others due to a shift in Scotland's overseas trade to larger and better-appointed harbours in the vicinity, Reformation St Andrews remained a large parish by the standards of sixteenth-century Scotland. It therefore offered a considerable challenge to the architects of the New Jerusalem.

Ministers of the Church such as James Melville had to hand three distinct weapons for enforcing their moral standards and their doctrines upon the Scots: certain teachings and traditions of the church; the active support of the secular authorities; and a new and ubiquitous hierarchy of church courts and jurisdictions. All were put to full use. John Calvin, whose example the Scottish Reformers chose to emulate, had been impressed by the evidence contained in the *Acts of the Apostles* and in certain of St Paul's *Epistles* that the first Christian churches had strictly controlled and vigorously censured the social behaviour of their members. In his *Ecclesiastical Ordinances* of 1541, as well as in later editions of his *Institutes of the Christian religion*, Biblical sanction was claimed for the office of 'elder', whom Calvin made responsible for overseeing the morals and manners of the community.[5]

But who, precisely, comprised the community? Here the example of the early church was less often cited. There were many in the Protestant movement who argued that, as in the time of the Apostles, only true believers should be considered full members of the church; and that therefore only they should be subject to ecclesiastical discipline. This was the stance adopted by Calvinist leaders in both the Dutch Republic and north-west Germany: only those who had placed themselves 'under the sweet yoke of our chief shepherd Jesus Christ' were liable to discipline.[6] But Calvin himself had vehemently opposed this view. For him, the Christian community embraced everyone, sinners and saved alike; and in Geneva he created a special tribunal called the *Consistoire*, composed of ministers and elders (some of them also magistrates), to interrogate and judge all who fell from doctrinal and moral purity. And those who erred, whoever they might be, were severely punished—whether for religious obstinacy (like Miguel Servetus, who was burned at the stake for his steadfast refusal to accept Calvin's teaching) or for moral turpitude (like those convicted of flagrant adultery, who were drowned).[7]

This uncompromising stance was fully endorsed by the leading Scottish Reformer, John Knox. Although during his ministry of the English Church in Frankfurt (1554–5) and Geneva (1556–8) his elders could only deal with the 'manners and disorders' of the small exile community, in a polemic written at Dieppe in 1559, just before he embarked for Scotland, Knox made a powerful defence of strong discipline, up to and including death for deviants, equally applied to all. And when, the following year, the 'face of a public kirk' was at least established in his homeland, Knox ensured that the Scots

Confession recognised 'Ecclesiastical discipline, uprightly ministered as God's word prescribed, whereby vice is repressed and virtue nourished' as one of the three 'notes, signs and assured tokens' whereby the true church may be 'known from that horrible harlot' the church of Rome.[8] The reasoning and the consequences were both spelled out in chapter seven of another of Knox's literary endeavours of 1560 entitled—perhaps ominously—*A First Book of Discipline*:

> As that no Commonwealth can flourish or long indure without good lawes and sharpe execution of the same, so neither can the Kirk of God be brought to purity neither yet be retained in the same without the order of ecclesiastical discipline, which stands in reproving and correcting of the faults which the civil sword either doth neglect or not punish: ... Drunkenness, excesse (be it in aparel or be it in eating and drinking), fornication, oppressing of the poore, ... wanton words and licentious living tending to slander, doe openly appertaine to the kirk of God to punish them, as God's word commands.

None were to escape scrutiny of their conduct for, the *Book* continued:

> To discipline must all the estates within this Realm be subject, as well the Rulers as they that are ruled: yea and the Preachers themselves, as welle as the poorest within the Kirk.[9]

It was to enforce a literal interpretation of Mosaic Law upon all Scots, and to prepare them for the second (and more glorious) coming of the Lord, that powerful new church courts were created. At the parish level a kirk-session, composed of the minister and a number of elders and deacons elected by the faithful, kept an eye on church fabric and finance, and administered poor relief, but spent most of its time on discipline. The records of almost every Scottish kirk-session, from the mid sixteenth to the mid eighteenth century, are filled with parishioners who manifestly failed to respect the Lord's Day; with neighbours who, before witnesses, quarrelled and assaulted each other either verbally or physically; and, above all, with couples who admitted, more or less reluctantly, their illicit sexual liaisons. But there were three eventualities which might cause a session to send one of its cases before a higher court— the local presbytery, where all the ministers of a given area met together primarily to supervise the morals and doctrines of the clergy. First, some offenders were referred to the presbytery because their transgression was particularly serious (any offence leading to sentence of excommunication was automatically referred). Second, others might be 'sent upstairs' because the offender (often a local landowner) either refused to accept the session's authority or repeated the crime frequently. Finally, others still might come before the presbytery because their case offered unusual difficulties.

A case of witchcraft uncovered in a remote parish of Orkney in 1649 may serve as an example of the first category. 'Margaret Greeg, a stranger of late come to the isle [Shapinsay]' was brought in by the local kirk-session for questioning because she was 'beginning to abuse the people in making them to think that she can tell them who it is that takes any thing from them that is stollen.' The implication was clear: 'The said Margaret is suspect of witchcraft', and she was accordingly referred to the presbytery for closer investigation.[10] An example of the second category occurs in the minutes of the kirk-session of Auchtermuchty in Fife, also in 1649. James Sibbald, a miller, was reported for carting a load of flour on the Sabbath. He appeared before the session, but with an ill grace, and was overheard in the anteroom 'saying "I defy the minister and you and all you session and all that ze can do ... I cair not for you".' For this evident insubordination he was referred to the presbytery, and 'depairted the session in a werrie disdainful way, muttering wordis quhilkis could not be heard'.[11] A splendid example of the third variety of presbytery disciplinary business—the 'difficult' case—is afforded by the remarkable saga of Janet Dick, whose apparent achievement of a virgin birth occupied the kirk-session of Airth and the presbytery of Stirling on several occasions between 1656 and 1668. Janet, a spinster, 'brought forth a bairn' and yet steadfastly denied ever engaging in sexual intercourse. Examination by midwives beforehand seemed to confirm her story. The kirk was not convinced, but even the most stringent questioning failed to break her story, so she was left 'lying under scandal' (a verdict which virtually deprived her of all civil rights) until the explanation was produced twelve years later. A local man, after being almost killed by a bolt of lightning, admitted that he had 'committed uncleanness' (as he put it) with the girl while she was so soundly asleep that she never woke up. The man was fined for his 'sin', and no cult of the Virgin Janet took root in the Central Lowlands.[12]

Janet Dick and her clandestine lover, like countless other inhabitants of seventeenth-century Scotland, never seem to have questioned the right of the church courts to judge and to punish them. Open contempt for the system, like that of James Sibbald, was rare; and it was seldom successful. Those who would not bend the knee were (except during the 1650s) eventually either imprisoned or forced to flee.[13] It is worth pausing a moment to wonder why.

No doubt there was an element of fear among most ordinary lay folk that resisting or refusing the commands of the church might lead to damnation; but that alone would probably not have been enough to secure obedience— it certainly did not in England.[14] In Scotland, however, fear was heavily reinforced by the comprehensive support for ecclesiastical justice provided by the secular authorities. It is true that the General Assembly failed to persuade the Scots Parliament in 1560 to give the *Book of Discipline* statutory backing; and that Parliament also declined a request in May 1562 to outlaw those 'horibill vices' described in *Leviticus* for which 'the eternal God in his Parliament hes pronounced death to be the punishment'.[15] But in 1563 incest and witchcraft were declared capital offences; while in 1567 'notoure and manifest adulterie' joined them, and fornicators were threatened with either a £40 fine or eight days in prison. In the same year, Parliament expressly recognised the kirk's jurisdiction in preaching of the Word, administration of the sacraments, and correction of manners; and between the 1570s and the 1690s ten separate Acts were passed to make blasphemy into a statutory offence, and fourteen to penalise sabbath-breach.[16]

Further down the judicial spectrum, but equally important, magistrates and landlords lent their evident support to the church courts by sitting on the local kirk-session. In most burghs the session elders normally included at least one of the town baillies, and sometimes the minutes note that a sentence was passed on offenders 'the baillies being present', since that made the decision immediately enforcable in both secular and ecclesiastical courts. Some urban parishes, indeed, openly reserved one or more places especially for their local law-officers.[17] The interlock of church and state was equally apparent in rural areas, not least because the internal divisions of each parish normally reflected the landholding patterns within it: elders were appointed for each barony, since that organism was the basic unit of economic and social life in early modern Scotland.[18] And, as in the towns, those exercising secular jurisdictions were encouraged to participate in the disciplinary work of the church. The acts of the kirk-session of the Gaelic-speaking parish of Cromdale, for example, drawn up in 1702 by the minister and elders 'and with them the laird of Grant, younger, of that ilk, as civil judge, to give his concurrence', ordained that 'In regard there are severall scandals committed within the bounds of this pariochen, therefore the civill judge, in the parish's presence, is to be intreated to every session, and his concurrence to suppress immorality is to be required by the minister and elders.'

And the secular courts returned the compliment: with very few exceptions, town magistrates, sheriffs and holders of heritable jurisdictions went out of their way to support the decisions and laws of the church courts. In the Baron Court of Stitchell, in 1660, for example:

> The said Barroun, takeing to his serious consideratioun how great a necessity Church Discypline of this Paroch has of the assistance and concurrence of the Civil Magistrat and helpe of his authority ... thairfor the said Barroun heirby judicially decernes and ordaines his ordnar officer of the Barroun [Court] to put in execution all Acts and Sentences of the Kirke Sessioun again all persouns whomsoever within this Barrouny and poynd for all penalty and fines to be imposed be them, and take the extract of the Kirke Session their Act for his warrand.[19]

But there was a price to be paid for this apparently perfect union of church and state: the kirk had to accept that it was usually inadvisable to follow the *Book of Discipline*'s injunction to proceed against 'all estates within this Realm' with equal energy. Although the General assembly in 1573 still insisted the 'great men offending in sick crymes as deserve sackcloath should receive the samein as weill as the poor', it rarely happened. After all, town magistrates and local landowners often possessed rights of patronage over the parish church and were sometimes impropriators of its tithes: their influence over the minister, and perhaps over some elders, should not be underestimated so their sins were usually either tacitly condoned or else privately settled. Thus in 1585 at Elgin although Provost James Douglas (an elder) confessed himself guilty of the sin of fornication, he was spared public penance in return for the cost of glazing a window in the church; while in Fife, somewhat later, although Lord Lindores was widely 'noted for his whoredom' and the laird of Kemback 'was said by some to be a great whoremaster', their respective sessions chose not to enquire more closely into the matter.

However these 'tactical concessions', as Bruce Lenman has pointed out, 'strengthened rather than weakened the system of Godly Discipline by making it more palatable to the ruling class.'[20] Just how essential secular support really was, whatever concessions it cost, emerged unmistakably in the 1650s when, during the occupation of Scotland by the army of the English Commonwealth, the civil authorities briefly withdrew their backing for ecclesiastical censure. In January 1652 all existing courts and jurisdictions in Scotland were abolished by decree of the conquerors and, in the subsequent judicial settlement, there was no place for either baron courts or church tribunals. In the summer of the following year, a session of the General Assembly was forcibly terminated by English troops and the ministers silenced and sent home. The significance of these events was not lost on contemporaries. In November 1653, for example, the kirk-session of Aberdeen was openly insulted by a servant to the Catholic Laird of Pitfodels:

> [Alexander Gordon] being demandit whairfoir he did not compeir sooner, he anserit: If it haid not bein to hold in the offiris paines, he had not compeirit now, nor at all. And, being demandit if he did acknowledge us to be ane judicatorie, he anserit: Unles we was authorized be the Comon wealth. And, being demandit again if he wes of our profession [sc. was he a Calvinist], he anserit: He came not to give ane acquittance, And all the whole tyme he carried himselff uncivillie and unbraidlinglie, thanking God that the tymes were not as formerlie.[21]

Such behaviour was only possible as long as the civil authorities in Scotland offered no support for church discipline. But, even before the Restoration, this policy was reversed and, from 1660 onwards, church courts everywhere in the kingdom could once more rely on the full support of statute, sheriff, baillie and baron in enforcing their will.[22]

All the above examples are taken from the system in its hey-day. They illustrate generalities that could be backed up by thousands of other cases, published and manuscript, almost identical in nature.[23] But how did it all begin? At what point did the new church courts, created after the Reformation, gain general acceptance; and when, precisely, did they first enter their symbiotic relationship with the established secular jurisdictions? The answer to this problem is not easy to provide, for the survival of the records of the church of Scotland is extremely uneven. In 1905, it was computed that documents from 16 synods, 84 presbyteries and 1,324 parishes of Scotland then survived. But in many of them sources began only in the eighteenth century, and some of those extant in 1905—including some of the earliest—

TABLE 1

SURVIVAL OF SCOTTISH CHURCH RECORDS, 1560–1700

Period	Kirk-session minutes surviving (in whole or in part)	Presbytery minutes surviving (in whole or in part)
1560–75	2	0
1576–1600	23	11
1601–25	70	23
1626–50	202	45
1651–75	352	62
1676–1700	527	82

have since disappeared.[24] By the end of 1979, the known survival of church records before 1700 was as given in Table 1.[25]

The parish of St Andrews in the later sixteenth century offers a unique glimpse of the process by which 'godly discipline' was first established in Scotland, both because its kirk-session register begins before any other—commencing, indeed, slightly before the Reformation itself—and continuing unbroken up to 1600, and because many of the events therein were also recorded and analysed in the *Diary* kept by one of its ministers, James Melville, during the 1580s and 1590s.[26] After 1600, there is a gap in the sources and, when the *Register* resumes in 1638, it is indistinguishable from those of other Lowland parishes from which the extracts printed above were taken.[27]

But this was not so in the beginning. It is true that the register of the kirk-session began on 27 October 1559, and that the session itself had probably been active for some weeks before that—perhaps since John Knox's triumphant return to the town late in June. But the early folios of the register contain a strange mixture of administrative, disciplinary and 'consistorial' business (the latter comprising matrimonial, testamentary and other matters previously heard by the Archbishop's 'commissary court'). There were two reasons for this. First, the session was obliged to deal, between 1561 and 1572, with a number of cases—124 in all—which arose from areas far outside the parish. Some came 'on appeal' from other kirk-sessions, some from parishes which lacked a kirk-session; others concerned misdemeanours of the clergy. Later, these cases would all have gone to the presbytery, but the presbytery of St Andrews was not established until 1581.[28] Instead, on the orders of the General Assembly, a number of 'superintendents' were appointed after 1560 to 'visit and plant kirks' in the dioceses of Scotland. John Winram, formerly a prior of the cathedral church of St Andrews and now a minister of the Reformed church in the burgh, was elected Superintendent for Fife and Perthshire in April 1561. His decisions as Superintendent were entered in the kirk-session's register. Only after he resigned his office eleven years later were the two jurisdictions separated.[29] A similar overlap of personnel explains the presence of 'consistorial' business in the register until 1564. Although on 24 August 1560 the Reformation Parliament abolished all papal authority in Scotland, papally-appointed bishops were permitted to continue their jurisdiction over matrimonial and other consistorial business, acting in their own names. Since some bishops did not subscribe to the Calvinist *Confession of Faith*, this situation was plainly unsatisfactory, and gradually the kirk-session in the chief town of each diocese, led by the 'superintendent' appointed for the area, took over the work.[30] This situation only changed with the creation of separate Commissary Courts, first at Edinburgh in 1564 (for Lothian and for appeals from elsewhere) and shortly afterwards at St Andrews.

The intermingling of consistorial, disciplinary and what later became presbytery matters in the same record renders the analysis of purely kirk-session business before 1573 difficult, though not impossible. It would seem that, until 1568, there were very few disciplinary items coming before the session (and all of them concerned sexual misconduct). This is not surprising. In the first place, until the fall of Mary Queen of Scots in June 1567, not all members of the town were subject to discipline, for attending Catholic worship that stopped short of the Mass was no crime. There were, as Gordon Donaldson has suggested, two churches in the kingdom between 1560 and 1567; and, although some Scots chose to belong to both, most regarded them as alternatives.[31]

Long before this, however, the kirk-session at St Andrews had begun to take cognizance of the offences later designated by Parliament as 'crimes'. The first two recorded cases in the *Register* (both from 1559) concerned adultery; in May 1560 we find the first punishment of fornication; and from the spring of 1568 a campaign to enforce proper observance of the Sabbath began.[32] There were also other efforts to enforce Reformation doctrine that went unrecorded in the *Register*. For example James Melville recalled seeing, as a student in 1571-2, 'a witche in St Andros, aginst the quhilk Mr Knox delt from pulpit, sche being set upe at a pillar befor him'. Shortly afterwards he watched her burn to death. But the *Register* says nothing of all this. At the same time, 'Mr Knox' also delivered a series of blistering sermons in the town church, execrating sin and commanding virtue, during which he 'was lyk to ding [smash] that pulpit in blads, and flie out of it'.[33] But again the *Register* is silent about trial and punishment. It was not until 1573 that the prosecution and recording of breaches of discipline became the norm.

There were several reasons for the change. On the national scene, the government had at last provided the reformed church with access to some of the wealth of the former establishment (by the Convention of Leith, January 1572), and had deprived of office all clerics who refused to accept the Confession of Faith (January 1573). Furthermore, the end of the civil war in the spring of 1573 ushered in a 'time of repose which God has granted us after our long troubles'.[34] In St Andrews itself, Winram resigned in 1572 and left the session free to pursue local control single-mindedly. Shortly afterwards the session ordained that where a servant was fined for some moral lapse, his or her master should be responsible for payment;[35] and henceforth there was less willingness to commute the normal penalties, imposed specifically to shame the transgressor, for money.[36]

TABLE 2
KIRK-SESSION CASES IN ST NINIANS PARISH, 1653–1719

Offence	Number of cases	Per cent
Sexual cases	307	57
Disorderly conduct	162	30
Enforcement/Authority	46	9
Other	20	4
Total	535	100

So it was in 1573 that the 'great work of discipline' really began in St Andrews. That year the *Register* commenced—significantly—with an injunction that all members of the session who missed a meeting should be fined 'wythout exceptioun of personis and forgeving to ony man', followed by a supplication to the magistrates that they would 'execut the actis and ordinances' of the session concerning fornicators, adulterers, sabbath-breakers and 'thame that ar warnit to compeir . . . and comperis not'.[37] It must have proved effective, because by 1600, some 1,716 parishioners had appeared before the session, an average of 61 per year. The analysis of their offences in Table 3, however, does not conform to the pattern that one might expect of an ecclesiastical court. Nor does it resemble the duties set out in the instructions issued to the elders of the urban parish of Stirling in 1600, which have been hailed as 'typical':

> to tak attendence to the maneris of the pepill . . . ; to attend quhat straingearis resortis to the toun, and to quhat effect; . . . [and to search for] any Jesuitis or seminarie Priestis . . . within this toun.[38]

For it is clear that in St Andrews 'the maneris of the pepill' occupied the lion's share of all attention, while the movement of 'straingearis' and papists scarcely received any. But St Andrews was by no means unqique. The few other parishes with surviving records from this period show almost exactly the same pattern. So do later ones. The disciplinary records of the Stirlingshire parish of St Ninians, for example, are shown in Table 2. The same may be also said of several Calvinist communities outside Scotland: at Nîmes in the south of France, where a kirk-session (*consistoire*) began work in 1561, four-fifths of all business handled concerned morals and the grim motto on the cover of one register read *Disciplina nervus ecclesiae*.[39] And, as Table 3 and Figure 1 show, the overall pattern of discipline in St Andrews was remarkably similar.[40]

TABLE 3
KIRK-SESSION CASES IN ST ANDREWS PARISH, 1573–1600

Offence	Number of offenders	Per cent
Sexual cases	986	57
Disorderly conduct	499	29
Enforcement/Authority	38	2
Other	193	11
Total	1716	99

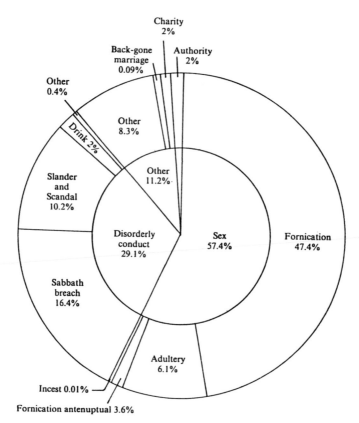

'Other' in the St Andrews records includes applications for poor relief (35 cases, almost all after 1597); the arrangement of baptisms for 21 illegitimate children or orphans; cases of infanticide (6) or manslaughter (8) making a brief appearance before going on to the civil courts; and the enforcement of marriage vows, about which one partner had had second thoughts (16 cases recorded—including one ingenious citizen in 1584 who successfully argued that 'he nevir maid promis of mareage ... bot onlie promittit to hir ane kow').[41] Few cases are recorded of 'testimonials' given to (or received from) god-fearing 'straingearis'; still less of suspected religious deviance, whether by witches or Catholics. As in seventeenth-century St Ninians—and most other parishes of the kingdom that have been studied—everything else paled before the apparent obsession of Scots Calvinists with sex.[42]

Most of the 986 sexual offenders hauled before the session were charged with fornication (sexual intercourse between two single persons)—813 cases— or 'fornication antenuptual' (intercourse between two persons whose marriage banns had been called but had not yet been wed)—63 cases. Adultery (105 offenders) and incest (5) were relatively rare, and bestiality and sodomy do not appear at all. Given that the entire adult population of the parish was probably under 2,000, and with around 32 offenders prosecuted for sexual misconduct annually, the chances of a lusty young person appearing before the session at some point was relatively high.[43]

Most of the fornicators arrived before the session in much the same way: a single woman was denounced by a neighbour or by an elder, either for having given birth or for being about to do so.

[10 August 1580] comperit Beteraige Bredfute and confessit and granted sche was deliverit off ane maiden bairne to James Wemis.

[31 August 1580] comperit Agnes Angous and confessit and granted hir to be wyth chylde to Jhone Buge younger, and submitted hir to the discipline off the kirk; and siclyk confessit this to be the thrid tyme she committed fornication.[44]

The session almost always picked on the woman first, because the accusation was so easy to prove: either a girl was pregnant and single or she was not. As the elders of Killearn in Stirlingshire smugly observed of a pregnant spinster: 'It is obvious that she has sinned, be the father who it will'.[45]

It was far less easy to establish the father's identity. Some girls refused to tell, although usually everyone knew who they had been seen with at the relevant time. Others named a man who denied the charge, and in such cases, the man was allowed to take an oath of innocence before the whole congregation during time of service. Normally he was allowed a week or so to peruse the oath, with its fearsome penalties for perjury:

Whereas I have been delated [reported] for fornication with X, I hereupon swear by the terrible and dreadful name of God the searcher of the secrets of all hearts, that I did never know the said X by having carnal dealings with her. And if this day I swear falsely, I do here before God's people in this congregation renounce my interest in Christ and my right to everlasting happiness in the life to come.[46]

This was usually enough to break the resistance of all but the totally innocent or the totally corrupt—and the kirk had no intention of allowing the latter to escape blameless. If a blatantly guilty man still seemed prepared to acquit himself on oath, the session could and did refuse him permission to do so, leaving him neither convicted nor acquitted but, as the phrase went, 'lying under scandal'. This, in effect, meant that a person could not go to church, could not leave their parish, and could not find work or receive poor relief. They also risked a summons to the local secular court for disturbing the peace.

One of the few alternative proofs to pregnancy that sexual misconduct had taken place was the discovery of a couple *in flagrante delicto*. In 1589, for example, James Meldrum delated his own wife for adultery with Nicholl Broun. The two parties named appeared before the session 'quha denyit the bill *simpliciter*' despite the fact that there were witnesses to the fact that Mr Broun had been 'fund, eftir ten houris at evin, hid secretele in James Meldrumis hous in this citee, behind ane bed heid'. The pair were therefore convicted, and condemned to appear in sackcloth before the congregation on Sunday in respect of their adultery, and before the magistates 'for the great sklander gevin by thame' in denying the charge.[47] Less spectacular behaviour could also draw unexpected attention to forbidden liaisons: a couple marching purposefully into the countryside at dusk might be followed and spied on; the moans of a couple who had left their bed too near an open window could attract the attention of bystanders; a careless boast of sexual prowess might be reported to the elders for further investigation.[48] But even these cases lacked that element of incontrovertible proof that pregnancy provided and, in the seventeenth century, the charge might have to be reduced from fornication to 'scandalous carriage'. But the St Andrews records scarcely mention this offence: under rigorous questioning, almost all of those accused eventually broke down and confessed.

The kirk disposed of a formidable arsenal of penalties against sexual offenders. Those guilty of lesser misdemeanours might receive a 'rebuke' in private from the session; those whose lapse was greater, but fell short of sexual intercourse, might be rebuked in public from the pulpit during church service. Parties to grosser offences, however, were each sentenced to pay a fine into the 'poor box' and to appear in church on successive Sundays on the so-called 'stool of repentance'. In most churches, this was a high, four-legged backless chair, like a modern bar-stool. In some parishes it was cleverly constructed so that it would topple over if the sinner failed to sit bolt upright; in others it was attached to a scaffold with several settings—the higher the setting, the worse the offence. 'The stool,' wrote an English visitor in 1635, 'is a public and eminent seat erected about two yards from the ground ... where the whole congregation may take notice' of the offenders. In some churches, he added incredulously, the stool was capable of holding 'six or eight persons'.[49] At Tyninghame, near Edinburgh, the cost of erecting a 'stool' was considerable: £8 to a joiner for the woodwork and £1 to a mason for the stone base. It was clearly a structure of substance.[50]

The usual penalty for fornication included three appearances on the stool on successive Sundays. If the sinner relapsed and fornicated again, six appearances were called for, and those who carried on in this way—referred to as 'trilapses', 'quadrilapses' and so on—were required to sit on the stool, clothed in sackcloth, for an indefinite number of times. While in public view, in this ungainly posture, the offenders were subjected to a lengthy rebuke by the minister. Afterwards they were fined. In St Andrews, until 1593, £2 Scots was normally the price of a simple fornication, double for a relapse and so on, each party paying the same penalty. Adultery, which led to appearances on the stool for up to nine months, and often a civil punishment, involved a fine of up to £100. These sums were large: average wages in Scotland were less than £1 a week, and the normal weekly collection in rural parishes might be counted in shillings rather than pounds. A few fornications and the odd adultery were therefore good news for the church treasurer, and indeed for the poor, who were dependent on alms from the session!

There were, however, other penalties. Those who showed no contrition, or who had no money for their fine, were imprisoned in the church steeple, receiving only bread and water, for up to a fortnight; those who were judged to be beyond redemption were banished—like Jonet Tod, 'ane common harlot ... nocht worthie of Christian society' who was expelled from St Andrews in 1598.[51] Those whose offence was aggravated were also ordered to stand in the 'jougs' at the Market Cross, pinioned for some hours while passers-by scorned or pelted them. On 19 December 1593, again in St Andrews, three women were condemned to be 'jokit' for two hours: one because she had been found guilty of fornication with the same person a second time; one because she had committed fornication while on poor relief ('being ane that ressavit the puir folkis almous'); the third because she had fornicated with several persons ('with Adam Duche ... and certane utheris filthelie, as wes delatit to the session').[52] Adulterers might be treated to the full range of these penalties. In December 1594, a St Andrews adulterer was 'jokit, cartit, and that throw the haill streitis of the town', before being taken to the North Haugh where 'ane great multitude of pepill' cast 'rottin eggis, filth and glar at him'. After that he was ducked in the wintery sea, and subsequently condemned to sit 'on the hichest degre of the penitent stuill' until 'the kirk be satisfeit'. After that, the magistrates took over: they banished him from the burgh.[53]

The only other offenders who regularly appeared on the stool of repentence were those found guilty of slander or insulting behaviour. In a society where people spent all their lives at close quarters, their every action surveyed by countless others, public reputation mattered far more than it does today. To allow an insult to pass unchallenged was, in effect, to admit that it was true. Accusations of misconduct were therefore always taken seriously, not least by the church, which encouraged its parishioners to take their slander to court for fear that otherwise they might settle the matter with fists or worse.[54]

The course of slander cases was as predictable as the sexual hearings. They normally began when a parishioner handed in a complaint that he or she had been maligned by another at a specified time and place. The party named was then called, and both persons involved were required to put down a deposit of £2—a precaution intended to discourage idle or malicious actions, for the party who lost the case also lost the deposit. At this point, either the slander was withdrawn and an apology publicly made, or else evidence was produced to justify it. Witnesses were called to speak of the character and reputation of someone accused of theft, witchcraft or some other crime, so that, in effect, a slander case was virtually a committal hearing on the crime mentioned in the slander. Many of the witchcraft cases heard by the secular courts of early modern Scotland began with an insult which was unsuccessfully challenged in a church court; they ended, normally, with a public burning for which church and state shared responsibility and costs.[55]

Other forms of slander or insulting behaviour, if proved, were likewise punished severely—although they stopped short of the death sentence. In 1579, John Scot was ordered 'in presens off the congregatioun off this citee, to sitt down upone his kneis, confes his offence maed agianis the said Jonett [his wife, whom he had falsely accused of adultery] and pronunce this wordis, haldand his awin tung in his hand: "fals tung, thow leid".' In 1594, a young man found to have threatened his father was condemned to 'compeir in sek claith, beir heddit, and beir futtit, upon the hichest degre of the penitent stuill, with ane hammer in the ane hand and ane stane in the uther hand, as tua instrumentis quhairwith he menassit his father, within ane papir writin in great letteris about his heid thir wordis: "BEHALD THE ONNATURALL SONE PUNISIT FOR PUTTING HAND IN HIS FATHER AND DISHONORING OF GOD IN HIM"'. After that he was, on successive days, to ask forgiveness of his father and of the church congregation, to stand in the jougs two hours, to be carted through the streets while his offence was proclaimed, and to receive solemn warning that 'If he evir offend aganis his father or mother heireftir, in word or deid, that member of his body quhairby he offendis salbe cuttit of from him, be it tung, hand or futt'.[56]

This was—and was meant to be—an exemplary sentence, to be carried out 'without mercy, in exampill to utheris to abstein fra the lyke'. But normally, non-sexual offenders were simply fined and rebuked. Most frequent in this category was 'sabbath breach', an offence committed by doing almost anything on a Sunday except going to church. People were fined for 'sleeping in the meadows in time of sermon', for selling or drinking ale on Sundays 'except it be for the satisfying of nature', as well as for travelling, arguing, or beating their wives (or servants) on the Lord's Day. But the commonest offence was working on Sundays: farmers struggling to harvest their crops while good weather lasted, and lax-fishers throwing their nets into the Tay whenever the salmon were running, all found themselves summoned to the session and fined if they had done it on the Sabbath.[57] To judge by the volume of surviving records, the kirk elders seem to have spent most of every Sunday on ceaseless patrol of their parishes, seeking out sinners and sluggards: 281 persons were accused of sabbath breach in St Andrews between 1573 and 1600.[58]

The offences dealt with by the kirk-session were thus mostly cut-and-dried: a pregnant spinster, a scandal uttered before witnesses, a man found sleeping outside during a church service, or staggering round the streets 'beastlie drunk'. There was no problem of proof, no point in denying guilt. And with the local laird or the bailies sitting on the session, there was little chance of escaping justice and no advantage in challenging the authority of the Court. And yet reluctance to 'submit to discipline' was understandably great. To avoid humiliation, some sat on the stool of repentance with their face covered; others carried swords and pistols.[59] Others tried to avoid coming at all—there were 38 cases of 'resistance to authority', ranging from arguments over whether the session's writ extended to a given area, to violent words exchanged between session and accused.[60] There was always, it is true, a hard core of parishioners who refused to accept the standards set by the session, and appeared several times before the court. Thus 81 persons appeared twice or more before the session between 1573 and 1600 for fornication (one person managed six appearances and another five), and seven persons appeared twice for adultery. One person even came three times. But by the time the *Register* closed, 'repeaters' such as these were virtually a thing of the past, and there were scarcely any cases outstanding in which those delated would not appear. It seemed as if, in St Andrews at least, 'all estates' had indeed become subject to discipline.

This changed situation of the 1590s deserves some futher attention. It would be wrong to suppose that the fluctuations in annual totals shown in the Appendix (pages 20–3 below) were solely the result of variations in offences committed—that the relative absence of sexual offences in the last decade of the century necessarily indicates a reduction of illicit liaisons. They *may* have reflected a new fear among the congregation, following the great plague of 1585–6, that God was not to be trifled with.[61] And, equally, they may have been the product of the undoubted changes in the priorities and activities of the ministers and the members of the session.[62]

In the first place, the clergy became steadily less tolerant of sin. Until his death in 1581, the minister was Robert Hamilton, an early Reformer in the town. James Melville, who had returned to Fife in 1580 both to teach at the university and to serve as the minister of an adjacent parish, was not impressed. 'Efter the first zeall of the Reformation, in Mr Knox and Mr Guidmans dayes', he wrote in his *Diary*, 'the cauldnes of Mr Robert Ham-iltones ministerie, and [the] ignorance and negligence of tham that sould haiff teatched theologie' caused great backsliding and disorder. 'Yea it was evin a pitie to sie that ignorance and profannes that was amangs tham.' But worse was to come. After Hamilton's death there was a hiatus: for more than three years there was no resident incumbent. So James Melville and his uncle Andrew, a Geneva-trained minister and the Principal of the 'New College' (sc. St Mary's), decided to help out by preaching at the town church and by stiffening the backbone of the session. The upsurge of business recorded in the *Register* in 1582–4 (see pp 20–3 below) is clearly a reflection of their efforts. But before long there was another reflection: some of their par-ishioners decided to drive the Melvilles out. For a 'grait space', wrote James, 'ther was na thing bot affixing of plackarts upon the Collage yett [gate], bosting with batoning, burning and chaffing out of the town'. James Melville confessed that he was afraid, but his uncle Andrew was made of sterner stuff. He passed immediately on to the offensive and accused the town magistrates of deliberately keeping the town church vacant, so that they could spend its revenues themselves on 'the goff, archerie, guid cheir etc'; and in his sermons he excoriated all who opposed him. From the pulpit one day he told James Learmonth of Balcomie, a somewhat dissolute gentleman who was identified as the author of one of the placards that threatened 'batoning', that he would be punished for his lechery by having no legitimate offspring, and for his threats by being one day beaten to death himself. (Both prophecies, we are assured, eventually came true.) On another occasion, one of Melville's tirades from the pulpit caused the town Provost to 'ryse out of his seatt in the middes of the sermont, and with sum muttering of words to go to the dure out throw the middes of the peiple'.[63]

Yet, in the end, Melville emerged clearly victorious. Before long, 'convicted in his conscience, the said Provest maid publict satisfaction be acknawlaging of his offence, and craving God and the congregation forgiffnes'; and the town council then agreed to the appointment of a new minister. Although plague struck the town with unusual severity in 1585–6, during which time (according to the session clerk) 'all gude ordour cessit in this citee', it merely

TABLE 4
ACTIVITY OF THE ST ANDREWS KIRK-SESSION

Session	Meetings	Session	Meetings
1573–4	27	1586–7	41
1574–5	20	1587–8	24
1575–6	14	1588–9	37
1576–7	18	1589–91*	49
1577–8	12	1591–3*	83
1578–9	23	1593–4	35
1579–81*	28	1594–5	17
1581–2	36	1595–7*	42
1582–3	36	1597–8	52
1583–4	45	1598–9	62
1584–5	31	1599–1600	23
1585–6	11		

* = session serving for two years

served as a prelude to a moral crusade in the town immediately afterwards.[64] The campaign began with the decision, on 19 October 1586, 'that ane generall delatioun be takin throch the haill town of the offendaris of Goddis Law' and was pressed home with rigour and determination by both ministers and elders for over a decade.[65]

Robert Bruce, minister from 1589, was (according to James Melville) 'maist confortable to the guid and godlie, and maist ferfull to the enemies ... The godlie, for his puissant and maist moving doctrine, lovit him; the worldings for his parentage and place reverenced him; and the enemies for bathe stude in aw of him'.[66] David Black, who came in 1590 as a second parish minister, was able to stop even the king in his tracks. The doubling of the permanent resident clergy of the time was also, of itself, an important stage in implementing godly rule. But the session, too, increased both the number of its meetings and the size of its membership. Although there were, in all, 812 meetings of the various elected sessions of St Andrews between 1573 and 1600, almost half of them took place in the 1590s. Moreover, in 1593, the 14 elders were increased to 39, and the quarters of the parish from 4 to 12.[67]

The explosion of disciplinary business during the 1590s (see p 23) was of course related both to the institution of new ministers and to the increased activity of the session; but perhaps of more importance was the presence among the elders of Andrew Melville, now Rector of the university and (in the words of R G Cant) 'the figure around whom the whole life of the city and university and most of that of Scotland revolved'.[68] He appeared on the session for the first time in January 1591, and was re-elected four times until October 1597.[69]

During the Melville years, 'profanation of the Lord's day' was rigorously punished: of the 281 sabbath-breakers hauled before the session between 1573 and 1600, no less than 191 (68 per cent) appeared after 1591. Likewise, of the 175 accused of slander and scandal, the majority—131 (75 per cent)—appeared during the last decade, and all but 4 of the 35 persons convicted of drunkenness and riot appeared after 1594. 'Swearing, blasphemy and cursing', which appear to have diminished according to the *Register*, were in fact dealt with after October 1596 in a different way. Each elder and deacon was now empowered to impose a summary fine on all who 'sueriis, banis or takis Godis name in vane' in their hearing. Those who refused to pay on the spot could have their goods impounded, and those who tried to oppose this could be 'incarcerat'. The new vigilantes were issued with a special purse in which to collect the fines, and from time to time the proceeds were paid over to the church treasurer.[70]

Sexual offenders were also dealt with differently under the new regime. The savage and exemplary penalties of 1593–4 for adultery and fornication have already been noted (pages 13–14 above). They did not stand alone. From 1593, all fornicators were required to pay punitive fines: the full rigour of the 1567 Statute was now to be enforced—£40 for the first offence, or 8 days in prison, and double for a relapse.[71] The records show that this penalty was exacted at first; but then something remarkable happened. Fornication in St Andrews seems to have ceased! Although 28 persons were disciplined in 1594 (which was itself a drop from the 50 to 60 persons annually of the pre-Melvillian era), there was only one each in 1595 and 1596. Adultery, too, almost disappeared from the *Register* between 1594 and 1597.

There are four possible explanations for this striking development. The first is that, with the penalties increased to such draconian levels, neighbours were reluctant to delate, or elders to prosecute, persons who were manifestly unable to pay such heavy fines.[72] But this ignores the fact that most fornication cases began with the birth of an illegitimate child, which was exceedingly difficult to conceal. Furthermore, 'concealing sin' was itself also liable to a heavy fine. The second possibility is that spinsters who suspected they were pregnant might leave the parish in good time, in order to avoid fine and humiliation. But this too, is rendered improbable by the common practice of kirk-sessions in sending back unmarried mothers to the parish where their 'sin' had been committed.[73] Third, it is conceivable that Melville and his fellow elders suddenly backed off in response to popular hostility to their policies. Certainly in the summer of 1592 there was a 'maist dangerus uproar and tumult of the peiple of St Andros against Mr Andro' following the accidental shooting of a local man in Butts Wynd by a college student practising archery. The 'wicked, malitius misrewlars of the town' [sc. the magistrates] seized the opportunity to attack Melville's main powerbase, ringing the town alarm bell and inciting the assembled multitude to break down the outer door of the College. A mob got as far as the main rooms, calling for fire, before the tumult was stilled. But the opposition endured. In 1597, one of Melville's most devoted followers was deliberately slain by a group of opponents as he walked in the country.[74] But had these unpleasant events led the session to reduce its vigour, the effect would have been visible in all areas of its disciplinary work; instead of which, although sexual cases dramatically diminished, other categories (as we have seen) soared.

So the most likely explanation for the relative absence of sexual offences in these years, improbable though it may seem, appears to be that fornication, adultery and the rest had become too dangerous a risk in St Andrews, and that a genuine 'reformation of manners' took place in the burgh.[75] There was certainly a similar change in the case of Sunday observance because, in the summer of 1600, the session proudly noted that 'the peopill convenis sua frequentlie to preaching that the kirk may nocht convenientlie containe thame', and the university chapel had to be opened as an overflow church for the town.[76]

By then, however, the Melvillian period in St Andrews was over. In 1596 and 1597 the extreme presbyterian party was defeated in the General Assembly; while David Black, having called the king's mother a whore and Elizabeth Tudor an atheist, was deprived of his ministry and Andrew Melville was dismissed as Rector and removed from the kirk-session. Their work, however, was not undone. The same General Assembly in 1596 ordered a session to be created in every parish of the kingdom, with order to 'strik nocht onlie upon gros sinnes, as hurdome, blodshed etc., bot upon all sinnes repugnant to the Word of God, as blasphemie of Gods nam, swearing in vean, banning, profaning the sabathe, disobedience to parents, idle unrewlie annes [ones] without calling, drunkards, and sic lyk ...' It seems a perfect description of the recent work of the St Andrews kirk-session, and now it was 'to be an universall rewll throuchout the realme'. James Melville noted it all in his journal with deep satisfaction.[77]

And, except during the Cromwellian occupation of the 1650s, the ecclesiastical tribunals of Scotland remained supreme until the mid eighteenth century when first a serious schism in the church (the 'Great Secession'), then spectacular improvements in transport, and finally industrial growth began to erode traditional society and its values.[78] Of course, the work of the church courts was seconded by the provision of sound Christian dogma and doctrine, over almost all the kingdom, via schools, universities, sermons and catechisms. And it was through education as well as discipline that most Scots came to accept that intercourse would take place only between married partners, and the practice of handfasting, whereby parties cohabited as soon as they were betrothed, entirely died out. Even insults came to be exchanged less readily, for slanderous accusations had become too expensive for rash utterance. But the sanction of the courts, lay and ecclesiastical, had played a crucial role.

Needless to say, Scotland was not alone in her attempt to enforce godly discipline and inward piety. Almost every state in Europe possessed some sort of Inquisition to enforce Christian standards of behaviour as well as Christian articles of belief: the 'bawdy courts' of England, the *Consistoire* in Geneva, the *Kyrkoråd* in Sweden, the Holy Office in Italy and Spain.[79] But where Scotland excelled them all was in the intensity of control exercised by her church courts. Even the tribunals of the Spanish Inquisition, each monitoring the actions of up to half a million people, only resolved 20 or 30 cases a year.[80] Most Scottish kirk-sessions, although they had seldom more than 3,000 parishioners, dealt with far more!

Thanks to this intensity, godly discipline had a further unexpected but highly significant influence on the long-term development of Scotland. In St Andrews, the session in the 1590s helped to turn a sort of 'Montaillou-sur-mer' into a strict, restrained and eminent university town. That achievement was never lost, and alongside the parallel work of the church courts in countless other parishes maintained thoughout most of the seventeenth century (and sometimes both before and after), it played a crucial part in grooming the kingdom for its future role as a major industrial power. By accustoming the work-force to social discipline, and by stressing the value of order, restraint and hard work, the Reformed Kirk unwittingly became the handmaiden of nascent capitalism. It may have tamed Scotland for another, higher, purpose; but Scotland was tamed all the same.[81]

APPENDIX

The disciplinary work of the St Andrews Kirk-session 1573–1600

I. SEXUAL OFFENCES

	FORNICATION		ANTE-NUPTUAL		ADULTERY		INCEST	
	M	F	M	F	M	F	M	F
1573	10	10	2	2	2	2	1	1
1574	2	3	1	2	5	4	0	0
1575	6	5	2	2	1	0	0	0
1576	3	4	0	0	0	0	0	0
1577	6	5	1	2	2	2	0	0
1578	2	7	0	0	0	0	0	0
1579	5	10	1	1	1	2	0	0
1580	15	18	0	1	0	2	0	0
1581	6	5	0	0	3	2	0	0
1582	12	12	4	4	1	0	0	0
1583	20	23	0	0	1	0	1	0
1584	40	41	2	3	5	4	0	0
1585	10	13	2	3	1	1	0	0
1586	18	23	1	1	0	1	1	1
1587	29	33	2	2	6	4	0	0
1588	20	20	2	2	1	1	0	0
1589	31	30	1	1	2	1	0	0
1590	33	38	1	2	4	4	0	0
1591	23	26	0	0	2	3	0	0
1592	11	14	1	0	3	2	0	0
1593	26	28	1	1	2	2	0	0
1594	12	16	0	0	1	1	0	0
1595	1	0	0	0	1	1	0	0
1596	1	0	1	1	0	1	0	0
1597	4	1	0	1	1	1	0	0
1598	14	16	0	0	2	2	0	0
1599	16	11	2	2	6	6	0	0
1600	13	12	2	1	1	2	0	0
Total	389	424	29	34	54	51	3	2
Total	813		63		105		5	

II. DISORDERLY CONDUCT

	SABBATH BREACH		SLANDER & SCANDAL		DRINK & RIOT		OTHER	
	M	F	M	F	M	F	M	F
1573	5	0	1	1	0	0	0	0
1574	27	0	0	1	1	0	0	0
1575	2	0	3	1	1	0	0	0
1576	20	2	1	2	0	0	0	0
1577	0	1	1	1	0	0	1	0
1578	0	0	0	0	2	0	0	0
1579	0	0	1	2	0	0	2	0
1580	0	0	1	1	0	0	0	0
1581	0	0	2	1	0	0	0	0
1582	22	0	2	0	0	0	0	0
1583	5	0	0	3	0	0	0	0
1584	0	0	2	1	0	0	0	0
1585	0	0	0	0	0	0	0	0
1586	0	0	1	1	0	0	0	0
1587	0	0	1	2	0	0	0	0
1588	0	0	2	0	0	0	0	0
1589	1	0	0	0	0	0	0	0
1590	5	0	3	6	0	0	0	0
1591	6	0	1	5	0	0	1	0
1592	1	0	1	1	0	0	0	0
1593	6	0	2	0	0	0	0	0
1594	37	5	8	0	10	0	0	0
1595	11	4	11	2	0	0	0	0
1596	13	1	6	2	6	0	0	0
1597	13	8	5	7	0	1	1	0
1598	17	3	18	7	10	0	0	0
1599	28	10	28	9	1	0	2	0
1600	26	2	17	1	3	0	1	0
Total	245	36	118	57	34	1	8	0
Total	281		175		35		8	

III. OTHER BUSINESS

	OTHER		CHARITY		MARRIAGE		AUTHORITY	
	M	F	M	F	M	F	M	F
1573	3	3	0	1	1	0	3	2
1574	10	1	0	0	0	0	1	0
1575	5	0	0	0	0	0	4	0
1576	2	2	0	0	0	0	0	1
1577	6	4	0	0	1	0	0	0
1578	0	2	0	0	1	0	0	0
1579	1	0	0	0	0	0	0	0
1580	1	0	0	0	0	0	0	0
1581	1	1	0	0	1	0	0	2
1582	3	4	0	0	0	0	2	0
1583	8	1	0	0	0	1	0	0
1584	0	4	0	0	1	0	0	0
1585	0	2	1	0	2	0	0	0
1586	1	4	0	0	0	0	1	0
1587	9	5	0	0	1	0	1	0
1588	2	3	1	0	0	0	0	0
1589	2	2	0	0	2	0	0	0
1590	3	1	0	0	0	2	0	0
1591	1	2	0	0	0	0	2	0
1592	3	3	0	0	0	1	0	0
1593	5	4	0	0	0	0	0	0
1594	2	0	0	0	0	0	2	0
1595	3	3	0	0	0	2	4	2
1596	0	1	0	0	0	0	4	1
1597	2	0	3	1	0	0	0	0
1598	4	2	1	0	0	0	2	0
1599	6	1	11	5	0	1	0	0
1600	3	1	6	5	0	0	1	0
Total	86	56	23	12	10	6	30	8
Total	142		35		16		38	

IV. ANNUAL TOTAL OF ALL BUSINESS

	ADMINISTRATIVE CASES	DISCIPLINE
1573	11	55
1574	12	60
1575	5	32
1576	5	37
1577	5	42
1578	2	14
1579	4	26
1580	1	39
1581	8	24
1582	13	67
1583	15	65
1584	20	103
1585	4	35
1586	12	51
1587	14	85
1588	10	54
1589	17	73
1590	11	102
1591	9	71
1592	2	41
1593	11	77
1594	10	94
1595	6	45
1596	14	38
1597	45	50
1598	50	102
1599	19	137
1600	26	97
Total	361	1716

NOTES

This paper was originally prepared for a workshop on the History of Crime organised by Jan Sundin and held at Stockholm in 1983. I should like to thank the other members of the workshop—Jan Sundin, Bruce Lenman, Ken Lockridge, Birgit Petersen, Heinz Schilling, Marja Taussi Sjöberg and Martin Vejbrink—for their invaluable assistance; and Jane Dawson, James K Cameron, Leah Leneman, R N Smart, T C Smout and David Underdown for further helpful suggestions. I am also most grateful to Nancy Wood for research assistance. Finally, I have learned much from the students of St Andrews University to whom I taught Scottish Reformation history, and in particular from James Pratt, who graduated in 1986 and was killed in a mountain accident only one year later. I would like to dedicate this paper to his memory.

1   *The Diary of Mr James Melvill, 1556–1601* (Edinburgh 1829: Bannatyne Club, vol XXXIV), pp 188–9 and 195. There is another edition of Melville's holograph manuscript (in the National Library of Scotland): R Pitcairn (ed). *The autobiography and diary of Mr James Melville* (Edinburgh 1842: Wodrow Society, vol III). All quotations that follow are, however, from the 1829 edition.

2   H Scott, *Fasti ecclesiae scotticanae*, V (Edinburgh 1925), p 177ff, gives the exact size of the parishes in and around St Andrews. Cameron was disjoined from St Andrews in 1646; Strathkinness and Boarhills in the nineteenth century. The parish of St Leonards, inside the burgh, was used by all members of the university and was entirely separate from St Andrews parish.

3   The first true census for the parishes of Fife, compiled in 1755, gave St Andrews a population of 5,877 persons: see J G Kyd, *Scottish Population statistics including Webster's analysis of the population since 1755* (Edinburgh 1952: Scottish History Society, third series, vol XL), pp 38–41, combined total for St Andrews and Cameron parishes. Attempting a back-projection from this figure is hazardous, but might be attempted along the following lines. Webster judged that the parish in 1755 possessed 1,177 'fighting men', aged between 18 and 56 years. The record of those who subscribed to the 1643 Solemn League and Covenant in the parish of St Andrews contains 985 names. Of these, 140 were members of the university and therefore belonged to the parish of St Leonards, reducing the total for St Andrews parish to 845. Since only adult males were included among the subscribers, it seems reasonable to suppose that the 845 might be roughly equated with Webster's category of 'fighting men'. Using Webster's carefully calculated ratio of fighting men to the total population, (1 : 5) a parish of some 4,250 is indicated for the year 1643. (See the list in St Andrews University Archives, Typ/BE.C43 TSS2: *A solemne League and Covenant* [Edinburgh 1643], 15–43.) Continuing backwards, the earliest surviving tax record for St Andrews, the burgh stent-roll for 1618, contained the names of 486 householders, but covers only the burgh, not the parish, and omits those who (like all university personnel) were exempt from taxation. If we assume 5 persons to have constituted the average household, the population of the burgh proper in 1618 may have approached 2,500. (St Andrews University Archives: MS B65/20/3.) Happily, these tentative calculations are supported by a letter from the ecclesiastical historian David Calderwood, written to the archbishop of St Andrews in 1615,

which claimed 'there are in fact more than 3,000 regular communicants' in the parish (quoted by D Hay Fleming [ed], *Register of the minister, elders and deacons of the Christian congregation of St Andrews, comprising the proceedings of the kirk-session and of the superintendent of Fife, Fothrik and Strathearn, 1559–1600* (2 vols, Edinburgh 1889–90: Scottish History Society, vols I–II), II, p lxxiv.

4   See J M Anderson (ed), *Early records of the university of St Andrews* (Edinburgh 1926: Scottish History Society, third series, vol III), pp 154–9 and 262–72, for matriculation and graduation rolls during the period 1556–65. These reveal that no graduation ceremony could be held in 1559–60, on account of the troubles, and record very few graduates from then until 1565. Matriculations were more or less halved during 1560–63, while in 1559 the record states '*Hoc anno, propter tumultus religionis ergo exortos, paucissimi scholastici ad hanc universitatem venerunt*' (p 266). The plague of 1585–6 is recorded in Melville's *Diary*, pp 148, 162.

5   John Calvin, *Institutes of the Christian Religion*, 4th edn (Geneva 1559: English translation by J T McNeill, London, 1961), Book IV, chap 12; and *Ordonnances ecclésiastiques* (Geneva 1541), chap 10, 1.

6   See A C Duke, 'The ambivalent face of Calvinism in the Netherlands, 1561–1618' in M Prestwich (ed), *International Calvinism 1541–1715* (Oxford 1985) pp 109–34, especially pp 130f; and H Schilling, 'Reformierte Kirchenzucht als Socialdisziplinierung. Die Tätigkeit des Emder Presbyteriums in den Jahren 1557–62' in W Ehbrecht and H Schilling (eds), *Niederlande und Nordwestdeutschland* (Cologne/Vienna 1983), pp 261–327.

7   See the accounts given by R M Kingdom, 'The control of morals in Calvin's Geneva' in L P Buck and J W Zophy (eds). *The social history of the Reformation* (Columbus 1972), pp 5–16; and E W Monter, 'The consistory of Geneva, 1559–69', *Bibliothèque d'humanisme et renaissance*, XXXVIII (1976), pp 467–84. See also the important discussion of J K Cameron, 'Scottish Calvinism and the principle of intolerance' in B A Gerrish and R Benedetto (eds), *Reformatio perennis: essays on Calvin and the Reformation in honor of F L Battles* (Pittsburgh 1981), pp 113–28.

8   'The forme of prayers and ministration of the sacraments' of 1556 was published in D Laing (ed), *The works of John Knox*, IV (Edinburgh 1855), 155–214—see especially pp 203–6: 'The order of ecclesiasticall discipline': and the 'Answer to a great nomber of blasphemous cavillations' of 1559, in *ibid*, vol V (Edinburgh 1856), pp 17–468—see pp 208–32 on the need to punish; the Scots 'Confession of faith', chapter XVIII, in W C Dickinson (ed), *John Knox's history of the Reformation in Scotland* (2 vols, Edinburgh 1949), vol II, pp 266–7. It is worth noting that both Luther and Calvin had seen only two (not three) 'marks' of the true church—right teaching of the gospel and right administration of the sacraments.

9   J K Cameron (ed), *The first book of discipline* (Edinburgh 1972), pp 165–6, 173: 'The Seventh head: of ecclesiastical discipline'.

10 Orkney church records (Orkney County Library, Kirkwall), 23/1, p 148: Minute of the kirk-session of Shapinsay, 24 June 1649. Mistress Greeg had correctly informed two people of the whereabouts of a blanket lost a long time before she came to the island: her success as a diviner was her undoing.

11 Quoted in J di Folco, 'Discipline and welfare in the mid seventeenth century Scots parish' *Records of the Scottish Church History Society*, XIX (1977), pp 169–83, at p 176. The burgh of Auchtermuchty was apparently riven by dissent throughout the 1640s and 1650s—among the elders, between the minister and some of

his elders, and between the session and a group of parishioners. See further details in *ibid*, pp 176–7.

12   Scottish Record Office, Edinburgh, [hereafter SRO] CH2/722/6, entries in the register of the presbytery of Stirling for 1 and 8 October 1656; 26 January 1659, 20 March 1661; and CH2/722/7, entries for 21 September 1664, and 29 April, 22 July, 22 August, 16 September, and 18 November 1668. This case was generously brought to my attention by Dr Stephen J Davies of Manchester Polytechnic.

13   See the example of an Edinburgh delinquent pursued in 1653–5 by letter to Aberdeenshire whither she had fled in hope of avoiding censure, in L M Smith, 'Scotland and Cromwell: a study in early modern government'. Unpublished PhD thesis, Oxford University, 1980, p 236. See also W Mackay (ed), *Records of the presbyteries of Inverness and Dingwall, 1643–1688* (Edinburgh 1896: Scottish History Society, vol XXIV), pp 60, 84: the case of William McPherson, in 1675, 'adulterer and thereafter fornicator in Inverness, haveing appeared several yeares *in sacco*, evidenceing his publick remorse for his said gross sins, supplicated the presbytery [of Inverness] to be absolved.' But the assembled ministers seemed to feel that a few further years in sackcloth were called for, and the petition was refused. So in 1677 the unfortunate man went away to Holland to become a soldier: possible death at the hands of the Catholic French must have appeared preferable to endless humiliation before his fellow-parishioners.

14   The most influential account of the 'bawdy courts' of Reformation England is that of C Hill, *Society and Puritanism in pre-revolutionary England* (London 1964), chap 8. Subsequent research, however, has not endorsed his negative, unsympathetic account. See, for example, P Collinson, *The religion of Protestants* (Oxford 1982), pp 62–70; R Houlbrooke, *Church courts and the people during the English Reformation, 1520–1570* (Oxford 1979); M J Ingram, *Church Courts, sex and marriage in England, 1570–1640* (Cambridge 1987); S Lander, 'Church courts and the Reformation in the diocese of Chichester 1500–1558' in C Haigh (ed), *The English Reformation revisited* (Cambridge 1987), chap 2; R B Manning, *Religion and society in Elizabethan Sussex* (Leicester 1969); R A Marchant, *The church under the Law: justice administration and discipline in the diocese of York, 1560–1640* (Cambridge 1972); and J A Sharpe, 'Crime and delinquency in an Essex parish 1600–1640' in J S Cockburn (ed), *Crime in England 1550–1800* (London 1975), chap 4.

15   Quoted in *Knox's History of the Reformation*, II, p 49. The petition continued with a vintage piece of Knoxian moral blackmail: 'and seing that kings are but His lieutenants, having no power to give life where [God] commands death, … so will He not fail to punish you for neglecting his judgements'.

16   Details from T Thomson (ed), *Acts of the Parliaments of Scotland*, II (Edinburgh 1814), p 539; III (Edinburgh 1814), pp 24–5, 38; and B Lenman and G Parker, 'The state, the community and the criminal law in early modern Europe' in V A C Gatrell, B Lenman and G Parker (eds), *Crime and the Law. The social history of crime in western Europe since 1500* (London 1980), pp 11–48, at p 37. Interestingly enough, persons convicted of sodomy and bestiality were also executed but without a statute to that effect ever having been passed! It was the opinion of one great eighteenth-century Scots lawyer that they were tried and condemned solely on the basis of the book of Leviticus: see J Erskine, *An institute of the laws of Scotland* (1773; revised edn, Edinburgh 1838), p 1105.

17   From 1599 onwards, for example, the kirk-session of Glasgow resolved that the persons elected as provost and bailies of the burgh should always be enrolled among the elders. See G Donaldson, *Scotland: James V–James VII* (Edinburgh 1971), p 225.

18 See S J Davies, 'Law and order in Stirlingshire, 1638–1747'. Unpublished PhD thesis, St Andrews University, 1983, chap 4. It is worth noting that the baron courts had also supported ecclesiastical jurisdiction *before* the Reformation. In 1529, for example, all tenants of the barony of Alloway were ordered to accept any censures imposed by the church within forty days, and anyone condemned by the church for adultery was automatically to lose their land (see M H B Sanderson, *Scottish rural society in the sixteenth century* [Edinburgh 1982], p 12). Statutes against adultery had also been passed, for example in 1551, but the penalty was only outlawry: see the important discussion in J Wormald, ' "Princes" and the regions in the Scottish Reformation' in N A T MacDougall (ed), *Church, Politics and Society: Scotland 1408–1929* (Edinburgh 1983) pp 65–84, especially at p 82 n 34.

19 SRO CH2/983/1, p 1: minutes of the parishes of Cromdale, Inverallen and Advie, 14 Dec. 1702; G and C B Gunn (eds), *Records of the Baron Court of Stitchill, 1655–1807* (Edinburgh 1905: Scottish History Society, vol L), p 21: declaration of 26 Nov. 1660—sc. directly after the restoration of Charles II. For further examples, and some excellent general remarks, see B P Lenman, 'The limits of godly discipline in the early modern period, with particular reference to England and Scotland' in K von Greyerz (ed), *Religion and society in early modern Europe 1500–1800* (London 1984), pp 124–45.

20 See the perceptive remarks of Lenman, 'The limits of godly discipline...' p 135f. The examples in the text come from I B Cowan, 'Church and society in Post-Reformation Scotland', *Records of the Scottish Church History Society*, XVII (1971), pp 185–201; and di Folco, 'Discipline and welfare', p 171.

21 J Stuart (ed), *Selections from the Records of the Kirk-session, presbytery and synod of Aberdeen* (Aberdeen 1846: Spalding Club, vol XV), p 121. Mr Gordon was sent to the presbytery and was there excommunicated for papism and disobedience.

22 On these policy changes see L M Smith, 'Scotland and Cromwell', chap 9; and *idem*, 'Sackcloth for the sinner or punishment for the crime? Church and secular courts in Cromwellian Scotland' in J Dwyer, R A Mason and A Murdoch (eds), *New perspectives on the politics and culture of early modern Scotland* (Edinburgh 1982), pp 116–32.

23 For three admirable studies of the working of the kirk in its prime, see D Henderson, *The Scottish ruling elder* (London 1935), especially pp 100–45; W R Foster, *The church before the Covenants 1596–1638* (Edinburgh 1972), chaps 4 and 5; and W H Makey, *The church and the Covenant, 1638–1651* (Edinburgh 1978), *passim*.

24 T Burns, *Church property: the benefice lectures* (Edinburgh 1905), pp 1–65 and 193–268 (a list of church records then extant).

25 Calculated from P Rayner, B Lenman and G Parker, *Handlist of records for the study of crime in early modern Scotland (to 1747)* (London 1982: List and Index Society, Special series, vol XVI), pp 158–259. These totals include only volumes deposited, in or before 1979, in the Scottish Record Office or in New Register House. It is thought that a further 130 or so kirk-session records dating from before 1750 are extant in private hands.

26 David Hay Fleming's edition of the Register (hereafter cited as *Register*: see full citation in note 3) omitted only some of the coarser exchanges between various sinners and the session. They were indicated by dots ... Volume I covers the years 1559–82 and Volume II covers 1582–1600.

27 Five volumes cover the period 1638–1706 in some 1600 folios: H M Register House, Edinburgh, OPR 453/5–9. See also the parallel to Melville's diary:

T McCrie (ed), *The Life of Mr Robert Blair, minister of St Andrews, containing his autobiography* (Edinburgh 1848: Wodrow Society, vol XIII). The original register for 1559–1600, filling some 300 folios, is still conserved at Holy Trinity church in St Andrews.

28   My thanks to Dr Jane Dawson, who communicated to me the results of her own research on the Reformation in St Andrews.

29   See *Register*, I, pp xxvii–xxxv for details. The work of the superintendents is covered by D G Mullan, *Episcopacy in Scotland: the history of an idea, 1560–1638* (Edinburgh 1986), chaps 2–3.

30   For details on the commissary courts before, during and after the Reformation, see G Donaldson, 'The Church Courts' in *An introduction to Scottish Legal History* (Edinburgh 1958: Stair Society, vol XX), pp 363–73. On page 366 there is an interesting analysis of the business handled by the commissary courts of Scotland in the first half of the sixteenth century: around one-third were appeals from lower courts and, of the rest, about one-third concerned wills, one-quarter broken contracts, and one-fifth church property. The role of sex and slander cases, which became the staple of church courts after the Reformation, was negligible before 1560. In England, however, over 80 per cent of the cases heard by the London Consistory Court between 1470 and 1516 concerned either sex or slander: see R Wunderli, *London church courts and society on the eve of the Reformation* (Cambridge, Mass., 1981), p 81.

31   G Donaldson, *The Scottish Reformation* (Cambridge 1960), chap 3. John Carswell was both superintendent of Argyll and apostolic bishop of the Isles: see D E Meek and J Kirk, 'John Carswell, superintendent of Argyll: a reassessment', *Records of the Scottish church history society*, XIX (1975), pp 1–22. For the hesitant installation of the Reformation in other towns of the kingdom, see I B Cowan, *The Scottish Reformation: church and society in sixteenth-century Scotland* (London 1982), chap 8; M Lynch, *Edinburgh and the Reformation* (Edinburgh 1981), *passim*; *idem*, 'From privy kirk to burgh church: an alternative view of the process of Protestantisation' in N A T MacDougall (ed), *Church, politics and society: Scotland 1408–1929* (Edinburgh 1983), chap 5; A White, 'The impact of the Reformation on a burgh community: the case of Aberdeen' in M Lynch (ed), *The early modern town in Scotland* (London 1987), chap 4; and C H Haws, *Scottish parish clergy at the Reformation, 1540–74* (Edinburgh 1972: Scottish Record Society, vol III).

32   *Register*, I, pp 5–6 (adultery: the second case, concerning William Rantoun and Margaret Aidnam, lasted several months because Rantoun accused his own wife of adultery. John Knox, as minister, pronounced sentence. See *ibid*, pp 18–27). See also *ibid*, p 36 (first fornication) and p 294ff (sabbath-breach).

33   *Diary of James Melville*, p 46 (on the witch) and p 26 (on Knox being virtually carried up into the pulpit, where he reached the height of his oratorical powers only after about half an hour of warming up).

34   See Donaldson, *Scottish Reformation*, pp 171, 176, 183.

35   *Register*, I, pp 377–8. The fine was to be half the hiring-fee agreed between master and servant; since servants made up the largest single category of sexual offenders, this measure was of considerable importance.

36   The General Assembly of the Church ordained in 1573 that no minister 'may dispence with the extremitie of sack-cloth prescryvit be the acts of the generall discipline, for any pecuniall sowme' (quoted *Register*, I, p lii).

37   *Register*, I, pp 373–4.

38   Quoted in Foster, *Church before the covenants*, p 72.

39 See the tables in S J Davies, 'Law and Order in Stirlingshire', chap 4. For the close resemblance between St Andrews and Nîmes, over 1,000 miles away, see the exemplary study of R A Mentzer, '*Disciplina nervus ecclesiae:* The Calvinist reform of morals at Nîmes', *The sixteenth century journal*, XVIII (1987), pp 89–115. There are further (somewhat fragmentary) data on southern French (and west German) Calvinist church courts in J Estèbe and B Vogler, 'La genèse d'une société protestante: étude comparée de quelques régistres consistoriaux languedociens et palatins vers 1600', *Annales: économies, sociétés, civilizations*, XXXI (1976), pp 362–88. A detailed analysis of the copious surviving records of the Geneva *Consistoire* would be of great interest. At present we have only the pioneering study of Monter, 'The consistory of Geneva'.

40 Calculated from *Register*, pp 373–943. Annual totals are given in the appendix, pp 20–3 above. The total in Table 3 excludes 361 items of administrative business handled during the period.

41 *Register*, I, pp 392–4. John Chaeplan *contra* Jonet Lawsoun, 19 May and 9 June 1584.

42 Generalisation based on the survey conducted by Rayner, Lenman and Parker for the *Handlist* (see note 25 above).

43 It might be supposed that the picture would be affected by the presence of numerous university students in the town; but this does not appear to have been the case, for all university persons were subject to the discipline of their own officers alone. Students therefore are very rarely found among those tried by the kirk-session.

44 *Register*, I, p 449.

45 Quoted by S J Davies, 'The courts and the Scottish Legal System, 1600–1747: the case of Stirlingshire' in Gatrell, Lenman and Parker, *Crime and the Law*, pp 120–54, at p 125.

46 The text of the oath was standard: see an example in Davies, 'Law and Order', chap 4.

47 *Register*, II, p 656.

48 See, for an example, *Register*, II, p 523: case of Christene Mwir, 18 March 1584, 'quha grantis that sche, the xvij day of Marche instant [sic], in the nicht, past outwith the South Gait Port of this citee, and thair committit the filthy crime of adultrie with James Neilsoun'. The record notes a previous adultery with Andrew, earl of Rothes, which produced a bastard child. The case was therefore referred to the presbytery. For some similar examples, see L Leneman and R Mitchison, 'Girls in trouble. The social and geographical setting of illegitimacy in early modern Scotland', *Journal of social history* vol 21, No. 3, 1988, pp 483–97; and G R Quaife, *Wanton wenches and wayward wives. Peasants and illicit sex in early seventeenth century England* (London 1979), pp 48–56.

49 Sir William Brereton, *Travels in Holland, the United Provinces, England, Scotland and Ireland* (London 1844: Chetham Society, vol. I), p 107. The Aberdeen 'stool' was certainly capable of seating seven at a time—women and men on alternate days of course (see the fascinating study of A I Ritchie, *Churches of St Baldred: Auldhame, Whitekirk, Tyninghame, Prestonkirk* [Edinburgh 1880], p 86).

50 Ritchie, *Churches of St Baldred*, p 86.

51 *Register*, II, p 850; see also the numerous index entries for 'imprisonment' on p 975.

52 *Register*, II, p 766. 'Jokin' seems to have been a penalty found especially suitable for women. At Tyninghame, a second set of jougs was erected by the magistrates at the church door, on the special request of the minister, because 'there war sae

many railers in the toun, especiallie women, and that they troublit the session sae aft'. See Ritchie, *Churches of St Baldred*, p 88.

53 *Register*, II, p 793. Cf. similar cases in March 1595 (p 794) and August 1596 (p 819).

54 It was the same in England: see J A Sharpe, *Defamation and sexual slander in early modern England: the church courts at York* (York 1980: Borthwick Papers, vol LVIII).

55 See a classic illustration in Ritchie, *Churches of St Baldred*, p 105: the bill for burning two witches on the sands at Kirkcaldy in 1633 was shared between the town (which paid £17 for 10 loads of coal, some tar and tows, and the executioner) and the kirk-session (which paid £17 for the other expenses). Although no witch-burnings are recorded in the St Andrews session register, one was burnt in 1571–2 (see p 8 above) and several women from Pittenweem were burnt at St Andrews in 1597 (see *Register*, II, p lxxviii).

56 *Register*, I, p 441: case of 24 September 1579 and II, pp 785–6: case of 17 April 1594.

57 *Register*, II, p lxxiif gives a fine selection of offences. See also the interesting paper by Leah Leneman, '"Prophaning" the Lord's Day. Sabbath breach in early modern Scotland', *History* (forthcoming).

58 It is an interesting curiosity that 245 of these offenders were men and only 36 were women. Since the same pattern appears in most other records subjected to analysis, it may be suggested that perhaps women were more disposed to respect the church's commands, in this respect, and to fulfil its requirements, than men. This phenomenon has been observed in other societies—see S H Brandes, *Migration, kinship and community: tradition and transition in a Spanish village* (London 1975), chap 8; and K V Thomas, 'Women and the Civil War Sects' in T S Aston (ed), *Crisis in Europe 1560–1660* (London 1965), chap 13—but not, so far as I am aware, in Scotland.

59 Stuart, *Selections from the records of the kirk-session of Aberdeen*, pp 62–3 (1608) and p 116 (1651) about covered faces; *Register*, II, p 806 (1595: 'na persoun sall cum to the stuill of repentance armit with sowrd nor gun'—nor indeed to the session). See also K M Brown, *Bloodfeud in Scotland, 1573–1625. Violence, justice and politics in an early modern society* (Edinburgh 1986), p 185f.

60 *Register*, II, pp 556–7 (James Lermonth, heir to the barony of Balcomie, alleged that he did not live in the parish of St Andrews, 28 April 1585; it was one of his many appearances for various forms of sexual misconduct. See also p 15 above); and II, pp 547–9 (Jhone Cambell's 'dispytful and opprobrius wordis' to the session in December 1584). Note also the similar tensions and abuse in Auchtermuchty, somewhat later, recorded by di Folco, 'Discipline and welfare', pp 176–7.

61 Professor David Underdown has pointed out to me that precisely this happened at Dorchester in the early seventeenth century: following a great natural catastrophe—a fire that burnt down the town in 1613—some of the same laymen who had previously resisted the work of their Puritan minister suddenly became pliant and pious. I am most grateful to Professor Underdown for this preview from his forthcoming book on early modern Dorchester.

62 See Gatrell, Lenman and Parker, *Crime and the Law*, pp 4, 49–75, and 190–237 on the methodological problems posed by 'labelling' and by 'panic prosecutions' in the historical study of crime.

63 *Diary of James Melvill*, pp 89–90. Calvin had also faced a determined group of opponents among the magistrates of Geneva in 1552–3, but they were vanquished: see E W Monter, *Calvin's Geneva* (New York 1967), pp 82–88.

64 *Register*, II, p 559 n 4.
65 *Diary of James Melvill*, p 182.
66 *Register*, p 576
67 *Ibid*, pp 760–1. In 1599 it was changed to 19 quarters, with one elder and one deacon each (p 904).
68 R G Cant, *The university of St Andrews. A short history* 2nd edn (Edinburgh 1970), p 52.
69 *Ibid*, pp 694–5, 760–1, 788–92, 801–4. Two of these Melvillian sessions continued in office for two years apiece.
70 *Ibid*, p 821; see also pp 929, 942, 943.
71 *Ibid*, p 767.
72 Similar considerations clearly operated in eighteenth-century England with regard to the game-laws, after poaching became a capital offence: see D Hay and others, *Albion's fatal tree. Crime and society in eighteenth-century England* (London 1975), and E P Thompson, *Whigs and hunters. The origin of the Black Act* (London 1975).
73 See some English examples of 'girls in trouble' fleeing from the hostile parish in which they lived in K E Wrightson, 'The nadir of English illegitimacy in the seventeenth century' in P Laslett, K Oosterveen and R M Smith (eds), *Bastardy in its comparative history* (London 1980), pp 176–91. There was at least one good reason for firmness: unless the father of a bastard could be found, the parish might become responsible for its upkeep.
74 *Diary of James Melvill*, p 206.
75 It is a remarkable fact that bastardy seems to have reached a peak in several other countries of western Europe at precisely this time: D Levine and K E Wrightson, 'The social context of illegitimacy in early modern England' in Laslett, Oosterveen and Smith, *Bastardy and its comparative history*, pp 158–75 (for England), and M del C González Muñoz, *La población de Talavera, siglos XVI–XX* (Madrid 1975), p 109 (for Spain) both found an 'explosion of illegitimacy' in the 1590s. It is difficult to be absolutely sure what happened in St Andrews at this time because there is no usable register of births.
76 *Register*, II, pp 925–6. See also Leneman, 'Prophaning the Lord's Day'. There is some debate about the likelihood of short-run 'reformations of manners' in early modern times, however. Contrast D Levine and K E Wrightson, *Poverty and piety in an English village: Terling 1525–1700* (London 1979), who clearly found something of the sort in the Essex parish that they studied, with M J Ingram, 'Religion, communities and moral discipline in sixteenth and seventeenth-century England: case studies' in von Greyerz, *Religion and society*, pp 177–93, who looked carefully for parallels in other parishes but failed to locate any.
77 See *Diary of James Melvill*, p 231, and Donaldson, *Scottish Reformation*, p 222.
78 See the pertinent remarks of L Leneman and R Mitchison 'Scottish illegitimacy ratios in the early modern period', *Economic History Review*, 2nd series XL (1987), pp 41–63. However, it may be rash to attribute the end of church discipline in the mid eighteenth century entirely to extrinsic changes in the intellectual environment, such as the Enlightenment. There may also have been a change in the attitudes of church leaders on the necessity for discipline, as appears to have happened in the Calvinist city of Emden at the same time: see the tantalising remarks of H Schilling, ' "History of Crime" or "History of sin"? Some reflections on the social history of early modern church discipline' in E Kouri and T Scott (eds), *Politics and society in reformation Europe* (London 1987), pp 289–310, at p 299.

79   For Sweden, see J Sundin, 'Control, punishment and reconciliation. A case study of parish justice in Sweden before 1850' in A Brändström and J Sundin (eds), *Tradition and transition. Studies in microdemography and social change* (Umeå 1981), pp 9–65; for Germany, see L J Abray, *The people's reformation: magistrates, clergy and commons in Strasbourg, 1500–1598* (Oxford 1985), chap 8; Schilling, 'Reformierte Kirchenzucht'; and the sources cited in the notes to *idem*, ' "History of Crime".'

80   See sources cited in G Henningsen, J Tedeschi and C Amiel (eds), *The Inquisition in early modern Europe. Studies on sources and methods* (Dekalb 1986), p 121f; and G Parker, 'Some recent work on the Inquisition in Spain and Italy', *Journal of Modern History*, LIV (1982), pp 519–32.

81   The crucial importance of 'fundamental discipline', involving both secular and ecclesiastical institutions, in preparing Europe for rapid social and economic change was first highlighted by Gerhard Oestreich. See his studies, posthumously published in *Strukturprobleme der Neuzeit* (Berlin 1980) and *Neostoicism and the early modern state* (Cambridge 1982). See also the interesting remarks of Schilling, ' "History of Crime" ', p 293ff, and of V A C Gatrell in Gatrell, Lenman and Parker, *Crime and the Law*, p 300.

Food and Hierarchy in Scotland, 1550–1650

A Gibson and T C Smout

Among the classes of document of which Scottish historians have hitherto
made little use are details of the food and drink available in such institutions
as the court, the universities and charitable hospitals, provided either by
descriptions of formal allowances, or from kitchen accounts. In this paper
we want to examine a small number of such documents, not in order to make
a comprehensive study of Scottish food in the early modern period, but rather
to demonstrate a few of the insights on social history that they can be made
to yield.

I

The first document relates to the court of James VI and Anne of Denmark
and illustrates the anthropologists' aphorism that 'food is not feed'.[1] Food,
in addition to providing nutrition, is a social cement; a measure of proximity
and distance in a hierarchy; a demonstration of power and dependency. Many
years ago the Bannatyne Club published a document entitled 'The estate of
the king and quenis majesties houshold reformit, begynnand on monunday
the first day of februare, 1590', which detailed all the members of the court
from the monarch to the stable boys and then proceeded to relate 'the nowmer
and names to be servit at tables, and quantitie of ordinar allowance'.[2] It was
obviously intended to be a new dining plan for the royal family now that the
king was entering upon the married state. The context indicates that the food
allowances mentioned were what was to be consumed per day. The list began
with the king and queen and went down through a series of tables until it
ended with the names of humble 'personis havand onlie allowance of breid
and drink', like the Belman of the Canongait and the cleaners: 'twa dichtaris
of the clois'. The document mentions three kitchens, one cooking for the
king's table, one for the queen's and a third for the court at large. It is possible
to interpret this in various ways, but it seems likely that meals were normally
taken in three or perhaps four rooms (apart from what might actually have

33

been consumed in the kitchens or distributed from them outside the palace). One room would be the king's chamber, where the royal couple ate, evidently at two tables, with their closest attendants, or perhaps sometimes the king dined alone, with the queen in a separate chamber.[3] One room would be the general hall of the king's household. A clear distinction between the chamber and the hall, between the lord's room and the servants', is visible in English royal and noble households from the fourteenth century. Finally, there was the queen's master's householders' hall, explicitly so mentioned in the document, and evidently containing two main tables. It was obviously convenient in several respects to lay out the king's and queen's households as distinct entities, especially when the formal details of a royal marriage with all its mutual rights and obligations were being described.

The amplitude of the king's majesty was instantly demonstrated by the list of the viands at the king's table: twelve and a half 'breids' (each wheaten loaf would have weighed 19 ounces); ten Scots pints of wine and twelve of ale (each Scots pint being the equivalent of three English or Imperial pints); two pieces of beef (since an animal was divided into 48 pieces and perhaps carried on it 200 to 250 lbs of edible meat, each piece would have amounted to about 4 or 5 lbs), two pieces of roast mutton, two pieces of boiled mutton, two quarters of lamb, three pieces of 'greit' veal, four pieces of game, two poultry and six chickens. The dishes at the queen's table were inferior only in the basic quantities of bread and drink: seven breads, five pints of wine, ten pints of ale. For meat, she had a quarter of beef (or six pieces when there was fish), a side of mutton, two whole lambs and a suckling calf, two beef tongues, seven pieces of game, four poultry or eight chickens, two capons, a goose, nine doves, as well as a salmon, 40 apples and 80–100 eggs. Her dishes, with fish, eggs and tongue, are more varied than those of her consort, as though certain foods were regarded as more female: we get the same hint in another context when the English traveller Richard James describes porridge, 'of oate meale floure boilde in water, which they eate with buttermilke or ale', as a dish eaten 'by the common people and schoole children at breakfast and by Ladies allso'.[4]

The dishes of the king and queen were not, of course, intended for their majesties' nourishment alone. Once tasted they were available to others in the court, perhaps sitting in inferior halls. The point of their own gargantuan allowances was to demonstrate the royal command over resources, which they were then free to eat, waste or give away to guests or to their dependants. It is clear from the document that the spare food from the royal dishes descended in a chain. On the king's side, there was a 'gentlemen servandis table' at which the sitters were given bread, wine, ale and the right 'to eate on the Kingis Majesties rest'; four men of rank sat there, the almoner, the cup-bearer, the carver and the sewar (an official who superintended the arrangement of the table, the seating of the guests and the tasting and serving of the dishes). In turn, they were served by five servants who were given bread and ale and the right to 'eate on the rest thairof'. We thus see a hierarchy of three tables. It was exactly the same on the queen's side, where 'the first table in the quenis maister houshaldis hall' was 'to eate on the quenis rest'. There were ten men here, including the carver, the preacher (who would have been the queen's private Lutheran chaplain brought over from Denmark under the terms of the marriage settlement), the secretary, the usher and the tailor. They were served by the queen's four pages, her three lackeys and two other people, who ate in turn on their rests. All, however, were given their own separate allowance of bread and ale, with wine to the second but not to the third table in each hierarchy. Thus the extraordinary quantities placed before the king and queen came to feed not two people but 30. Substantial quantities must nevertheless have been left over when they had finished.

Apart from the royal tables and their dependants there was, within the household, a series of other tables not eating the king and queen's left-over food but being provided directly from the kitchens, though each in turn with their own attendants that ate from their rests. It is not usually possible to see in what room they were situated, but perhaps that is not an important detail. The 'table for the Duke of Lennox and the master of the household' was apparently the most prestigious of these. It seated twelve important courtiers, faced with a generous allowance of bread, wine, ale, beef, veal, mutton, lamb, grouse and various types of poultry, with the additional note that 'upoun the fishe day, 18 or 20 dishe as they may be had'. It is not clear from this document whether at court the old medieval principle of three fish days a week and a month of fish days in Lent, was still being followed in its old strictness (as it certainly was in the universities), but it is plain here and elsewhere in the document that at least there still were regular fish days. In both quantity and variety of food the table of the Duke of Lennox exceeded all others except that of the royal couple.

It is possible to calculate that if all the food available to this table had been consumed by the twelve men entitled to be there, they would have eaten in the region of 10,000 calories a day, or about three times as much as is regarded as necessary to keep a very active, healthy man at the peak of physical condition. They were, however, served by another ten people, who had bread and ale and the right to 'eate on the rest theirof': dividing it between 22 mouths who bring the daily allowance down to about 6,000 calories. One can only conclude that, as with the royal table, there must have been a great deal to be disposed of elsewhere even when these had all been satisfied.

There were another seven identifiable tables in the royal household fed directly from the kitchens, mostly with servants who consumed their rests; the king's valets and ushers (eleven served by six); the king's pages of the stable (five served by one); the master porter and his four aides; the viol players (four served by one); the officers of the king's house (sixteen served by six); the queen's ladies and gentlewomen (eight served by twelve); finally, a second table in the queen's master's householders' hall, sitting fifteen, with no note of servants. There was clearly a distinction between those who were given wine and ale and those who only had ale: in the foregoing seven tables only the tables of the master porter, the musicians and the queen's ladies were provided with wine. On the other hand, roasted mutton, veal, fowls, beef and boiled mutton penetrated right down to the second table in the queen's master's householders' hall, at which were seated the goldsmith, the furrier, three servants or boys of the Danish chaplain and others at the bottom of this particular pecking order.

All these tables, moreover, at least where there is any opportunity of measuring the calorie intake, were over-providing for those seated and those attending. For example, the table of the queen's ladies and gentlewomen in fact entertained seven ladies and a man: perhaps in deference to their assumed lighter heads, the allowance of wine was only about half that served at the Duke of Lennox's table. But the amount of food (bread, ale, wine, beef, mutton, veal, chickens, doves) shared just among the people at this table would have provided about 10,000 calories each, dropping to about 5,000 if the attendants (both men and women) from the satellite table are added. A 'very active woman' needs (on modern calculations) only 2,500 calories a day, so once more they were being allowed about twice as much as they needed. A final example is the more humble table of the king's pages of the stable, where four pages, their 'maister' and their servant, had bread, ale, beef and boiled and roasted mutton: still this amounted to more than 5,000 calories a day, far in excess of any possible needs.

In these tables we have, so far, accounted for 142 people entitled to full meals within the royal household and suggested that, on average, they were receiving about twice as much food as they would need for nutritional purposes: therefore what was carried away from the tables should have been able to provide for nearly as many people again (it is conventional to allow for about 10 per cent waste in calculations of this kind). We may now certainly add in some of the cooks: we know that eight served in the queen's kitchen (she brought her own Danish cook, Hans), and though special food allowances were not made for them, it is inconceivable that they did not eat from all that was carried back and forth of their own making. Next, 30 names are given 'of personis havand onlie allowance of breid and drink'—invariably a 'bread' and a pint of ale; some of these were also on the kitchen staff ('four turnbrochies in the Kingis and Court kitchene') and whatever their formal allowance may have been, it would be unlikely that they did not also eat from the left-over food of the rest of the court. Indeed, their allowance of bread and ale, amounting to about 1,550 calories, would have been insufficient to keep them alive in the absence of extra food that they would either have had to obtain from the royal kitchens or to purchase from somewhere else.

However, even if this extra 38 are added to the original 142, there would probably be enough food left over to feed another 50–70 individuals; who received it we cannot tell. Some may have been casual guests; it is not clear from the document what arrangement, if any, was to be made for entertaining visitors, or how numerous they might have been. Some may have been relations of the cooks and servants who took food home. Some may have been attached to the court but not formally named among those entitled to be fed: the full list of his majesty's household, which precedes the list of food allowances, includes characters like the 'trumpettouris' and 'palfurmers viij in nowmer, of quhom he that keipis the camel is ane', and these cannot be identified by name among those at the tables or given bread and ale. There is no sign that the kings of Scotland habitually relieved a string of poor men who waited at the kitchens for the left-overs, as were the arrangements, for instance, at the court of English mediaeval kings, certainly from the thirteenth century onwards; but there is a possibility that they did so.[5]

When the 'food-chain' that we have posited is represented diagramatically (see Figure 1), one or two features stand out. There is some subtlety in a hierarchic arrangement where the Duke of Lennox, who was the king's cousin, the Master of the Stable, the Master of the Works and certain other officials who sat at this table, and the highborn ladies who were the queen's attendants, were not expected to eat food picked over by their majesties, but, the 'gentleman servandis', such as the carver and the cup-bearer and certain of those in the queen's master householder's hall (including, significantly, both the tailor and the preacher), while at least as well provided with meat and wine as the highest courtiers, were expected to eat the king's and queen's rests. This surely emphasised the way in which the second group were the direct creatures of the royal couple. On the other hand, by getting wine where the lesser courtiers (like the stable staff, the goldsmith and the furrier) only got ale, this group's superiority over the lesser courtiers was emphasised, even though the latter obtained their food straight from the kitchens like the Duke of Lennox. The only recipients of wine in this system who seem at first sight inappropriate are the master porter and the viol players: but the master porter was probably responsible for providing it to the court, and it was better that he had to drink it. The musicians had perhaps established an international principle that no-one could be expected to play courtly music on ale alone.

However one considers the matter, it is hard to imagine that any members of James VI's court were undernourished and clear that those at the top of the food chain had endless opportunity for overindulgence. The pattern of hierarchy, hospitality and gluttony was repeated, to a greater or lesser degree, throughout the landed classes in Lowlands and Highlands alike. To take just one example at the lower end of the scale, the English traveller Fynes Moryson, in the Borders in 1598, was:

> at a Knight's house who had many servants to attend him, that brought in his meate with their heads covered with blew caps, the Table being more than halfe furnished with great platters of porredge [pottage], each having a little peece of sodden meate: And when the Table was served, the servants did sit downe with us, but the upper messe in steede of porredge, had a Pullet with some prunes in the broth . . . The Scots, living then in factions, used to keepe many followers, and so consumed their revenew of victuals . . .[6]

This was modest enough, but demonstrated exactly the same sense of a communal 'court' differentiated by the menu as did the royal household.

Interestingly, too, as late as 1737 Sir Archibald Grant of Monymusk (another man of limited means and pretensions) enjoyed for his dinner a leg of mutton and cold roast beef, the remains of which were then passed down to a 'second table', and finally to the nursery after the second table had taken its fill: but the 'servants' were to dine on 'two roots of tongues sheeps

The Royal Kitchens

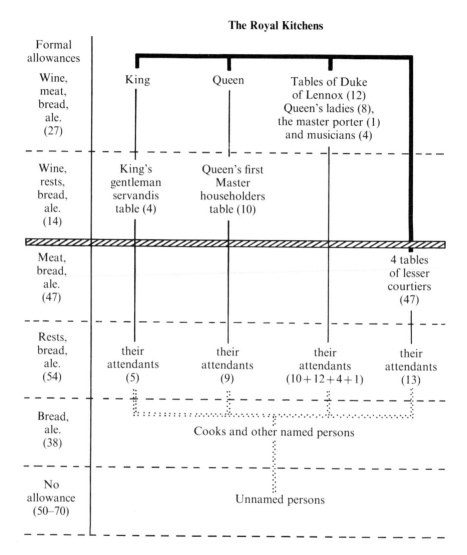

Formal allowances			
Wine, meat, bread, ale. (27)	King	Queen	Tables of Duke of Lennox (12) Queen's ladies (8), the master porter (1) and musicians (4)
Wine, rests, bread, ale. (14)	King's gentleman servandis table (4)	Queen's first Master householders table (10)	
Meat, bread, ale. (47)			4 tables of lesser courtiers (47)
Rests, bread, ale. (54)	their attendants (5)	their attendants (9)	their attendants (10+12+4+1) their attendants (13)
Bread, ale. (38)		Cooks and other named persons	
No allowance (50–70)		Unnamed persons	

▬▬ indicates untouched meat arriving from the kitchens

─── indicates formal arrangement to pass on left-over food ('rests')

······ indicates probable informal arrangement to pass on left-over food

Figures in brackets are the number of individuals fed at each level

▨▨▨ indicates level above which wine was served

FIGURE 1   The food chain at the royal court.

puddings' and did not enjoy the better meat. It was another food chain, demonstrating hierarchy and dependency at a more humble level, but in manner otherwise reminiscent of James VI's court a century and a half before.[7]

It was, of course, possible to regard the sixteenth-century use of food in great houses from the disapproving standpoint of the moralist. Thus Hector Boece in 1527 compared the ancient times when 'our elderis had sobriete' and 'plente with sufficence' with modern days where 'we have ebriete and dronkinness . . . immoderat cursis with superfluite: as he war maist noble and honest that culd devore and swelly maist'. Modern man, he says, searches out delicate courses that provoke the stomach to hold more than it can digest:

> Throw quhilk we ingorge and fillis our self, day and nicht, sa full of metis and drinkis, that we can nochte abstene, quhill our wambe be sa swon, that it is unabil to ony virtewis occupation.[8]

Boece was a university principal and it is interesting to see whether in the post-Reformation Scottish colleges there is less evidence of overindulgence than in the hierarchies of the royal court and landed families. Our second set of documents, therefore, focuses on academic life.

II

Three of the five Scottish universities left quite detailed accounts of what was provided at their tables. Let us consider first King's College, Aberdeen, Boece's old university, whose 'Liber Rationum' describes in detail the food provided for the masters, students and servants between 1579 and 1653: total provision and cost are given for most of the period, but only occasionally is it possible to relate consumption to the number of people provided for.[9]

One such occasion was the latter part of May, 1650: the fare provided on Tuesday, 21 May is typical. It was taken in three meals. Breakfast consisted of wheat bread at the high table, oat bread for everyone else, and ale. Lunch was, similarly, wheat bread and oat bread; the eleven sitters at high table demolished two legs of lamb; the twelve sitters at the second table demolished two more legs; the six pantrymen ate a fifth leg: there were, in addition, twenty bursars and four servants who did not appear to have had meat at this meal, but who could share in the 84 haddock, one and a half salmon, broth and 4.5 pints of plumdames (prunes) available to the whole pantry. No drink is recorded, but some must surely have been taken. At supper seventeen dined at high table and there were now 21 bursars—otherwise the number of sitters was the same and totalled 60 individuals: between them (without any indication as to how this was shared out) they ate a lamb 'and three legs', 3 salmon and another 4.4 pints of plumdames: again the high table had wheat bread, everyone else had oatbread and ale was universally distributed.

It is most unlikely that anyone went to bed hungry at Aberdeen, but the calculation of the nutritional content is, in this case, impossible, partly because the size of the wheat or oaten loaves is unknown except for the bursars. In their case, it appears that the oatbread allowance alone amounted to 21 oz and would have provided over 2,000 calories. As boys aged 15 need only about 2,880 calories, more than two-thirds of their energy requirements were being met from oats, before they even began to devour the fish, lamb and ale. There are in these accounts also occasional references to the provision of small quantities of milk and eggs, but none whatever to fresh vegetables. There must surely have been some provision of the latter from the college garden: one can make the same assumptions about the royal court, where greenstuffs and milk are also not allowed for.

One sees here at Aberdeen some differences and similarities to what went on at court and in landed households. Firstly, there was no question of anyone in university life being entitled to wine: ale was everyone's drink, teacher, student and servant alike. Secondly, the equivalent in the college to the wine/ale distinction at court was a wheat-bread/oat-bread distinction: that marked the main status division in the academic hierarchy. Thirdly, more food was provided than those formally entitled to sit at table were ever likely to eat.

Glasgow University was another institution that left excellent food records and in this case provided a hint as to where the extra food went. In 1602 Privy Council took it upon themselves to lay down the food allowances 'for halding of the commoun table within the College'.[10] The general resemblance to Aberdeen is clear. The first 'meis' was to consist of the five masters, who breakfasted on a white loaf of one pound in weight, with the remains of yesterday's meat, and a Scots pint of ale, shared among all five; dinner was 'ordinarlie quhyt breid aneuch', with five chopins of ale of a higher quality than the common ale of the town, a dish of brose, another of skink or kail soups, a piece of boiled mutton, another of beef, a roast of veal or mutton with a fowl or cony or a pair of doves or chickens, 'or uther siclyk secund rost'; supper was the same as dinner. On fish days they breakfasted on eggs, 'with breid and drink sufficient'; this was to be followed by a dinner and a supper of soup, eggs, 'thrie disch of weill grathit fisch or uther equivalent' at both meals, and bread and drink as before. Again, they seem remarkably well provided for. The bursars on the flesh days had an oat loaf in the soup in place of a wheaten loaf and at dinner 'tua ait laiffis amang four, ane dische of kaill or bruise, ane peice of beif, ane quart of aill', with supper the same. On fish days they did without soup at breakfast, and at dinner and supper had their usual bread and drink with 'ane dische of kaill, ane of eggis, another of fishe'. Food again illustrated and maintained hierarchy, but even the inferior quality and choice of the bursars' menu probably left them well fed.

For a period in mid-century it is possible to examine at Glasgow from the provision accounts in the university archives, not merely what they were entitled to have but what was placed before the staff and students day by day and week by week.[11] These are most useful when the number of those seated at the common table is known. In October 1641 a report was presented by the university commissioners naming the principal, five regents, ten bursars and four servants so entitled to meals, and at this period the college diet books provide further information about boarders. From 19 November to 18 December, 1640, and from 3 May to 2 June, 1641, we have analysed the kitchen accounts to see what was formally provided for the people concerned (see Appendix).

We know from other documents that arrangements were made at Glasgow for those non-bursar students who boarded with the masters and paid appropriate fees to be allowed to sit at the masters' table, while those who paid smaller fees were allowed to sit with the bursars.[12] The college probably contained 20 or 30 boarder students apart from the bursars and although they did not have to dine at the common table they were encouraged to do so. There were also, interestingly, penalties for taking food from the room.

The items on the menu are much as one would expect from the regulations of 1602; rather more calories came from wheat bread than from oatbread: some 40 per cent of the energy requirements came from meat (again, it would be more for the academics, less for the students): the most important meat was beef, with substantial amounts of poultry and mutton, a little veal and pigeon meat: sometimes they are extra items, not detailed here, like larks. Fish, surprisingly, provided a very insubstantial part of the energy—the tradition of fish days had well and truly fallen by the wayside by 1640. Butter, milk and eggs (but not cheese) were all present in fair quantities, though in volumetric terms over ten times as much beer and ale was provided as milk. There were very few frills, such as sugar or candied fruit (which are found in noble household accounts of the seventeenth century), though there were both raisins and plumdames to ease the bowels. Once again there are no purchases of any other fruit or fresh vegetables, but we must assume the college gardens came to the rescue. Otherwise it appears to have been an excellent diet (see Appendix). It also seems to have been a generous one, for with some 3,700 calories apparently provided daily for sedentary academics and young teenagers who can hardly have been expected to need over 3,000, it would not entirely have escaped Boece's censures.

At St Andrews University there are similar voluminous records both of food entitlements and of kitchen accounts: the diet books of St Leonard's College, for example, run from 1586 to 1743 (with some gaps), listing all the food that was taken from the kitchens into the dining hall.[13] They still await detailed analysis by historians. The first significant document for our purposes, however, is part of a proposal for reformation of the university by George Buchanan, dated between 1563 and 1567.[14] It may be taken to represent the Protestant ideal of what the eating arrangements should be in an academic institution. In the 'college of humanities' the Principal and his two servants were to share daily two Scots quarts of ale, a quantity of wheat bread, a quarter of mutton or equivalent fish: there is an interesting note that if the Principal was married he was entitled to put a boarder in his place at meals, to eat this allowance. The regents also obtained ale, wheat bread and mutton, with fish and eggs or herring on fish days—somewhat less in quantity, but still providing by modern calculations an adequate 3,200 calories a day on meat days. Finally, the bursars were given 'ane bread and ane pynt of ale on the day, (and) the sext part of ane quarter of mouton': probably about two-thirds of what the regents were eating, but also adequate fare. Since the type of bread is not specified as wheat, we are probably justified in the light of later evidence in thinking that oaten bread was intended for the bursars. Thus we see that while Buchanan did not wish the college to go hungry, he fully maintained the mediaeval notion that both the quantity and type of food were markers of hierarchy (the Principal is allowed more than the regents, the regents than the bursars, the bursars were not allowed wheat bread). On the other hand there was to be no superfluity and the food appears exceptionally plain for all.

The reality, as we might expect, diverged from this plan. Examination of the St Leonard's College diet books, 4 February to 4 May, 1588 (but excluding Lent) show, indeed, a large consumption of ale and of wheaten and oaten loaves (about 60 per cent of the bread was in wheat loaves). Of the meat, however, the lowly-esteemed mutton to which Buchanan had expected the college to confine itself, provided only about 7 per cent by volume; nearly two-thirds was fresh beef, 15 per cent salted beef and almost as much veal; there was also a little poultry. The predominance of beef over mutton however, may be related to the fact that it was the spring season when mutton was often difficult to procure. The fish days, which were at this time three in each week, were dominated by a diet of whiting, followed by cod, codling and mussels and a little turbot, skate, salmon, scallops and dried fish: of herring, which Buchanan had expected them to eat, there is only a trace. There are also eggs, vinegar, butter, milk (but by volume much less than a tenth of the ale supplied), occasionally pasties, regularly figs and prunes. It is, unfortunately, impossible to provide a convincing picture of how many people were expected to eat this food, so the extent of its abundance can only be guessed at. Our calculations suggest that about 30 per cent of the calories over the 49 day period came from meat and a little over 50 per cent from bread and ale. The different proportions from Glasgow relate both to the seaside location of St Andrews and the fact that formal fish days no longer applied in Glasgow at the later period.

The St Leonard's diet book should be considered along with a document of 1597 that was produced for government commissioners as a statement of what the university considered necessary for its provisioning.[15] As usual, this is not so detailed or unambiguous as one could wish, but it makes clear a number of points. Firstly, it confirms the distinction between wheat-bread-eating masters and regents and oat-bread-eating bursars. Beef was provided in equal quantities for both divisions, but was in any case less important than mutton. Indeed, the main difference between the diet of the regents and the bursars lay not in the type of food, but the relative quantities of mutton and fish allowed: the regents were to receive £43.10s.0d. Scots worth of mutton a year, the bursars only £14.10s.0d., the regents were to receive £21.15s.8d. worth of fish and eggs a year, the bursars a mere £3.3s.8d. Yet calculations of energy values for what each received on meat days (it is not possible to do the same for fish days) point to a daily allowance of about 4,900 calories for the regents and 4,000 for the bursars. These are so high that they must be intended also to feed people not mentioned at all on the entitlement list—no doubt, as at Glasgow University, paying boarders, either of high degree, who would eat wheat bread with the masters, or of lower degree, who would eat oat bread with the bursars.

III

We have considered the world of courtly power and the world of learning: let us in conclusion glance at the world of charitable giving, represented by the arrangements made for orphans at Hutchesone's Hospital, Glasgow, in 1649.[16] We do not know how typical this orphanage was of such institutions, but comparable data from eighteenth-century children's hospitals are in line with the impression conveyed.[17] The 'orders set down by the committee for planting the poor' in the hospital were explicit: in a memorandum headed 'for the young ones', it was stated that preference would be given to orphans who would 'eitt and bed within the hous'. They were to be accommodated 'in the hous quhair the schoole now is', in 'two rooms and two beds in each': elsewhere it is stated that there were to be twelve children at the school, so the children must have slept three to a bed.

The specifications for their diet were equally clear:

> each of them to have ane peck of meill weikle . . . ane herring to ilk ane of thame ewerie vther nicht. It is thought they would have kaill, and so for this must have two peckis of grottis in the monethe and a schilling in that tyme for the kaill and also a leg of beife in the monthe . . . it is thought meit that they be small drink browne to them, about twelfe pennies the pynt, by some neighbour, quhairof they must have four pyntis each day.

A modern orphanage would be alarmed in particular by the absence of milk (perhaps one should say, the substitution of beer for milk): but in terms of calorie intake, our calculations suggest that there was more than enough energy in the diet. The children were under 14; boys aged 9–11 are today held to need 2,280 calories, girls 2,050; this diet produced about 2,800 calories. Even allowing for 10 per cent wastage it appears generous enough to leave a margin over of at least 200 calories per child. There is a servant mentioned in the memorandum—'they must have one quha will mak thair meit and wash their cloathes, quha must have food and rayment, and theirfor at leist must have 4s. per diem, and that scho be tain speciall notice of to be trustie'. Despite the explicit mention of a money wage for her to buy food, it appears possible that she could supplement this from the surplus provisions of her charges if she chose to do so.

In conclusion, the diets we have considered run to a certain pattern. Firstly, even the meanest provided more than enough calories for those named in the entitlement. Secondly, the quantities provided are often so greatly in excess of what was nutritionally necessary as to indicate that others, generally not named in the entitlement lists, were feeding from the provisions. In the case of the court, it would be guests, no doubt, the lowest servants and the hangers-on; in the universities the fee-paying 'boarders'; in the orphanage possibly the housekeeper. Finally, everywhere, except in the orphanage, food was used to reinforce and emphasise hierarchy, most elaborately in the royal court, but equally clearly in the universities to mark the difference between the bursars and servants on the one side and the rest of the academic community on the other.

To the anthropologist, 'in establishing precisely who eats what and with whom commensality is one of the most powerful ways of defining and differentiating social groups'.[18] In sixteenth and seventeenth-century Scotland it was clearly so: a man or woman at court was or was not worth his or her wine; a man or boy at university was or was not worth his wheaten loaf. Today, also, it is clearly so, though the forms change. Not everyone receives an invitation to sherry with the Principal, and those who accept do not generally go to quench their thirst.[19]

NOTES

1   Mary Douglas, *In the Active Voice* (London 1982), p 117.
2   *Papers Relative to the Marriage of King James the Sixth of Scotland, with the Princess Anna of Denmark* (Bannatyne Club, Edinburgh 1828), pp 23–38.
3   David Starkey, *The Reign of Henry VIII: Personalities and Politics* (London 1985), p. 26, provides a contemporary illustration of Henry VIII dining without his queen: it is unclear how far this might have been due to his peculiar domestic problems rather than general practice at the English Court.
4   'Richard James, 1592–1638: description of Shetland, Orkney and the Highlands of Scotland', *Orkney Miscellany*, vol I (1953), pp 53–4. His account, despite the title, refers here more generally to Scotland.
5   Chris Given-Wilson, *The Royal Household and the King's Affinity* (London 1986).
6   P Hume Brown (ed), *Early Travellers in Scotland* (Edinburgh 1891), pp 88–9.
7   SRO: Grant of Monymusk Muniments, GD345/925.
8   P Hume Brown (ed), *Scotland before 1700 from Contemporary Documents*, p 102.
9   Aberdeen University Library MSS K.2: extracts printed in Cosmo Innes, *Fasti Aberdonenses* (Spalding Club, Aberdeen 1854), pp 578–99.
10 *Register of the Privy Council of Scotland*, Vol VI, *1599–1604* (Edinburgh 1884), p 452.
11 Glasgow University Archives, MSS 26732–3: Schedule and accounts for boarders.
12 James Coutts, *A History of the University of Glasgow* (Glasgow 1909), p 81.
13 St Andrews University Library MSS: Diet books of St Leonards College.
14 'The opinion of George Buchanan concerning the reformation of the University of St Andrews', *The Bannatyne Miscellany*, vol II (Bannatyne Club, Edinburgh 1836), pp 87–9.
15 National Library of Scotland: Crawfurd and Balcarres MSS: Untitled University of St Andrews diet account, 1597.
16 J D Marwick (ed), *Extracts from the Records of the Burgh of Glasgow, 1630–1662*, (Scottish Burgh Records Society, Glasgow 1881), pp 178–9.
17 J Richards, 'Some notes on the early history of the Dean Orphan Hospital *Book of the Old Edinburgh Club*, vol 27 (1949), pp 155–68; E S Towill, 'The minutes of the Merchant Maiden Hospital', *Book of the Old Edinburgh Club*, vol 29 (1956), pp 1–92.
18 Gillian Feeley-Harnick, *The Lord's Table: Eucharist and Passover in Early Christianity*, (Philadelphia 1981), p 11, quoted in Gwen K Neville, *Kingship and Pilgrimage: Rituals of Reunion in American Protestant Culture* (Oxford 1987), p 72.
19 The authors would like to express their thanks to their colleagues, Dr Chris Given-Wilson and Dr Richard Fardon, for their advice and comments on this paper. The research was undertaken with assistance from a grant by the ESRC as part of a wider study on prices, wages and food in Scotland, 1580–1780.

APPENDIX

Diet at the Common Table of the College of Glasgow, 1640–41

Establishing the nutritional content and value of early diets is far from straight-forward. Even the most detailed diet accounts seldom define precisely how much of each food was provided. Just how large, for instance, were the chickens, doves, herrings or eggs taken to the table? How much did the 'portions' or 'pieces' of beef, mutton, veal or lamb weigh? Even when the weight of an item is specified, it is not always possible to be sure what system of weight was being used. Scotland had its Troy and Tron systems; the 'Tron' pound varied from place to place but was generally some 25 per cent heavier than a pound 'Troy', which itself was some 10 per cent heavier than a pound imperial Avoirdupois. All the diets considered in this paper have necessitated some assumptions, and although there is generally some evidence on which to base these, in some cases they still amount to little more than educated guesses. The following analysis of the diet accounts available for the College of Glasgow in 1640–41 illustrates the nature of some of these assumptions.

Equally problematical is just how appropriate for these early diets are the modern calculations regarding the nutritional content of food. There is, of course, no alter-native to these nor any way of realistically modifying them to meet the requirements of early foodstuffs. What, for instance, might be the nutritional difference between modern beef, mutton, chicken or eggs and their ancient counterparts? Given the predominance of grain foods in many early diets, this is a particularly important consideration with regard to wheat and oat bread, oatmeal and ale. We know that methods of preparation can substantially alter the nutritional content of these foods. Take, for instance, the effect of milling on the composition of wheat flour. If an extraction rate of 85 per cent is used wheat flour will contain about 89mg of Vitamin B_1 per 100 grammes of flour; alter the extraction rate to 70 per cent and there will remain only 20mg per 100 grammes.[1] This reduction will cut the amount of niacin available by half and the amount of calcium by a quarter. The calorific content of the flour is, however, little affected by such a change. Perhaps equally important is the variety of grain used; decades of scientific breeding and the importation of foreign strains may have substantially altered the nutritional content of wheat, oats and barley. It is, however, quite impossible to isolate any such changes (let alone quantify them) and there is no alternative but to take the modern tables of food composition at face value.[2]

Such uncertainties leave our nutritional calculations with inherent limitations. Precisely what confidence limits should be placed on our estimates cannot be deter-mined, but the authors believe that they provide an acceptable general guide to the quantity and nutritional quality of the food provided at the various institutions considered. Readers may, however, draw their own conclusions from the following illustrative analysis of the diet provided at the College of Glasgow in 1640–41.

---

[1] S Davidson, R Passmore, J F Brock and A S Truswell, *Human Nutrition and Dietetics* (6th edition, Edinburgh 1975), pp 198–200.

[2] Throughout this study nutritional information has been extracted from A A Paul and D A T Southgate, *McCance and Widdowson's The Composition of Foods*, 4th edition, Ministry of Agriculture, Fisheries and Food and the Medical Research Council, HMSO, London 1978.

Four account books in Glasgow University's archives provide details on the food provided at the 'Common Table' of the College between 1626 and 1646.[3] These are day-by-day accounts of the food purchased for the 'Common Table'; but whilst they list the boarders present, an accurate analysis of the diet is impossible as the Principal, the masters, the bursars, and probably the principal servants also ate at the Common Table—and their numbers are not specified. Fortunately, however, a 'Report concerning the Universitie of Glasgow'[4] presented by the Commissioners of Visitation at Holyrood in October 1641, provides a list of the members of the college present during the academic year 1640–41. This recorded their annual fees and the cost of their board which, in Scots money, were as follows:

	Fee	'for his table'
The Principal	£1,200	£40 quarterly
To each of five Regents	£1,000	£40 quarterly
To each of ten bursars	—	£18 quarterly
The Economus	£104	£32 quarterly
The Cook	£40	£12 quarterly
The Porter	£40	£12 quarterly
The Foreman of the Kitchen	£40	£12 quarterly

This, with details on the attendance of boarders available in the diet accounts themselves, allows the numbers eating at the 'Common Table' to be established for the academic year 1640–41.

This use of the term 'Common Table' does not imply that all ate at the one table, or that the diet was the same for all. In fact, it is likely that there were at least two tables at this time. There were certainly two tables in 1608; at that time student boarders who paid at the same rate as the masters sat at the same table with them, and others who could not afford so much might sit with the bursars and partake of the same fare with them.[5] An agreement drawn up in 1608 between the College and Andrew Herbertsoun, a burgess of Glasgow, gives a general impression of the food presented to the two tables.[6] He was to provide the masters 'and utheris that payis as they pay' with:

At nyne houris upone the flesh dayis viz. Sonday Monounday Tyisday Wedinsday and Furisday . . . ane soup of fyne quheit breid or ane portioun of cauld meit as best may be had with sum dry breid and drink; at twelf houris the said Andro . . . sall serve thame in broois skink sodden beif and muttoun the best in the mercat, roistit muttoun or veill as the commoditie of the sessoun of the yeir sall serve, with ane foull or the equivalent theirof, with gud quheit breid the best in the mercat without scairstie, and gud staill aill aucht or ten dayis auld that sall be bettir nor the haill aill in the Toun, and at supper sicklyke; And on the

3 GUA 26730–26732; Schedule of Boarders in the College and Accounts relative to them, 1626–1633, 1633–1640 and 1640–1646. GUA 26733; Accounts for the provisions, etc, for the Boarders at the Common Table, 1639–46.

4 'Report concerning the Universitie of Glasgow by the Commissioners of Visitation 1641, the State of Revenue, etc.' printed in *Munimenta Alme Universitatis Glasguensis* (Glasgow 1854), vol II, pp 457–61.

5 J Coutts, *A History of the University of Glasgow* (Glasgow 1909), pp 80–1.

6 'Contract with Andrew Herbertsoun touching the Boarding of the Masters and Bursars', printed in *Mumimenta Alme Universitatis Glasguensis* (Glasgow, 1854), vol III, pp 519–22. This seems to reflect quite closely the provisions 'for halding of the commoun table within the College' laid down in 1602 by the Privy Council.

fische dayis the said Andro sall furneis everie ane in the morning ane callour fresch eg with sum cauld meit or milk and breid and sum dry breid and drink, at noone kaill and eggis herring and thrie course of fische gif thai may be had, or the equivalent thairof in breid and milk fryouris with dry breid as of befoir, and at supper sicklyke.

The bursars, meanwhile, had to make do with a distinctly less varied and less appetising diet:

The Bursouris on the flesche dayis in the morning everie thrie of thame ane soup of ait breid and ane drink, at noone broois with ane tailye of fresche beif with sufficient breid and aill to drink, at evening on the said manner ane tailye of fresch beif to everie mess. On fische dayis breid and drink as on the flesche dayis, at disjoone ane eg, at noone eggis herring and ane uthir course, at evening sicklyke.

Once again, therefore, the social hierarchy of an institution was being reflected and emphasised by the provision of food to individuals within it. This almost certainly remained true in 1640–41, but it is only possible to establish an overall average diet at the 'common Table'. Some must have fared better than others (the Principal and regents did, after all, pay twice as much 'for their table' than the bursars), but this distinction cannot be pursued.

The accounts for two periods during the academic year have been considered; from 19 November to 18 December (with 28 November excluded because of a gap in the accounts), and from 3 May to 2 June 1641. The number of students in attendance varied from one week to the next, but over the 60 days covered by these accounts there was a total of 1,993 man-days to be provided for. (Individuals had to be away for more than eight days to qualify for a reduction in the cost of their board; shorter absences would presumably not be noted in the accounts and thus this 1,993 man-days represents a maximum demand on the food provided at the 'Common Table'.)

Table I describes the total provision of food to these men and boys over this 60-day period. The assumptions necessary to convert the often vague statements of quantity into utilisable weights and measures, as given in Table I, fall into a number of categories:

Wheat Bread: Although the actual weight of each loaf was not given, the cost of each was recorded on the charge side of the accounts. Throughout November and December 1640 each loaf cost 1s.6d. From 3–10 May 1641 each cost 1s.8d., and from 11 May–2 June each cost 1s.10d. The Town Council in Glasgow set the price of bread in October 1640 at 13 oz (Tron) for 10d. If we may presume that this price applied to the College in November and December of that year then each loaf bought by the College would have weighed 23.4 oz Tron or 31 oz Imperial Avoirdupois. McCance and Widdowson's values for 'wholemeal' bread have been used.

Oat Bread: Again the weight of each loaf was not given. However, the charge side of the accounts show that each boll of oatmeal was baked into, on average, 243.2 loaves. If we may presume the boll to have weighed 8 stone Troy (as it was to be defined by parliament later in the century) then each loaf would have contained 8.42 oz Troy, or 9 oz Imperial Avoirdupois, of oatmeal. How much the actual loaves weighed once

TABLE I
THE PROVISION OF FOOD AT THE 'COMMON TABLE' OVER SIXTY DAYS IN 1640 AND 1641

	Assumptions	Total Provision
	all figures in Imperial Avoirdupois	
829 loaves wheat bread	each loaf weighs 31 oz	25,699 oz
1,310 loaves oat bread	each loaf contains 9 oz oatmeal	11,790 oz
942 pints ale	each pint contains 60 fl oz	56,520 fl oz
775 pints beer	each pint contains 60 fl oz	46,500 fl oz
$340\frac{1}{2}$ portions mutton	each portion weighs 42 oz	14,301 oz
342 portions beef	each portion weighs 75 oz	25,650 oz
63 portions veal	each portion weighs 42 oz	2,646 oz
20 portions lamb	each portion weighs 42 oz	840 oz
103 fowls	each fowl provides 80 oz flesh	8,240 oz
140 chickens	each chicken provides 32 oz flesh	4,480 oz
20 doves	each dove provides 16 oz flesh	320 oz
1,688 eggs	each egg weighs 2 oz	3,376 oz
303 herrings	each herring provides 4 oz flesh	1,212 oz
126 portions 'hardfish'	each portion weighs 32 oz	4,032 oz
159 pints milk	each pint contains 60 fl oz	9,540 fl oz
64 lb (Tron) butter	each lb weighs 21.2 oz	1,358 oz
$62\frac{1}{2}$ lb plumdamas	each lb (Tron) weighs 21.2 oz	1,326 oz
12 lb raisins	each lb (Tron) weighs 21.2 oz	255 oz
4 tongues		
4 wild fowls		
80s.0d. worth of salmon	indefinable, but	
5s.4d. worth of 'fresh fish'	minimal, nutritional	
2s.8d. worth of trout	contribution to diet.	
41s.4d. worth of wine		
$1\frac{1}{2}$ pints of French wine		
$\frac{1}{2}$ pint of Seck		

baked remains unknown, but as they would have contained little else but oatmeal and water we may presume the oatbread to have had approximately the same nutritional value as the oatmeal from which it was made.

Ale and Beer: Although the charge side of the accounts show that each boll of malt was brewed into 11 gallons 3 pints (273 English pints) of ale this is little help in establishing the nutritional quality of the ale relative to modern brews. We have taken ale to be comparable to McCance and Widdowson's 'pale ale' and the beer, which was probably a stronger brew, to be equivalent to their 'bitter'. The Scottish pint was very nearly equivalent to three modern English pints and thus contained 60 fluid ounces.

Meat: The charge side of the accounts list the beef carcases purchased and note the number of 'portions' into which they were cut. From young beef carcases an average of $32\frac{1}{2}$ portions were cut, with a range of 28 to 48. The other, unspecified, carcases provided an average of 52 portions each, with a range of 43 to 80 portions.

Cattle in early modern Scotland were much smaller than their modern counterparts; the best available estimate is that they provided about 240 lbs of meat and edible fat. This would suggest that each portion weighed about $4\frac{1}{2}$ lbs or 72 ounces.

Mutton, lamb and veal were also accounted for in portions—but here there is no internal evidence on their size. Quite often, however, early diet accounts show mutton to have been cut into 9 portions; these were presumably particular joints. The best

TABLE II

AVERAGE DAILY NUTRITIONAL VALUE OF DIET

			Energy kcal	Protein g	Fat g	Carbo-hydrate g	Calcium mg	Iron mg	Vit A µg	Vit B1 mg	Vit B2 mg	Niacin mg	Vit C mg
Wheat Bread	(30)	12.89 oz	789.7	32.2	9.9	152.8	84.1	9.16	0.0	9.54	0.26	20.50	0.0
Oat Bread	(17)	5.92 oz	672.5	20.8	14.6	122.1	92.2	6.86	0.0	0.83	0.18	6.39	0.0
Ale	(894)	28.36 fl oz	201.4	1.7	Tr.	13.0	80.5	Tr.	0.0	Tr.	0.28	2.55	0.0
Beer	(893)	23.33 fl oz	212.1	2.1	Tr.	15.2	73.0	Tr.	Tr.	Tr.	0.23	3.97	0.0
Mutton	(A)	7.18 oz	351.9	27.2	27.1	0.0	10.2	2.10	Tr.	0.15	0.36	13.17	0.0
Beef	(B)	12.87 oz	560.3	51.4	39.3	0.0	20.7	5.38	Tr.	0.20	0.59	23.38	0.0
Veal	(B)	1.33 oz	65.8	9.0	3.3	0.0	4.0	0.45	Tr.	0.02	0.08	3.91	0.0
Lamb	(A)	0.42 oz	20.7	1.6	1.6	0.0	0.6	0.12	Tr.	0.01	0.02	0.77	0.0
Fowl	(322)	4.13 oz	253.2	26.5	16.4	0.0	10.5	0.95	Tr.	Tr.	Tr.	4.92	0.0
Chicken	(322)	2.25 oz	137.7	14.4	8.9	0.0	5.7	0.52	Tr.	Tr.	Tr.	2.67	0.0
Dove	(338)	0.16 oz	10.5	1.3	0.6	0.0	0.7	0.88	Tr.	Tr.	Tr.	0.64	0.0
Egg	(169)	1.69 oz	70.6	5.9	5.2	Tr.	25.0	0.96	67.2	0.03	0.22	1.76	Tr.
Herring	(485)	0.61 oz	34.3	3.5	2.2	0.0	5.7	0.17	8.4	Tr.	0.03	1.34	Tr.
Hardfish	(448)	2.02 oz	45.3	10.5	0.3	0.0	8.0	0.22	Tr.	0.04	0.04	2.75	0.0
Milk	(124)	4.79 fl oz	88.2	4.5	5.2	6.4	162.8	0.05	52.5	0.05	0.24	1.15	9.6
Butter	(140)	0.68 oz	142.9	0.1	15.8	Tr.	2.9	0.03	190.2	Tr.	Tr.	0.02	Tr.
Plumdamas	(718)	0.67 oz	5.8	0.1	Tr.	1.5	0.3	0.07	34.0	0.02	0.01	0.07	0.5
Raisins	(809)	0.13 oz	8.2	Tr.	Tr.	2.1	8.4	0.05	1.0	Tr.	Tr.	0.02	Tr.
Total			3671.1	212.8	150.4	313.1	595.3	27.97	353.3	10.89	2.54	89.98	10.1

available estimate regarding the size of mutton carcases is that they provided about
$23\frac{1}{2}$ lbs of meat and edible fat. This would suggest that each of the portions weighed
something like 42 ounces. In the absence of any better estimate this has also been
used as the weight of lamb and veal portions.

The composition of early breeds was certainly different to that of modern breeds;
they had, for instance, considerably less edible fat on their carcases. Taking early beef
and mutton carcases to contain about 85 per cent lean meat and 15 per cent edible
fat, McCance and Widdowson's figures on the nutritional content of lean and fat
beef and mutton have been used to estimate the nutritional value of the beef, veal,
mutton and lamb.

The amount of meat provided by the fowls, chickens, doves and eggs has been
estimated from modern parallels. A fowl is taken to provide 5 lbs of flesh, a chicken
2 lbs, and a dove just 1 lb. McCance and Widdowson's figures for chicken have been
used for the first two items, their figures for pigeon for the last. Eggs are taken to
weigh 2 ounces each.

Fish: Herring we presume to have provided 4 ounces of flesh each. The 'hardfish'
were probably dried cod; a dozen were purchased by the college in 1640–41 and these
were cut into 4 portions each. Presuming the cod to have provided 8 lbs of flesh then
each piece would have weighed 2 lb. McCance and Widdowson provide figures on
the nutritional composition of both herring and cod.

Milk and Butter: The Scots pint was very nearly equal to three modern English pints
and thus was 60 fluid ounces. The butter was explicitly stated to have been weighed
by the Tron pound. This probably weighed 21.22 oz Imperial Avoirdupois.

Plumdamas and Raisins: Here we can only presume the Tron pound to have been
used. Information on their nutritional value has been taken from McCance and
Widdowson's figures for damsons and raisins respectively.

On the basis of these estimates it finally becomes possible to make some general
estimate of the nutritional quality of the diet at Glasgow in 1640–41. This can be
compared with the DHSS 'Recommended Daily Amounts of Nutrients' as given in
Table III. In terms of energy the diet was over generous by perhaps some 25 per cent.
In fact the diet exceeded requirements in all aspects except for Vitamin A and Vitamin
C. This may be as much a consequence of the scope of the accounts as the failure of

TABLE III

DHSS RECOMMENDED DAILY AMOUNTS OF NUTRIENTS

	Energy kcal	Protein g	Calcium mg	Iron mg	Vit A µg	Vit B_1 mg	Vit B_2 mg	Niacin mg	Vit C mg
BOYS									
12–14	2,640	66	700	12	725	1.1	1.4	16	25
15–17	2,880	72	600	12	750	1.5	1.7	19	30
MEN									
18–34 Sedentary	2,510	62	500	10	750	1.0	1.6	18	30
18–34 Moderately Active	2,900	72	500	10	750	1.2	1.6	18	30
35–64 Sedentary	2,400	60	500	10	750	1.0	1.6	18	30
35–64 Moderately Active	2,750	69	500	10	750	1.1	1.6	18	30

the diet itself. Both Vitamin A and Vitamin C are to be found in greens and vegetables. These are just the sort of items that would have been produced in the college gardens and may thus have been excluded from the accounts. It is worth noting that the 1608 contract with Andrew Herbertsoun mentions the provision of kaill—it does seem likely that it was still available in 1640–41. As little as 4 ounces of kaill would have more than fulfilled Vitamin C requirements. This would still have left the diet perhaps some 25 per cent deficient in Vitamin A, but this was a vitamin particularly con-centrated in offal and, as the body can store it over many months, the occasional dish of liver, haggis or the like would have easily made up all Vitamin A requirements. It does seem as if the masters and students fared very well indeed.

Debtors, Imprisonment and the Privilege of Girth

Lorna Ewan

The right of Sanctuary, or, as it was known in Scotland, the Privilege of Girth, has been romanticised by many writers, not least the idealistic Victor Hugo.[1] In pre-Reformation Europe, however, the 'Sanctuary' played an entirely functional role in the judicial process. In general terms a person who had committed, or was suspected of having committed, a crime, could take refuge in a church or area of consecrated ground. There followed a period of grace, usually forty days, during which the official legal procedures could be set in motion. At a time when justice was often a private and personal matter the existence of sanctuaries enabled 'an alleged offender to escape his private avengers and ultimately seek refuge in public hands'.[2]

Throughout Europe the concept of sanctuary, as a recognised component of the law, was largely rejected around the time of the Reformation; Francis I abolished the Right throughout France in 1539, the Papacy withdrew it from assassins, heretics, traitors, brigands, and those who stole from churches or on highways in 1591, whilst in England an act of Henry VIII, passed in 1540, so prescribed the function of sanctuary it was rendered invalid.[3] However, in Scotland the Right of Sanctuary, as a legally recognised institution, was retained at Holyrood in Edinburgh. This was no archaic legislative relic, but a privilege which featured in the judicial procedure until the late nineteenth century. The reasons for this conscious retention of a system, which had been discarded throughout the rest of Europe must be sought in the Scottish attitude towards debt and indebtedness—after the Reformation only debtors could claim the Right of Girth and seek asylum at Holyrood.

The Scots have long invoked their God to forgive them their debts as they forgive their debtors, but until the Victorian era the sin was not to be *in* debt but to be unable or unwilling to pay. That there should ever have been any shame attached to the mere fact of being in debt is in itself remarkable. The concept of credit—deferred payment or over-trading—exists in the most primitive, non-monetary economies.[4] To lend goods and services and, with more sophistication, currency, without an immediate return but with the promise of repayment is an essential component of any but the crudest 'immediate exchange' system. Thus indebtedness, be it in cash or kind, is an inevitable feature of life in societies dependent on agriculture for food and on the use of raw materials for other industries; 'In a world where seasons are uncertain and six months intervene between sowing and harvest, the need of advances was not the invention of man; it was inherent to the nature of things'.[5] This intrinsic facet of life has long been recognised and understood, not least by the authors of the Old Testament; both biblical law and the prophets were concerned with protecting debtors especially in times of shortage following crop failures.[6]

For the Scots, the vocabulary of debt was so widely understood and accepted, that in 1596 the parish minister of Kilrunny in Fife was able to expound the doctrine of the Covenant in the form of a corporate catechism, specifically 'for the use of the people',[7] structured as a metaphor using the idea and vocabulary of debt: '. . . for Chryst is the Cautioner of the Covenant and Contract for us, an sa principall deatter, taking the sam upon him to satisfie in all whar we ar unable'.[8] It is surely implicit that the minister was able to assume complete comprehension of the terminology by his congregation before employing it to teach what was, after all, a fundamentally important element of his theology.

Credit, and therefore debt, was certainly neither new nor strange to the people of Scotland. Credit was an inevitable and essential lubricant to the agrarian economy of the time, exposed as it was to the 'recurrent hazzards of the calendar, many seasonal disasters and long waiting periods: one had to plough before one could sow, sow before one could reap, and so it went on, interminably'.[9] This need for credit permeated the complete social spectrum. Although incurred for different reasons and in different ways by each social group, debts were ubiquitous, expected and accepted.[10] Every tenant or labourer, artisan or merchant, minister or laird, owed or was owed either goods, money or service at some time in his life. From testamentary evidence alone it is clear that very few people died without debts 'restand awand be or to'. For example, of 120 seventeeth- and eighteenth-century testaments relating to the Grandtully estates in Perthshire only nine did not record any unresolved transactions in the testator's estate.[11] Similarly, 200 seventeenth-century testaments, examined from the Panmure estates in Forfarshire, indicated that 69 per cent of the testators died as creditors and 70 per cent as debtors.[12] Furthermore, the ever litigious Scots were seldom slow to claim against tardy debtors in the Commissary and Sheriff Courts—a vast corpus of evidence from the consequent processes substantiates the impression that indebtedness was an everyday occurrence. From the small claims court of the Dunkeld Commissariot alone, 12,811 processes have survived from the period 1680 to 1765.[13] A sample of these taken across the entire period indicated that many of the processes contained multiple claims, the average being 3.85. Although this can only provide a very rough guide these figures suggest that around 50,000 claims were made in the area over the period—approximately 580 each year.

As these documents merely represent those processes which have survived, do not include claims for debts of over £40 Scots, and exclude all those debt/credit transactions which were settled without recourse to law, they only reflect one tiny thread in a vast and complex network of indebtedness. This network extended across class boundaries and throughout both town and country. The nature of the transactions did, however, tend to change from one end of the social spectrum to the other; amongst the less well-off debts were often both incurred and ultimately paid in kind, whilst the wealthy generally employed bonds and bills of exchange.

This is not to suggest that debts were not frequently incurred across social boundaries. It was by no means uncommon to find tacksmen and tenants lending to their laird. Wadsetting was often the vehicle for such loans. This was a type of mortgage in which land was allocated as security in return for a sum of capital and low annual interest payments. As the redemption of a wadset necessarily involved repaying the capital this was one of the few ways in which landownership could move down the social hierarchy—the impecunious debtor could often be persuaded to convert the wadset into a feu for a relatively small payment.[14] Contracts of bond[15] were, on the other hand, largely, but by no means exclusively confined to transactions between members of the upper classes. Tenants could hold land by 'bond and tack' and often borrowed and lent by bond; of the 120 testaments examined which related to the Grandtully estates 15 contained bond transactions concerning tenants or sub-tenants. The practice was sufficiently frequent for some loans to be specified as being 'without bond'.[16]

References to indebtedness, by bond, between members of the nobility are legion. Some landed families succeeded or failed according to their money-lending skills; the 1st Earl of Dundonald, William Cochrane 'was making advances to impecunious noblemen'[17] during the 1640s and 1650s. By 1726 John, Earl of Dundonald, was owed, at least, £55,164.13s.4d. Scots, by other members of the nobility, in bonds dating from as far back as 1678.[18] Reflecting that the total hard currency of Scotland was believed, by contemporaries, to be around £9,600,000 Scots when funds were being raised for the ill-fated Darien scheme,[19] Dundonald's credit holding was indeed remarkable, and he was by no means alone. The significance of such credit holdings was not in the fact of their existence, nor in their size, but in the need for such a facility.

The ability and possibility to borrow was essential to lairds and their immediate subordinates, the tacksmen, factors, etc. Estates could not be run without credit, 'all estates accumulated debts, sometimes so heavy as to tie up the whole rental . . . on a sample of nine estates, on all except one, the value of the estate, at twenty years purchase, was less than the total creditors' claims'.[20] In general, however, as long as the interest was paid, creditors would not call in their capital. In 1673, for example, Sir Thomas Steuart of Grandtully was owed £12,900.6s.6d. Scots in 56 outstanding bonds,[21] but his main concern was with the annual-rent (the term for interest payments in Scotland).[22]

The practice of lending at interest—usury or ockery in Scotland—had long been condemned by the clergy and was illegal until 1587. Apparently straightforward theft was hardly felt to be more of a transgression:

Thay sine aganis the comand [8th commandment] that comittis thift or okker or ressis fra oders throw power and strintht . . .Thay that holdis thair seruandis feis fra thayme thay that denisz thair dettis and wil noth pay thair crediturs/thay that will not help thair nichtburs in thair necessite ad will notht len to thayme in thair mister without okker money or service or reward.[23]

Nevertheless, as early as c1425 the Scottish parliament, presumably recognising the need for credit facilities, enacted legislation which specified that if a usurer desisted and repented no penalty would be inflicted and usurers would normally be convicted posthumously.[24] The law-makers were in a difficult position; being sufficiently sophisticated to appreciate the need for credit, in order to enable trade to grow and flourish, whilst still having to condemn usury as an immoral and, therefore, illegal practice for as long as the church and the pious stood out against it.

To the church anyone was 'an usurer that by contracte taketh but one penny over and above the principall in respecte of tyme, and [is a] deadly synner before God'.[25] Time was thought to belong to God alone and, therefore, could not be sold, but it was. Under every conceivable disguise and using every possible surrogate, interest was charged. Fictitious partnerships, excessive security, interest paid in kind or personal labour and even deliberate error were all common means of exacting usury. It could even be disguised as 'full board': 'a man who is possessed of an hundred golden or sun crowns, will lend them to a merchant, for which the merchant will maintain him for a whole year in his house, and at his table, and at the end of the year will return him his money'.[26]

Usury seems to have been ubiquitous in Scotland, both geographically and socially and both before and after its legalisation. However, the vast majority of these transactions were not made with a professional money-lender but with people who made their living by other means—people who would lend at interest when they could. Ockery was, for the most part, a 'bye-employment' rather than a profession. The Privy Council Register of 1611 substantiates this view.[27] Of 31 prosecutions for ockery in Perth the professions of those charged were listed as:

Burgess	1
Cordiner	1
Lister	1
Baxter	2
Tailor	2
Not specified	2
Weaver	2
Maltman	3
Widow	3
Skinner	6
Merchant	8

It is also interesting to note that in the same year eight ministers were summoned in front of the Privy Council, elsewhere in Scotland, on charges of ockery.[28] The crime certainly seems to have been both habitual and ineradicable in the Scottish populace. After its legalisation the continuing condemnation of usury was more apparent than real. In 1616, the presumably rather disheartened cleric, Wolfgang Musculus, commented that 'the Diuines shall reforme Vsurie when Physicians have cured the Gout: the sinne and the disease as both incurable'.[29]

Lending and borrowing was such a common occurrence that irrespective of its form, indebtedness was an unquestioned and accepted feature of the economy at all levels. Until it became apparent that the debtor was unable or unwilling to repay his debts he remained part of the vast economic matrix. However, once the debtor had either to seek refuge from his creditors or succumb to the judicial process, Scotland's unique approach to debtors as a criminal group becomes apparent.

The Debtors Act of 1880 saw the final abolition of imprisonment for civil debt in Scotland (imprisonment for debts of less than £8.6s.8d. had been abandoned some 45 years earlier). This abrogation of arrest for civil, non-fraudulent debt marked the end of a fascinating sequence of legislation. The legal position of the debtor had become characterised by what seemed, superficially, to be an inconsistency in the law. The division was encapsulated in Bell's dictum pertaining to debtors, 'The spirit of the law in Scotland is mild, in regard to the imprisonment of debtors: while it is sufficiently vigilant to prevent fraudulent absconding'.[30] There was certainly a substantial body of law which discouraged creditors from having their debtors incarcerated; from 1654 onwards there had been rigorous attempts to moderate the laws against debtors.[31] Cromwell and his council were particularly active in providing relief for debtors but most significant was the 'Act of Grace', passed by parliament in 1696. This stated that:

> Creditors imprisoning debtors who cannot aliment themselves must provide an aliment of at least 3s. a day or consent to their liberation, if they refuse the magistrate w(i)t(h)in 10 days [will] set the prisoners at liberty w(i)t(h)out being liable for the debts.[32]

The basic principle of this Act remained in law until 1880; although by the time Howard visited Scotland's prisons in the 1770s the magistrates usually ordered an alimentation payment of 6d. (sterling) per day. After 1825 the incarcerating creditor was bound to pay a deposit for any aliment ordered; the award of aliment depending on the status of the prisoner. Once the deposit of 10s. was spent the debtor was freed if no further sum had been lodged.[33]

A further deterrent to the incarceration of debtors was the additional charge for 'caption'—the warrant for the apprehension of a debtor—which was paid by the creditor to the gaolers. This fee varied but was commonly 2s.6d. or 5s. (sterling) or, as in the Edinburgh Tolbooth 6d. per £1 of debt.[34] Furthermore, by the process of *cessio bonorum*[35] a debtor could obtain his liberty after one month in prison by surrendering all his effects to be divided among his creditors. Later, if the debtor's circumstances improved, his belongings might still be subject to the claims of his creditors.

This was sensible as well as compassionate legislation. A debtor could rarely hope to improve his affairs from inside a prison whilst a creditor could always use alternative law to prosecute for payment; very different from the English situation where a debtor was imprisoned until he had paid 20s. in the pound.[36] English law never supposed that a man could not pay what he owed.[37] This led to the establishment of institutions such as the King's Bench prison which was populated entirely with debtors who often languished there for the remainder of their life.

The Act of Grace must also have gone a long way towards preventing 'vexatious litigation'; there was little point in having to support your debtor in prison if there was no prospect of ever being paid—however much personal animosity might be involved. Although Howard and other commentators saw Scotland's law on debtors as compassionate, self-interest was probably the main motivating force behind the Act of Grace. Parliament was clearly determined that neither the exchequer nor the royal burghs should pay for the upkeep of debtors and indirectly was attempting to reduce the prison population. In fact, the Act operated so as to mitigate the law of imprisonment for debt. The state clearly preferred creditors to utilise the alternative legislation available which enabled them to poind[38] for debts and distrain goods and land. Parliament was, however, always aware of its own interests, declaring no less than three times that it would be usurious, and hence illegal, for creditors not to grant to their debtors the 'retention of a proportion of their annual rents for payment of taxation'.[39] Also, as long as a debtor had other goods or lands his horses and oxen which he used for ploughing could not be poinded by his creditors.[40] The authorities had no desire to swell the number of destitute people.

If debtors were actually imprisoned, despite the legislative discouragement, the second half of Bell's dictum on the law relating to debt, that 'it is sufficiently vigilant to prevent fraudulent absconding' is seen to reflect a particularly harsh piece of legislation. Although debtors could be scourged or put in the stocks, long periods of imprisonment were, particularly prior to the Act of Grace, also a common punishment for the impecunious debtor. This in itself was not unusual but in the case of debtors it was specified, in law, that they would be allowed no fresh air or excercise. Known as *squalor carceris* the law specified that,

> After a debtor is imprisoned, he ought not to be indulged with the benefit of the air, nor even under a guard; for Creditors have an interest, that their debtors be kept under close confinement, that by *squalor carceris* they may be brought to pay their debt.[41]

The evils of this legislation were undoubtedly compounded by the fact that in the event of a debtor escaping, his gaoler—and through him the magistrate who issued the warrant—was responsible for the debts of the escaped prisoner. As this remained on the statute books until 1839 debtors were frequently, 'consigned to the closest and most severe confinement . . . often crowded together in a close and fetid room which [they were] never allowed to quit'.[42] This then was the other side of the coin; for those debtors who were imprisoned despite the Act of Grace and subsequent related legislation, captivity was peculiarly horrible.

For some hard pressed debtors there was an option. If it could be attained the privilege of sanctuary offered some degree of refuge. A person retiring to sanctuary was automatically protected from diligence for the first twenty-four hours after his arrival. During that time he had to be booked into the sanctuary and obtain an official protection which in 1800 cost two guineas. Describing this process in 1801 Peter Halkerston, then bailie of the abbey and sanctuary, wrote 'When a protection is demanded it is always granted and upon production thereof, the officers of the jurisdiction, the constables of the bounds, the Abbey guards and the whole inhabitants are bound to turn out and protect the debtor'.[43]

Sanctuary had not always functioned so smoothly. Little is known about the actual workings of the original Right of Sanctuary or, as it was known in Scotland, *Girth*. The privilege was certainly not originally intended for, or used by, debtors although ultimately its use became exclusively theirs. The Right of Girth had ancient origins. Skene suggests it was already an accepted system by the sixth century AD.[44] Initially it was a privilege extended only to those who had killed someone, enabling them to flee to designated areas of royal or ecclesiastical lands. There, 'the shedder of blood could obtain . . . not only protection but fair trial and restriction of the range of the blood feud from which he fled'.[45] At face value this may seem to provide a loophole through which felons could escape, but in fact it was a means of ensuring non-partisan trial in an age of often local, biased and all too swift 'justice'. For pursuers to violate sanctuary was in Celtic society a capital crime.[46]

All parish churches were considered to offer some degree of sanctuary. In theory the extent of such sanctuaries was limited to the Frith stool which stood beside the altar; anyone sitting on the stool was under the protection of the Mother Church. In practice, however, the extent of Sanctuary was much greater, often including the kirkyard and beyond, figuratively described as 'being within the shadow of the Frith Stool'.[47] The right of sanctuary provided in such situations seems to have been fairly ineffectual, often being violated by those who had no fear of the penalties of sacrilege. The most infamous of such violations occurred when John Comyn was murdered, in Greyfriars Church, Dumfries, by Robert the Bruce and his compatriots in 1306. The violation was recorded by Barbour,

> He mysdyd thair gretly but wer
> That gave na gryth to the awter[48]

There was also a certain number of places which were granted the right of sanctuary by the sovereign—The Great Right. This was a special privilege bestowed by the king on religious houses of his choice. It could encapsulate substantial areas of land around these establishments where fugitives could seek the 'King's Peace'. The functioning of the Right of Girth in these places was dependent on the presence of the religious household which was required to shelter and feed refugees.

The sites themselves were sometimes chosen because of a personal preference of the sovereign[49] but there also seems to have been some conscious attempt to provide a good coverage of the country basing the sanctuaries around main lines of communication. Such sites included the richly endowed hospital at Soutra, the monks' cell at Lesmahagow, the Preceptory at Torphichen, the ancient monastery at Dull, and St Duthac's in Tain. Records of the endowment of sanctuaries survive from the reign of David I but even by then the privilege seems to have been a long established concept.

In addition to ecclesiastical sites the Great Right could be bestowed on royal lands and residences. The evidence is scant but it seems likely that the right of sanctuary was bestowed wherever the royal court happened to be. This would ensure that the king was not deprived of the assistance or advice of his subjects should any civil action be brought against them.[50] The only royal sanctuary to endure, after the Reformation, was Holyrood.

The extent of areas designated as sanctuaries was usually marked by girth crosses and/or chains. Relics of the system have survived as place-names, such as Cross-chain Hill and Girthgate at Soutra, or are still extant, like the impressive girth cross at Dull or the remnants of the sanctuary wall of Holyrood. Others feature in the documentary record in some way: the girth cross which used to stand at the foot of the Canongate in Edinburgh, marking the boundary of the Holyrood sanctuary, was recorded for its alternative use as a place of execution. In July 1600 Robert Birrel noted that, 'Johne Kiriland of Waristone murderit be hes awin wyff and servant man, and her nurische being also upone the conspiracy. The said gentilwoman being apprehendit, scho was tane to the girth crosse upon the 5 day of Julii, and her heid struck fra her bodie at the Cannagait fit . . .'.[51]

Another noteworthy monument was Macduff's Cross which stood near Newburgh in Fife. It is supposed to have been a memorial to the defeat of Macbeth which, as it marked the restoration of an exiled king, conferred peculiar privileges on the clan Macduff, 'whose valour contributed to that event'.[52] Whether or not this was the reason for its foundation the area certainly acted as a 'family' sanctuary.

> The Croce of the Clan Makduffe dividis Stratherne fra Fife abone the Newburgh beside Lundoris. The quhilk had privilege and liberty of girth, in sik sort that when ony man-slayer, being within the ninth degree of kin and bluid to Makduffe sumtime Earle of Fife, came to that Croce and gave nine kye and ane Colpindach [a young ox or cow], he was free of the slaughter committed by him.[53]

This privilege was certainly taken advantage of by those who fell within its jurisdiction, Sir Alexander de Moravia being only one of many recorded to have claimed its use, when he was accused of the murder of William de Spaldyne in December 1391.[54]

The sanctuary offered by the Cross of Macduff seems to have been both more comprehensive and less democratic than that available elsewhere. In other places where the privilege of the Great Right had been bestowed the only 'man-slayers' who could seek asylum were those who could claim 'Slaughter on suddenty'. This was a killing which had occurred in the midst of a violent quarrel or in a hot-blooded moment, otherwise known as 'chaud melle'. Of course any killer could claim 'chaud melle' and later when tried be found guilty of forethought murder.

Inside Sanctuary the Master of the Girth was responsible for the health, safety and welfare of fugitives. He had, nonetheless, a responsibility to the Crown, to support and maintain law and order, such that on receipt of a charge from the appropriate court he would relinquish the accused. Before doing so, however, the Master would demand adequate security (caution) for the fugitive's life and limb.[55] In this way the Great Right enabled the processes of law to function without the intervention of those attempting to 'take the law into their own hands'. Once under trial the accused would be convicted or aquitted under the normal rulings of the law.

From the records of the canons of Holyrood, it is clear that the privilege of girth was extended to all classes of men. At the time of David I, a charter was granted to the canons of Holyrood which indicated that if sanctuary was sought by someone whose right to the privilege was in doubt he could undergo 'ordeal by fire' or 'ordeal by water'. The former, endured only by the landed classes 'necessitated walking barefoot and blindfolded over red-hot plough-shares', the latter, undertaken by peasants involved the fugitive being bound hand and foot before being thrown into water; unlike the unfortunate 'witches' of later centuries, if he floated the refugee was judged to be innocent.[56]

It is also apparent that the Master of Girth was bound to apply the rules of sanctuary equally to both masters and servants requiring him as it did.

> . . . to deliver the runaway serf to his owner; but equally . . . to protect the fugitive from violence . . . the law recognising that the master had the right to take the serf out of Sanctuary, and to compel him to return to his home and servitude, but insisting that he had no right to mutilate or kill his serf, provided that any master who exercised his right to claim his runaway serf, must swear, before removing him from Sanctuary, that he would not punish the serf in life or limb.[57]

Erskine suggests that under Roman law sanctuaries were, in fact, originally intended as a means of protecting slaves from the severity of their masters.[58]

The efficacy of this endeavour towards equality in the eyes of the law cannot be judged. When it did operate as intended the Great Right of Sanctuary was undoubtedly an antidote to violence and disorder and must have defused many a volatile situation. Unfortunately the early records are too sparse to give any useful indication of the extent to which the Right was respected, violated or, indeed, used. Once again the most infamous of the violations involved the Comyns and the Bruce: having fled to sanctuary at Tain, Bruce's Queen and daughter were forcibly removed by the Earl William of Ross.[59] One of the few records of the use of sanctuary by an impoverished and probably indebted man can be gleaned from the Lord High Treasurer's Accounts for James IV, 'Item, to ane pure wyff at had hir husband in girtht in Torpechin, in elimise [alms], xiiiis'.[60]

Precisely when the Right of Girth was extended to debtors is uncertain. Erskine seems to suggest that since the establishment of Christianity, debtors have always had the right to flee from the effects of their creditors' diligence to the refuge of sanctuary.[61] At any rate, legislation during the reign of Alexander II indicates this probably happened by the end of the thirteenth century.[62]

Although the Reformation saw the abolition of religious sanctuaries, those in royal precincts continued to function. In practice this meant that only Holyrood remained in use. This may have been related to the absence of the King after 1603, the protection of his advisers no longer being necessary as it was in a peripatetic and Scottish based court. Thus, although the legal status of the Holyrood sanctuary was diminished, most of the changes applied to intentional lawbreakers and offenders in a capital crime; for the civil[63] debtor it remained a place of refuge.

The offered asylum was not, of course, without penalties. Until the Act of Grace was passed debtors retiring to sanctuary had no means of support, and on arrival any money in their possession was taken to pay creditors and the protection fee. In 1531, John Scot, 'a man neither polished by learning, nor accustomed to business, nor sufficiently shrewd for practising deceit',[64] was, as litigant in a defeated case, rendered bankrupt. He was shrewd enough, however, to take refuge at Holyrood but having no money could not subsist. In this instance the King, hearing of his case, intervened and ordered Scot confined for thirty days with only bread and water—it seems that Scot actually fasted for the thirty days, but his ultimate fate is unknown. This case was undoubtedly only recorded because of the King's intervention; for the destitute without support from friends or relatives, lack of food, clothing and shelter must have been a common problem. Subsequent changes in legislation support this view.

The provision of aliment to debtors in the Act of Grace applied not only to prisoners but also to those who had fled to sanctuary and,

> there is no instance on record of the Court of Session having refused the prayer of any person in sanctuary who sued for the benefit of the Act of Grace.[65]

Having claimed the benefit of the Act of Grace all the inhabitants were bound, when desired, to execute a disposition *omnium bonorum* 'for behoof of all his creditors'.[66] If this was refused, and for as long as it was not fulfilled, then the debtor was not entitled to aliment. This was equivalent to the process of *cessio bonorum* required from imprisoned debtors.

Gradually the privilege of girth began to weaken, in fact if not in principle—particularly when the means of apprehending a debtor altered to allow the creditor to breach the sanctuary boundaries:

> According to the regular form, the messenger-at-arms touches the debtor's shoulder with his baton; after which he is held in law to be in custody; and should he thereafter escape and take refuge in the sanctuary, the messenger may follow and seize him there, and take him to prison.[67]

For those who did attain sanctuary there must often have been a degree of permanency about the situation. Walter Scott's description of Whitefriars Sanctuary, although imaginary, may well have been based on the circumstances prevailing at Holyrood and a knowledge of its past.

> The ancient sanctuary at Whitefriars lay considerably lower than the elevated terraces and gardens of the Temple, and was therefore generally involved in the damps and fogs arising from the Thames. The brick buildings by which it was occupied crowded closely on each other, for, in a place so rarely privileged, every foot of ground was valuable; but erected in many cases by persons whose funds were inadequate to their speculations, the houses were generally insufficient, and exhibited the lamentable signs of having become ruinous while they were yet new. The wailing of children, the scolding of their mothers, the miserable exhibition of ragged linens hung from the windows to dry, spoke the wants and distresses of the wretched inhabitants.[68]

Although, as ever, verbose, Scott draws a vivid picture. Holyrood, like Whitefriars, must have been a remarkably unhealthy place; at the bottom of the hill, receiving all the rubbish and sewage of the growing town—disease would have been rife.[69]

The extent of the privilege did, however, cover a circuit of about four and a quarter miles including Arthur's Seat and Salisbury Crags (Fig. 1), thus enabling refugees to take advantage of a substantial area of open countryside. Compared with the filth and confinement endured by those imprisoned under the regime imposed by *squalor carcercis*, Halkerston suggests that those in sanctuary enjoyed the benefit of comfortable lodgings, salubrious air, and of 'extensive and romantic walks'.[70] Halkerston's remarks notwithstanding, much of the area, as today, would not have invited long-term residence.

There are indications that some residents did stay in the sanctuary on a semi-permanent basis; following the abolition of the right of sanctuary in England, soon after the Reformation, Holyrood was seldom without distinguished English characters, 'some of them gaunt, oldish gentlemen, seemingly brokendown men of fashion, wearing big gold spectacles, who now drew out existence here in defiance of creditors'.[71] Holyrood certainly continued to offer asylum to refugees from the upper echelons of society until well into the nineteenth century. For three years between 1793 and 1795 Charles-Philippe, Comte d'Artois, the younger brother of Louis XVI, lived within the Abbey bounds being under threat of arrest for debts outstanding in England.[72] Also, it is clear that the privilege was still fully functional when Halkerston, then bailie of the Abbey, was writing in 1820 although there is little to indicate whether or not the less well off could still seek refuge there.[73] With the protection fee at two guineas the truly destitute would have been unable to remain within the refuge for more than the preliminary and gratuitous twenty-four hours. Even for the 'better off' debtor it would be unwise to assume that taking the option of sanctuary was then, or had ever been, either easy or appealing. A debtor could travel outside the sanctuary limits on Sundays, when apprehension by creditors was illegal,[74] although there is evidence that

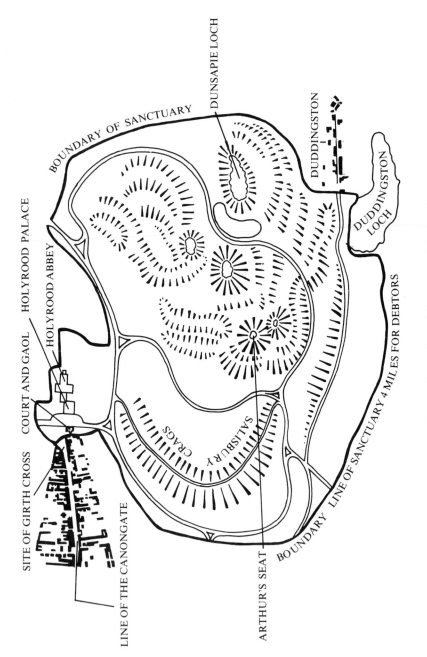

FIGURE 1 Holyrood Sanctuary, Edinburgh.

to leave sanctuary at all could be unwise: on 21 July 1709 the Court of Session heard a complaint from

> a party . . . that he had been inticed on a Sunday by one of his creditors to come out of the abbay . . . and been detained by him at his house, under pretence of communing, till the clock struck 12 at night, and then taken caption by a messenger, who the creditor had ready at hand . . .[75]

Ironically, there was even a prison within the sanctuary precincts for those who incurred debts during their stay in Holyrood.[76]

Following the Debtors (Scotland) Act of 1880 when imprisonment for debt became almost entirely unknown as a penalty, sanctuary too became obsolete although, technically, it remained in law. It will probably never be possible to establish the extent to which sanctuary was utilised by the debtors of Scotland but its very existence, and persistence, in the judicial system across so many centuries does invite the conclusion that it was seen as an important element of justice. This view is compounded by the frequency with which it features in the legislation. Even after the Reformation when its significance might have been expected to diminish, major bodies of law such as the Act of Grace indicate the continuing importance of sanctuary, specifically at Holyrood, and in relation to indebtedness. Debtors were not seen as criminals in the same way as other felons, debt was something which could catch up with anyone, from any section of society and in any part of the country. People lent and borrowed freely, often without caution (security) or with inadequate caution. The actual act of lending could be as much a social or diplomatic act as it was an economic transaction, concerned as much with cementing relationships and social dependencies as with rates of return.[77] The concept of Sanctuary, as it related to debtors, was simply a component part of this overall approach to indebtedness.

NOTES

1   As exemplified in Hugo's novel about fifteenth-century Paris, *Notre-Dame de Paris.*
2   M R Weisser, *Crime and Punishment in Early Modern Europe* (Bristol 1979), p 55.
3   Although the 1540 Act was repealed in 1603 and common law restored, sanctuary was finally abolished as a legal institution in 1623–4; '. . . certain so called sanctuaries existed till the eighteenth century, which gave practical immunity to fraudulent debtors and even to criminals. They existed in spite of statutes passed to suppress them, and did not wholly disappear till the arm of the law was strengthened by the establishment of an efficient police system'. W S Holdsworth, *A History of English Law* (London 1903), vol III, p 306.
4   R Firth, 'Capital, Saving and Credit in Peasant Societies: A Viewpoint from Economic Anthropology' in R Firth & B S Yamey (eds), *Capital, Saving and Credit in Peasant Societies* (London 1964).
5   R H Tawney, in his introduction to Thomas Wilson's *Discourse upon Usury* (London 1925), p 19.
6   J Hastings (ed), *A Dictionary of the Bible* (Edinburgh 1898), vol I, p 579.
7   R Pitcairn (ed), 'Autobiography and Diary of James Melvill' in *Woodrow Soc* vol II (Edinburgh 1842), p 362. See also R Mitchison, *Lordship to Patronage: Scotland 1603–1745* (London 1984), p 27.
8   Pitcairn, *Diary of James Melvill*, p 365.
9   F Braudel, *The Wheels of Commerce* (London 1979) p 562.
10 For a complete classification of debts, types and reasons for incurrence see L Ewan, thesis on Indebtedness in Scotland (in preparation).
11 Scottish Record Office (SRO), CC7/6.
12 I D & K A Whyte, 'Debit and Credit, Poverty and Prosperity in a Seventeenth-Century Scottish Rural Community' (unpublished Conference Paper 1984) p 8.
13 SRO CC17/7/2–3.
14 B Lenman, *An Economic History of Modern Scotland 1660–1976* (London 1977), p 32.
15 'Bond is the name used to describe the deed (or clause or clauses in a deed) by which an obligation is undertaken. This obligation may be of any kind, as to pay, or to do, or to abstain from doing'. From J L Wark, *Encyclopaedia of the Laws of Scotland* vol 8 (Edinburgh 1929), p 300.
16 SRO, CC7/6.
17 S G Checkland, *Scottish Banking: A History 1695–1973* (London 1975), p 7.
18 From 'An Inventory of Debts due to the deceast Johne Earle of Dundonald', SRO GD233/108/1/1.
19 Lenman, *Economic History*, p 50.
20 J Grant Michie (ed), 'Records of Invercauld 1547–1828' in *New Spalding Club* (Aberdeen 1901).
21 SRO GD121/45/241/16.
22 Ironically, his nephew Colonel John Steuart was to be imprisoned by his creditors some years later; W Fraser (ed), *The Red Book of Grandtully* (2 vols, Edinburgh 1868) vol II, p clxxxix.
23 J Gaw, Richt Way to the Kingdom of Heuine (c1533), in *Scottish Text Society* (STS) (Edinburgh 1888).
24 *Acts of the Parliaments of Scotland* (APS) 2 Reg Maj, vol I, p 618 c 46 (Edinburgh 1814–75).
25 T Wilson, *A Discourse upon Usury* (1572), R Tawney (ed).

26 As noted by Estienne Perlin in 1551–2 in P Hume Brown, *Early Travellers in Scotland* (Edinburgh 1891), p 77. The frequent occurrence of this sort of loan is substantiated by Fynes Moryson in 1598 when he comments, '. . . I have found that for the lending of sixtie pound, there wanted not good citizens who would give the lender a faire chamber and a good dyet as long as he would lend them the money'. *ibid*, p 81.

27 *Register of the Privy Council of Scotland* (1610–13) vol IX, p 348.

28 J Wormald, *Court Kirk and Community* (London 1981), p 126.

29 T Adams, *The Soules of Sicknesse* (London 1616), p 28.

30 G J Bell, *Principles of the Law of Scotland* 5th edn, sect 2315 (Edinburgh 1860).

31 *APS* vol VI ii (1654) 822 b, (1656) 759 a, 759 b, 760 a, 762 b.

32 *APS* General Index and vol X, (1696) p 66 c 32.

33 J Cameron, *Prisons and Punishment in Scotland* (Edinburgh 1983), p 62.

34 Cameron, *Prisons and Punishment*, p 61, and J Neild, State of *Prisons in England, Scotland and Wales* (London 1812), p 300.

35 *Cessio bonorum*: The ceding or making over of a person's property and effects to his creditors.

36 J Howard, *State of the Prisons in England and Wales with an Account of some Foreign Prisons 1777/1780 and 1784* (London 1929) p 147.

37 P Halkerston, *A Treatise on the History, Law and Privileges of the Palace and Sanctuary of Holyroodhouse* (Edinburgh 1801), p 50.

38 Poinding was a diligence or form of law by which a creditor could endeavour to make good his payment. As the earliest diligence recognised in the law of Scotland poinding enabled a debtor's moveables to be directly transferred to a creditor. Letters of poinding could be used to remove goods from a debtor's lands and have them carried to the market cross of the head burgh of the sheriffdom where they were then sold.

39 *APS* vol IX (1690) p 236 b; vol X (1698) p 130 b; vol XI (1702) p 21 b.

40 *APS* vol II (1503) p 246 c 50; vol III (1581) p 217 c 14.

41 J Erskine, *Principles of the Law of Scotland* 21st edn, quoting Act of Session 14 June 1771.

42 J J Gurney, *Notes on a visit made to some of the Prisons in Scotland and Northern England* (London 1819), pp 107–8.

43 P Halkerston, *Treatise on Holyrood*, p 56.

44 W F Skene, *Celtic Scotland* (3 vols, Edinburgh 1880), vol II, pp 65–6.

45 A Hannah, 'The Sanctuary of Holyrood', *Old Edinburgh Club*, vol XV (1927), p 56.

46 Hannah, 'Sanctuary of Holyrood', pp 56–7.

47 P H R Mackay, *Sanctuary and the Privilege of St John* (Edinburgh 1976), p 5.

48 J Barbour, *The Bruce c*1374, STS (Edinburgh 1894) vol I, ii, p 44 (gryth and awter translating as girth and alter respectively).

49 One example of this occurred when Malcolm IV bestowed the Great Right on Innerleithen Church after his dead son had lain there overnight.

50 P Halkerston, *Treatise on Holyrood*, p 42, and J Erskine, *Institute of the Law of Scotland* (Edinburgh 1773), vol 4, p 25.

51 R Birrel, 'Diary of Robert Birrel from 1532 until 1605', in J G Dayell (ed) *Fragments of Scottish History* (Edinburgh 1798), p 49.

52 G Chalmers, *Caledonia* (5 vols, Edinburgh 1824), vol II, p 466.

53 J Skene, 'De Verborum Significatione' quoted in *Liber Insule Missarum, Bannatyne Club* (Edinburgh 1847), pp xii–xiii.

54 *Liber Insule Missarum*, p xiii.

55 Mackay, *Sanctuary*, p 8.

56   Hannah, 'Sanctuary of Holyrood', p 59.
57   Mackay, *Sanctuary*, pp 8–9. This egalitarian ruling dates from the thirteenth century hence the use of the term 'serf'. In *Lectures of Scotch Legal Antiquities* Cosmo Innes noted that 'The last claim of neyfship or serfdom proved in a Scottish Court was 1364' (Edinburgh 1872), p 159, indicating that the term was in use until at least half way through the fourteenth century.
58   Erskine, *Institute* IV, pp 812–3.
59   G W S Barrow, *Robert Bruce* (Edinburgh 1976), pp 228–9.
60   J Balfour (ed), *Accounts of the Lord High Treasurer of Scotland* (Edinburgh 1902) vol IV, 1507–1513, p 189.
61   Erskine, *Institute* IV, pp 812–3.
62   *APS* Alexander II, vol I, p 401 c 9.
63   J L Wark, *Encyclopaedia of the Laws of Scotland* (11 vols, Edinburgh 1927) After the Reformation, 'The right of Sanctuary afforded protection to civil debtors only, and did not extend to debtors of the King, or to criminals (including fraudulent bankrupts), or to persons under diligence for performance of a fact within their power.' vol 8, p 40.
64   Hannah, 'Sanctuary of Holyrood', p 61.
65   *ibid*, p 84.
66   Wark, *Laws of Scotland* pp 8, 38. *Omnium bonorum*: a disposition conveying all the granter's goods of every description.
67   W Bell, *Dictionary and Digest of the Law of Scotland* (Edinburgh 1838).
68   W Scott, *Fortunes of Nigel* (Edinburgh 1831) p 198.
69   I H Adams, *The Making of Urban Scotland* (London 1978), pp 133–4, for a discussion of early sewage disposal in Edinburgh.
70   P Halkerston, Note Respecting the Sanctuary of Holyroodhouse in *A Translation and Explanation of the Technical Terms and Phrases used in Mr Erskine's Institute of the Law of Scotland* (Edinburgh 1820), p 94.
71   R Chambers, *Domestic Annals of Scotland*, 2nd edn (Edinburgh 1859), vol 1, p 97.
72   A J Mackenzie Stuart, 'A Royal Debtor at Holyrood', *Stair Soc*, Miscellany One (1971), pp 193–201.
73   With the rising price of the protection fee and, almost certainly, the effects of changing social attitudes, few of the truly destitute were claiming the Right of Sanctuary by the nineteenth century. However, it is interesting to note that Peter Halkerston, as bailie of the Abbey and Sanctuary, was still attempting to reduce the protection fee as late as 1801. He also mentions a register of those who had sought and been granted Sanctuary at Holyrood—no evidence of such a list being extant has been found.
74   Mackenzie Stuart, 'Royal Debtor', p 194.
75   Lord H H Kames, *The Decisions of the Court of Session from its first Institution to the present time* (Edinburgh, 1791) vol I, p 361.
76   Neild, *State of the Prisons*, p 199. In 1688 an attempt was made to have a prisoner there transported to another prison but the action was defeated 'because then his other creditors might have arrested him, which they could not do in the abbey', from Kames, *Decisions of the Court of Session*, vol I, p 361.
77   R A Dodgshon, 'Highland Chiefdoms, 1500–1745: A Study in Redistributive Exchange' (Unpublished Conference Paper 1985), p 15.

The Scottish Farming Township
As Metaphor

Robert A Dodgshon

Studies of how early farming townships were organised have mostly assumed a pragmatically-worked landscape, one in which the practical character of clearing the wood, dividing out the land or ploughing the soil mattered above all else. Communities are effectively seen as responding to needs and functions in a direct, uncomplicated way rather than conceiving them through hidden concepts of order. Yet any familiarity with anthropological studies of peasant societies suggests that such a mundane approach neglects what could be a vital dimension. Put simply, early farming communities will not have approached the laying out of their townships or routines of husbandry in a matter-of-fact way but would have been informed by concepts about how best to organise their world so as to sustain the continuing abundance of plants, animals and the community itself. As G C Homans made clear in his discussion of the English medieval village,[1] these concepts were not based on the teaching of the church but were rooted in customary beliefs that approached the problem of abundance and fertility in a seemingly more direct way. Indeed, such beliefs could serve as a source of order, transforming townships into symbolic landscapes rich in signs and meanings.

I want to argue that our understanding of pre-Improvement farming townships in Scotland can be enhanced by taking a similar approach. Even during the early modern period, 1500–1750, we can recover practices and rituals that seemingly charged their layout and sense of order with a quite different meaning to that which we might expect in a purely Euclidean world. In fact, for areas like eastern and north-eastern Scotland, the range and legibility of these practices and rituals suggests we may be dealing with the ingredients of a once unified cosmology. Their survival in such a coherent form raises further questions about the regional culture of these areas, suggesting that recent debate over the Picts as 'a conserving culture' may have long-term implications for the understanding of local culture.[2]

The problem can be introduced through evidence for the practice of sun-division. This was a means of dividing townships between landholders that was prevalent throughout eastern and north-eastern Scotland during the

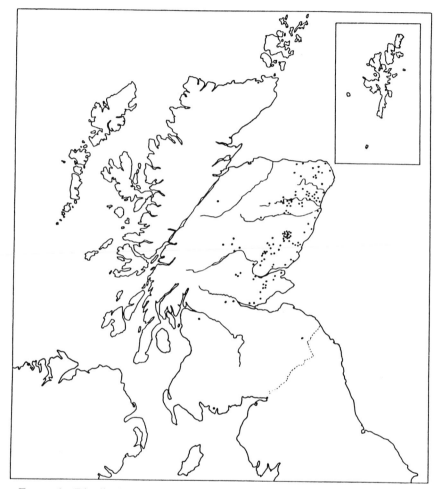

FIGURE 1   Distribution of references to solarem/umbralem and sunny/shadow
shares. Reprinted from Dodgshon, Scandinavian solskifte and the sun-wise
division of land in eastern Scotland, p 6.

medieval and early modern periods. By it, landholders had their holdings or
shares designated as the sunny or shadow portions of the township. Those
holding the sunny portion were allocated land lying towards the south and
east of the township whilst those holding the shadow portion were allocated
land lying to the north and west. Such a scheme could be employed to divide
a township into runrig strips or into separate, discrete holdings.

   A review of evidence for the practice provided three main conclusions.
First, when mapped, references to sunny and shadow shares appear concentrated in eastern and north-eastern Scotland (Fig. 1). Second, the Scottish
material removed any ambiguity that might still remain about the authenticity

of the practice in Britain. This was an important point of conclusion as English evidence for the sun-division had been treated sceptically, with some writers seeing medieval references to land lying versus solem and versus umbram as referring to land lying towards the south and north respectively. No such doubt can exist over equivalent Scottish references. Not only do we find the terms sunny and shadow being freely used in translation for the Latin forms of solarem and umbralem, but we also find instances in which their meaning is made fully explicit. Some charters, for instance, refer to the sunny and shadow portions of a township as lying runrig, or intermixed with one another in the form of strips. In this sort of context, such references cannot possibly have been used to denote whether one share was actually more sunny or more shady than another or more southerly or northerly than another in an absolute sense. Set within a runrig layout, their use can only be to establish the relative ordering of land during its allocation. Any ambiguity that might still remain in the interpretation of such terms can be removed by looking at early law texts, such as T Craig's *Jus Feudale* or J Erskine's *Principles of the Law of Scotland*. In them, we find the principles behind a sun-division fully explained, with the terms sunny and shadow being used to determine the order in which land was allocated. Appropriately, such divisions were to begin at dawn, in the east of the township and work their way round the township in a sunwise direction, doling out strips of land to the sunny half, then, the shadow half in strict sequence. The third conclusion concerned the relationship between the sun-division of townships and the use of schemes based around over [upper]/nether, east/west, fore/back and mor/beag [great/ little]. Those based around over [upper]/nether, east/west and fore/back occur alongside the sun-division of townships in eastern and north-eastern Scotland but, in addition, are to be found widely throughout southern Scotland as well as in the far north. The use of divisions based around mor/beag occur throughout the Highlands. There are good reasons for seeing these different forms as equivalent to each other, variants of the same basic scheme. Not only do we find law books treating designations like east/west and fore/back as identical to sunny/shadow forms, but more revealing still, we find townships divided into east/west shares in one source being described as divided into sunny/shadow or upper/nether shares in another.[3]

Viewed in association with the wider and equivalent use of share designations like east/west, over/nether or mor/beag, sun-division constitutes strong evidence for the former use of dual classificatory schemes. In their original form, such schemes fused society and the world around it into a single scheme of classificatory order, creating a conceptual world of two interlocking halves or moieties. As R Wagner has pointed out, such a scheme provided cultures with a basis for internal differentiation but—through its stress on categorical opposition—it also stressed the interdependence of the two halves.[4] The categorical order embodied in such a scheme was invariably expressed through the spatial ordering of society, with the two symbolic categories into which society was divided being spatially-opposed through relational oppositions like east/west, nether/upper and so on. To judge from the available literature, we can expect any one of three possibilities: either a society could divide itself internally between opposed territories, paired settlements or between halves within a single settlement. As a classificatory scheme that arranged society's perception of the cosmos within the same framework of order as society itself, so that the divisions within society embodied the divisions within the universe at large, it follows that the order mapped into settlement or territory also symbolised these wider divisions. In effect, each mapping served as a microcosm of their macrocosm, replicating the given order of the latter in the earthly world of the former. It is for this reason that a widespread feature of dual classificatory schemes was the way settlements were ordered through relational oppositions that had as much to do with the categorical differentiation between what was above/below (i.e. sky/earth, upper/lower, white/black, day/night and sunny/shadow) as with what lay around (i.e. east/west). Indeed, the dual ordering of settlement embodied all these different forms of categorical opposition at one and the same time, being a real-world representation of all that was upper/lower, east/west, fore/back and so on.

There is certainly a case for seeing tribal groups in dark-age Scotland— including those of eastern and north-eastern Scotland—as ordered through dual classificatory schemes.[5] Their fusion of social and natural order and their categorical sub-division of this fused order into two opposed halves would have had considerable implications for the ordering of space and settlement, hints of which occur in contemporary sources. Of course, by the late fifteenth century, when we first see relational oppositions like sunny/ shadow, east/west or mor/beag being used to divide townships, we are confronted with the residual traces of such a system, a survival only of the procedures by which it was mapped into space and territory. Admittedly, their treatment as equivalent forms even to the extent of being interchangeable in the designation of particular examples preserves the spirit of their original compound meaning. However, the order into which townships were being cast by such procedures now reflected the need to differentiate between the holdings of landowners or tenants and no longer had anything to do with the dual ordering of society. The mere fact that society faced a continuing need to distinguish between holdings or townships may in itself have been sufficient to ensure the continuing use of these archaic ordering procedures despite the substantive change in their social context. However, we must not be too hasty in reducing practices like sun-division solely to procedure, one sustained by a combination of practical need and inertia rather than any ongoing belief in its symbolism.[6] We have to consider the question of whether, quite apart from its initial links to the dual organisation of society, it continued to serve as a vehicle for other forms of meaning.

If we examine the anthropological literature on pre-modern communities, we find that symbolic order is shaped as much by their ideas on how their universe or cosmos came into being and sustained itself (= creation myths) as by their sense of classificatory order, the former providing theme and concept and the latter providing a structure of relationships. Furthermore, we also find that many cultures were just as concerned to symbolise their settlements through the concepts of the former as through the order provided

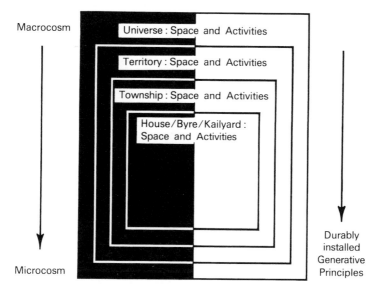

FIGURE 2   Diagrammatic representation of how the same principles of order can be expressed at different scales and through different dimensions of activity.

by the latter so that in every sense, their settlements became a microcosm of their macrocosm.[7] More was involved than a simple concordance of form between their earthly and heavenly worlds. What P Bourdieu calls 'durably installed generative principles' are used to shape everyday practices in a manner consistent with their concept of the universe so that different scales of order and different activities become homologous, each capable of serving as a metaphor for one another.[8] The product is a richly symbolic landscape (see Fig. 2). To reconstruct it in a projective or Euclidean sense is to transform it into a different kind of space, to emasculate the meaning which early communities themselves attached to it. As A Gurevich put it in a discussion of time and space in medieval Scandinavia: 'time and space in their perception were not *a priori* concepts existing before or outside experience' but drew their meaning from the substance of life, a meaning that was wholly ordered and symbolic.[9]

Informed by such work, I want to argue that the reason why schemes of land division rooted in dual classificatory order were carried forward in Scotland, long after the dual organisation of society had faded, was because they gave support to popular ongoing creation myths. In particular, I want to argue that those forms based on the use of sunny/shadow shares provide us with an entrée to this aspect of the problem simply because their relationship to prevailing creation myths appear more legible. Apart from its concentration in eastern and north-eastern Scotland, what stands out about the use of sunny/shadow shares is that as well as expressing a clear sense of relational order, it was also a form of share designation that was pivoted around a powerful symbolic subject, one that figures prominently in many primitive creation myths. Patently, this focus on the sun as a source of ordination extends and reinforces the symbolism embodied in the sun-wise execution of land allocation. In making this point, I am not suggesting that sunny/shadow shares differed in meaning from other forms of share designation. Their equivalency in early law books and their occasional interchangeability in practice would seem to rule out such an assumption. Indeed, it is more likely that for communities who made use of them, forms based on east/west, fore/back or mor/beag shares were charged with the same meaning as sunny/shadow shares, being different ways of expressing the polarities of the sun's movement. Set in this wider context, the significance of sun-division derives from its greater legibility to us as a symbolic ordering of land allocation not its individuality.

More to the point, I want to argue that it helps bring into focus a popular concept of abundance and fertility. This concept provided the peasant mind with a paradigm of order. Only by establishing an accordance between this conceptual order on the one hand and the actual organisation of the township and its activities on the other, effectively turning cosmography into geography, could communities assure themselves of fertility and abundance. At its core lay the idea of the sun as a source of fertility and abundance, a fairly obvious piece of symbolism in an agricultural society especially one whose growing season was short and risk-laden. From this central concept, farming communities derived two forms of order. First, there was the ordination provided by the sun's differentiation of the world into sunny/shadow, light/dark, fore/back and over/nether spaces. Second, there was a symbolism of movement. Studies of cosmographies in which the sun had a prominent role, such as E Turville-Petre's work on Norse cosmologies,[10] stress the fascination provided by this movement. The sun is not seen as a static symbol of fertility. It rose in the east, journeyed rapidly across the sky to disappear in the west, only to re-appear in the east the next day. Coupled with its equally vital shortening then lengthening journey between winter and summer, this provided the basis for a ritual of fertility based on a ritual of movement. To harness its powers, one had to establish an accordance with this clear ordination of time and space, starting in the east at dawn and working sun-wise around to the west by sunset.

The use of a sun-division to organise townships clearly demonstrates how such a concept could be used to both order and symbolise space. Where used to create a runrig layout, its effect on the peasant mind must have been profound and enduring with the entire arable of the township cast into a mosaic of differentiated but inter-dependent space through the imagery of sunny and shadow shares. The ritual that accompanied such divisions, with landholders starting in the east at dawn and working their way sun-wise round the township, is equally revealing. It proclaims that here was a ritual of movement or process, not a static pattern of fixed relational order. Conveniently, one of the few available descriptions of how an early division was actually executed, that involving the division of land at Liston in Stirlingshire in 1485, talks about landholders having to 'gang to the estfeld at dawn'.[11]

The procedure with which sun-divisions were executed has implications for how we interpret particular variants of the practice, or those based on sunny/ shadow, over/nether and easter/wester ploughs.[12] Though not evidenced explicitly, there is surely every reason to suppose that not only were these shares divided out in a sun-wise fashion, but there must have been—by virtue of the same symbolism—a sun-wise ploughing of the township, though an alternative might have been to establish a metaphor of the sun's movement by means of a token ritual before the first spring ploughing.[13] Though he does not link it to his evidence for the sun-division of land, Homans refers to a fifteenth-century English ritual whereby the plough was led sun-wise round a fire prior to the first spring ploughing. Though explicit evidence for the ploughing of land in a sun-wise manner in Scotland is lacking, there are indications that other forms of farm activity were associated with token rituals based on a sun-wise movement. A Carmichael, for instance, provides a number of Highland examples, with tasks like preparing the seed, harvesting and grinding the grain all involving a ritual of sun-wise movement designed to ensure abundance.[14] Comparable rituals were embedded in the routines of stock husbandry. They included the widely-reported practice of farmers driv- ing their stock between two fires or sun-wise around one. Such fires were called need fires, meaning they were started by rubbing sticks together, and were intended for 'the curing of cattell' or their protection against disease.[15]

This last example introduces an extra dimension to the problem. In addition to rituals based on sun-wise movement, the sun could also be symbolised through the use of fire. Significantly, the areas in which we find sun-division being practised are also areas for which the practice of fire rituals is par- ticularly-well documented over the sixteenth and seventeenth centuries. The extent to which fire rituals were practised and the extent to which they were seen as an alternative form of belief is underlined by the 1581 Act of Par- liament which specifically tried to control customary forms of symbolic belief like fire rituals and well dressings.[16] The fire rituals referred to here had a standard form. At a set time of the year, but mostly on either 1 May (Beltane), mid-summer (that is, St John's or St Peter's eve), St Michael's eve at the end of September or even in November, a district bon-fire (or bone-fire) was constructed on a local hill top. As well as being—in itself—a focus of ritual behaviour, with farmers and their families doing cermonial circuits of the fire in a sun-wise direction, it was also a source of symbolic meaning. After completing their circuit of the bon-fire, farmers took a lighted branch or clavie and returned to their farms where, in the company of their family and servants, they went on a sun-wise circuit of their arable fields, then their byres and houses—ritually re-lighting the hearth fire for the year in the latter— before finally planting the clavie in their kailyard. A full description of the custom was published for Moray by Lachlan Shaw[17] and for the Highlands by Martin Martin.[18] It is also mentioned in both Presbytery and Kirk Session records. A 1583 entry in the Stirling Presbytery records clearly felt that the Act of two years earlier needed reinforcement. Under the heading 'Ben fyris', it acknowledged the 'grit abuse and superstititioun usit be sindrie and dyvers persones within the bounds of the prebytery in setting further of ben fyres midsomer evin last' and reminded congregations that it was now unlawful.[19] In fact, despite the 1581 Act, the Church struggled long to eradicate the practice. At Dingwall, a 1655 declaration by the Presbytery required 'severall bretherin' to inform their congregations that they must 'desist of the superstitious abuse used on St Johnes day by burneing torches thro ther cornes, and fyres in thair townes and thaire after fixing thair staiks in thair kailyeards',[20] the declaration being repeated in 1671.[21] Even in the eighteenth century, local kirk sessions were still passing local acts against it. In 1704, the kirk session of Inveravon passed an 'Act against Clavies', stating that whereas 'it hath been the Custom and practice of many in this parish of Inveravirne to goe about yr folds & cornes with kindled Torches of ffirr, superstitiouslie & Idolouslie ascribing yt power to the fire of sanctifieing yr Cornes & cattell', those now found guilty of the practice were to be censured.[22] At Deskford, the minister was still warning 'the more ignorant and weak part of the parish' against the burning of fires as late as 1774.[23] The Church though, could be ambivalent. In Durris parish (Kincardineshire), fire rituals had made the transition from being a practice to be outlawed to being worthy of preservation, with the local kirk sessions actually supervising a bequest of 1787 that provided food for herdsmen involved in the building of mid-summer fires on Cairn-shee.[24]

The symbolism behind such fire rituals is well conveyed by G MacKay Brown in his *An Orkney Tapestry*. On midsummer eve, or Johnsmas, he wrote, 'fire answered fire from the hilltops, till all Orkney was a dapple of flame and shadow'. Each peasant took a torch of burning heather from the fire down to his own croft where he carried it slowly round his fields, barn and house so that 'he claimed a share of the sun's bounty for his family and stock'.[25] In reply to those who would dismiss MacKay's words as embroidering a rather empty ritual, it is worth noting that precisely what troubled the clergy about fire rituals is the fact that they were far from being empty of meaning. Admittedly, it was only one of a handful of popular customs which the kirk sessions were anxious to suppress because they were considered 'superstitious and heathenish practices'. The others included guizers[26] and well gatherings.[27] In their place, it offered its own interpretation of abundance and scarcity, with the Presbyteries regularly instructing congregations to pray in thanks for abundant harvests.[28]

Given official hostility towards them, it is tempting to argue that fire rituals were a socially marginal practice to be placed in the same category as witchcraft. This however, would be to miss an essential point. Witchcraft and fire rituals display an interesting polarity. Fire rituals were based on the assumption that a sun-wise ritual of movement conferred abundance. With witchcraft, the opposite was assumed, with the ritual of anti-sun-wise movement, widdershins or widdersonnes, inducing scarcity and infertility. When Janet Forsyth was charged with witchcraft at Westray in Orkney, 1629, the case against her rested on the fact that she had walked around a neighbour's best corn stacks 'contrair to the sun's cours' with the result that the corns from these stacks now 'laickit the substance'.[29] Likewise, we can only admire the conceptual mastery of an Aberdeenshire woman, Janet Wishert, who in

1597 was charged with going to the township's cornfields before sun-rise to check which way the corn was growing. What did she mean? If it 'growis withersonnes', she pleaded, it will be a year of scarcity, but when 'it growis sonegatis about', it will be a year of abundance.[30] Encapsulated in these two instances of reported witchcraft is the belief that to order things sunwise ensured abundance whereas to do things in reverse was to risk scarcity and disorder. One is reminded of what M Eliade said about the Vikings when they first landed in Iceland.[31] Their first act was to integrate their new space into their cosmography, an act which meant getting rid of its chaos by reducing it to their conceptual order of things. For the Vikings, this meant bounding their new territory with fire in a sun-wise ritual of movement. The same idea recurs in Gurevitch's work on medieval Scandinavia: the process of putting the world in order, separating earth and heaven, day and night, 'was at the same time a process of settling farmsteads and creating once and for all a definite topography of the universe', a topography that was characterised as much by its mythological and religious meaning as by its geographical meaning.[32]

The challenge posed by these various mental structures and ritual practices is whether we have any grounds for linking them together as the differentiated components of a once unified scheme of cosmology. Their homologous form and concept is undoubtedly suggestive. There is also little doubt that even as late as the seventeenth century, the various elements were not wholly detached but existed within the mind of individual or local communities. The evidence for Pitcaple (Aberdeenshire) illustrates the extent to which the different forms of symbolism and ritualistic expression may have existed side-by-side. Many of Pitcaple's townships appear divided into sunny and shadow shares so that their occupiers would have been imbued with a sun-based ordering of property, one executed through a sun-wise movement around the township.[33] In some cases, townships were organised around a distinction between sunny and shadow ploughs[34] so that there is also the possibility that ploughing was at some point associated with a ritual that symbolically replicated the sun's movement or invoked its life conferring powers. That such a sun-wise organisation of farm space and activity may have been linked with the use of fire to symbolise the power of the sun is, of course, implied by the ritualistic drawing of a fire from a community bon-fire and its sun-wise circuit around the fields and byre. The Pitcaple area was associated with such bon-fires[35] though a search of its kirk session records yielded no direct mention of them.[36] However, there were other dimensions to the symbolic use of fire. In 1686, on the same day that the Pitcaple barony court ratified the Act of Parliament requiring all tenants to live peaceably, 'free of all fanatical disorders', it set a fine of £20 Scots for outgoing tenants or others who 'drown out their fyres at their removeall' requiring them instead 'to leave the samen burning'.[37] The only possible explanation for such a by-law was that local communities perceived a link between a hearth fire re-lit annually by the township's bon-fire and the farm's fertility, so much so that extinguishing and re-lighting it at any other time threatened this vital link. An equally interesting entry is contained in the barony court records of nearby Leys. In 1628, its barony court had to decide how tenants should pay their reeking hens, a render that occurs widely in the north-east. Talking about all the townships of the barony, it declared that those of the east and west grounds should pay them in alternate years.[38] Clearly, the organisation of townships—whether in the form of east/west or sunny/shadow shares—was intertwined with customary practice, seemingly serving to give the latter form. It is also worth adding that a reeking hen was a render of a hen paid by each dwelling from which smoke issued, a choice piece of symbolism in a society which apparently attached meaning to the fire of a farmstead. Though its integral character must remain only an hypothesis, we can clearly fuse these various practices and rituals together into a single system of belief and behaviour, one whose effect was to create—in the mind of the ordinary peasant—a symbolic ordering of both activities and landscape (see Fig. 3).

The anthropologist, M Sahlins, has argued that cultural practices represent the way in which cultures conceive and symbolise their problems rather than the undiluted product or 'dependent variable of an inescapable practical logic'.[39] In the foregoing essay, I have tried to show that we cannot begin to understand how some early farming communities in Scotland organised their townships without first heeding his point. Viewed over the sixteenth and seventeenth centuries, areas like eastern and north-eastern Scotland can be associated with a range of practices whose observance served to create a symbolic landscape out of the farms and fields that students of rural history— the present author included—have too easily seen in terms solely of appearances. We need to see practices like the sun-division of land and fire rituals as being more than empty procedures or gestures for those who sustained them. Indeed, given the case for seeing divisions based on east/west, fore/back, over/nether and mor/beag as equivalent to those developed around sunny/shadow shares and given the widespread nature of both fire rituals and rituals of sun-wise movement, there are good reasons for arguing that this conclusion may extend far beyond the areas characterised by the explicit use of a sun-division. In a world of recurrent scarcities and famine, such practices acted out a concept of how these vagaries of farm output could be countered. Fertility and abundance were to do with observing a proper order of things, both in the laying out of the township and when performing the regular tasks of husbandry. In short, it was to do with the way the world of the township was symbolised, with the meaning that was attached to its organisation. Whilst it may be difficult to establish whether the different forms of symbolic expression were practised in the same township at the same time, this does not mean that they should be treated as incoherent, or without connection. Arguably, the way each worked towards an homologous form of order suggests they were rooted in, or devolved from, a coherent concept, one whose reconstruction may possibly provide us with the outlines of a peasant cosmology.

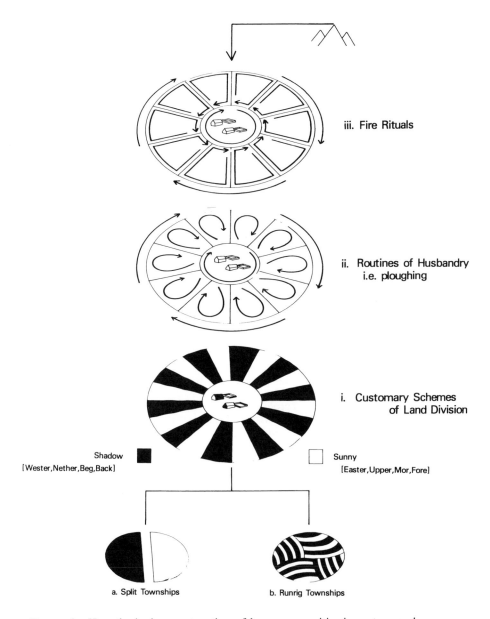

iii. Fire Rituals

ii. Routines of Husbandry
i.e. ploughing

i. Customary Schemes
of Land Division

Shadow
[Wester,Nether,Beg,Back]

Sunny
[Easter,Upper,Mor,Fore]

a. Split Townships

b. Runrig Townships

FIGURE 3   Hypothesised reconstruction of how communities in eastern and
north-eastern Scotland may have mapped their concept of the macrocosmos
into the organisation of their microcosmos, or their township and its everyday
routines.

NOTES

1   G C Homans, *English villagers in the thirteenth century* (Cambridge, Mass, 1941), especially pp 353–81.

2   The description of the Picts as a 'conserving culture' is taken from C Thomas, 'The interpretation of the Pictish symbols', *Archaeological Jnl*, 120 (1963), p 68. For a recent and highly relevant discussion of Pictish cosmology that bears out their description as 'a conserving society', see A Jackson, *The symbol stones of Scotland* (Stromness 1984), especially pp 120–43. What Jackson has to say on pp 218–9 has a considerable bearing on my subsequent discussion.

3   For a fuller review of this evidence, see R A Dodgshon, 'Scandinavian solskifte and the sun-wise division of land in eastern Scotland', *Scottish studies*, 19 (1975), pp 1–14.

4   R Wagner, *The invention of culture*, 2nd edn (Chicago 1981), p 116.

5   R A Dodgshon, 'Symbolic classification and the development of early celtic landscape', *Cosmos* 1 (1985), pp 61–83. The original version of this article was presented as a paper to a conference on 'Duality' held at Stirling University, 1984. It took account of A Jackson's 'Pictish social structure and symbol stones', *Scottish studies* 15 (1971), pp 121–40 but not of his more extended and authoritative discussion of Pictish dual organisation that was published in his *Symbol stones of Scotland*, 1984.

6   What follows should be seen as an extension of Dodgshon, 'Symbolic classification', 78–9.

7   For comment on this aspect, see M Eliade, *The myth of the eternal return or cosmos and history*, English edition (Princeton 1954), pp 6–34; P Wheatley, *The pivot of the four quarters* (Edinburgh 1971), especially pp 436–51.

8   P Bourdieu, *Outline of a theory of practice*, English edition (1977), pp 98–158.

9   A Y Gurevich, 'Space and time in the weltmodell of the old Scandinavian peoples', *Medieval Scandinavia*, 2 (1969), p 52.

10   E O G Turville-Petre, 'Fertility of beast and soil in old Norse literature', in E C Polome (ed), *Old Norse literature and mythology* (Austin 1969), p 245.

11   HMC, *Report on mss in various collections*, 5 (1909), pp 80–2. The Liston division has considerable interest. The commencement of its division in the east at dawn and the description of its major field units in terms like over field and nether field suggests it was conceived in the terms made clear by law books like Craig's *Jus Feudale*. Yet the division appears to have had the purpose of casting the township into red and white portions. A comparable division of townships into red and white sections occurs in SRO GD80/194, a list of services due from part of the Macpherson of Cluny estate. In fact, colour classification (invariably red, white or black) was a feature of dual or symbolic systems of classification and certainly features in Jackson's reconstruction of Pictish cosmology, *Symbol stones of Scotland*, pp 218–9.

12   Typical is the reference amongst the Lord Forbes Collection to the 'shadow plough of the manor of Thanistoun' in 1597, SRO GD52/1629, and amongst the Huntly Muniments to 'the wester plough of Tillycairn', SRO GD312/30/13.

13   Homans, *English villagers*, p 36.

14   A Carmichael, *Carmina gadelica*, vol 1. *Hymns and incantations* (Edinburgh 1928), pp 195, 243 and 249.

15   Examples of need fire for 'the curing of cattell' are detailed in *Extracts from the Presbytery book of Strathbogie*, Spalding club (Aberdeen 1843), pp 51 and 105.

16   *Acts of Parliament of Scotland*, vol 3 (Edinburgh 1814), p 212.

17 L Shaw, *The history of the province of Moray* (Edinburgh 1774), p 241. Shaw distinguishes between Beltane and mid-summer fires, the former involving a ritual movement around a fire and the latter a movement of a fire sun-wise round the fields. There is also relevant comment concerning the symbolisation of the sun on p 238. A more comprehensive attempt to schedule the various forms of fire ritual is provided by M Macleod Banks, *British calendar customs, Scotland,* vols 2 (London 1939) and 3 (London 1941).

18 M Martin, *A Description of the Western islands of Scotland,* 2nd edn (London 1716), pp 116–7. Martin described the practice as having died out during the mid seventeenth century.

19 J Kirk (ed), *Stirling Presbytery records,* Scottish history society, 4th series, 17 (1981), pp 84. An attempt to control 'the superstitious onbigging of mid-sommer fyris' at Elgin in 1591 also referred back to the 1581 Act, threatening those who ignored the warning with being put 'in sakecloth three seuerall Sondays vpoun the stuill of repentance besydis the kingis penaltie', see W Cramond, *The records of Elgin 1234–1800,* New spalding club (Aberdeen 1908), vol 2, pp 17–19.

20 W Mackay (ed), *Extracts from the presbytery records of Inverness and Dingwall from 1638 to 1688,* Scottish history society, first series, 24 (1896), p 268.

21 Ibid, p 323.

22 Scottish record office (hereafter SRO), CH2/191, vol 2, p 38.

23 W Cramond, *The church and churchyard of Deskford including extracts from the kirk sessions of Deskford* (Banff 1885), p 23.

24 A Macdonald, 'Midsummer bon-fires', *Folklore,* 15 (1904), pp 350–1.

25 G Mackay Brown, *An Orkney tapestry* (London 1973), p 129.

26 A good instance of the church acting against guizers—those who 'disguise themselves in the habit of ane other sex men in women's clothing and women taking on men's apparell'—is given in W Cramond (ed), *Extracts from the records of the synod of Moray* (Elgin 1906), p 133. Good references also occur in SRO CH2/217, vol 1.

27 Cramond, *Records of the synod of Moray,* p 69, includes an inspection of the kirk session records of Kingussie, 1643, which reported that it 'fand no censure of haunters and repairers to superstitious wells and places because the minister alledged all were guilty'. See also W Cramond (ed) *The presbytery of Fordyce* (Banff 1885), p 40.

28 Typical examples can be found in ibid, p 219; SRO CH2/971, parish of Clatt, vol 1, 1699; CH2/191, parish of Inveravon, vol 3, 1727 and 1750, the reference in 1727, p 156, talking about 'a day of thanksgivings to God in the province for his greate mercy in giving a plentifull cropt after the greate scarcity that the land laboured under in the last season'.

29 N W Thomas (ed), *County folklore,* vol 3, *printed extracts no 5, examples of printed folklore concerning the Orkney and Shetland islands.* Publications of the folklore society, 49 (published 1903 for 1901), p 77.

30 *Miscellany of the Spalding club,* 1 (Aberdeen 1841), p 96.

31 Eliade, *Myth of the eternal return,* p 10.

32 Gurevitch, 'Space and time', p 45.

33 SRO GD108/15, 21–2 and 28 provide examples like the 'half shadow lands of Auchtquhorsk', 1555, and the 'sunny half lands of Creichmond, Rombekendill, Ardeherauld and Ardibuk', 1588.

34 SRO GD108/17 and 25 provide examples like the 'scheddow pleuche lands of Glak', 1558/9, and 'sone pleuch of Glak', 1597/8.

35   J M McPherson, *Primitive beliefs in the north-east of Scotland* (London 1929), pp 6 and 8.
36   SRO CH2/527/1.
37   SRO GD108/49, 13 May 1686.
38   'Extracts from the court books of the baronies of Skene, Leys and Whithaugh 1613–87', in *Miscellany of Spalding club*, vol 5 (Aberdeen 1852), p 224.
39   M Sahlins, *Culture and practical reason* (Chicago 1976), p 206.

The Geographical Mobility of Women in Early Modern Scotland

Ian D Whyte and Kathleen A Whyte

INTRODUCTION

Historical sources relating to pre-industrial European societies are heavily biased towards documenting the activities and concerns of men. Until recently Scottish historiography has followed a similar path. However, social historians in many countries are beginning to redress the balance by studying the roles of women within the family, the community and society at large.[1] These new approaches have only just begun to influence Scottish social history.[2]

The lack of attention paid to women has been a characteristic of research into migration and population mobility in pre-industrial Europe. This is partly a function of the available data. Many sources which contain information on migration, such as apprenticeship records, are almost exclusively male-oriented.[3] Other types of records, such as court depositions, include some women but are heavily biased towards men.[4] Nevertheless, it is clear from many studies that the movements of women formed an important element in population mobility in the past. In his pioneering study of migration patterns in nineteenth-century Britain Ravenstein put forward a number of 'laws' of migration—more strictly hypotheses.[5] One of these was that women were more migratory than men within their county of origin but that men formed a greater proportion of long-distance migrants. Thus Ravenstein established that women were an important element in migratory populations. He also indicated that their migratory patterns—and hence possibly the reasons for their movement—were different from those of men. While the importance of female migration in the mid nineteenth century is readily discernible from census records it is harder to establish its significance in earlier times.

Some aspects of female migration have been explored for England and other countries in the early modern period.[6] Marriage distances have frequently been used as a surrogate measure of the degree of social interaction between communities.[7] Despite this, female mobility has rarely been accorded specific attention and there are indications that its scale and importance may have been underestimated.[8] Studies of population mobility in early modern Scotland have been limited until recently, but it has now been shown that the Scots, notably migratory in the nineteenth and twentieth centuries, were also highly mobile in earlier times.[9]

Within the space available it is impossible to consider every aspect of female mobility in early modern Scotland. Marriage mobility was undoubtedly an important element in the turnover of the rural population,[10] while the temporary migration of young girls from the Highlands to help with the Lowland harvest became increasingly important during the eighteenth century.[11] However, the contribution of women towards these types of population movement in Scotland has already received some attention. Instead, this essay will focus on the female contribution to three aspects of geographical mobility within Scotland which have been shown by previous research to have been important in other early modern west European societies: migration to the towns, the mobility of servants, and vagrancy.

Migration to the larger towns has been identified as an important influence on the social structures of both source areas and destinations. Urban in-migration was vital in allowing large towns and cities to maintain their populations and increase in size.[12] Equally important were its effects on rural areas, draining off surplus population in a relationship which could have both a positive and a parasitic side.[13] Scotland has often been viewed as a country in which towns had a comparatively small impact during early modern times. Recently, however, the rate of urban growth in Scotland from the sixteenth to the eighteenth centuries has been re-assessed and it is clear that, by the later eighteenth century, Scotland was one of the most highly urbanised countries in Europe.[14] This suggests that the scale and importance of migration to the towns, including the influx of women as domestic servants, has been underestimated.[15]

The localised but frequently-repeated moves of domestic and farm servants from one short-term contract to another was one of the most significant influences behind the high levels of turnover of the rural population in England.[16] Similar patterns of service existed in Lowland Scotland in early modern times and, indeed, farm service remained important into the twentieth century long after the system had declined south of the Border.[17] Servants also existed in the Highlands during the seventeenth and eighteenth centuries although less is known about their characteristics. Service of this kind appears to have been as usual in Scotland for women as for men, but the contribution of women to patterns of servant mobility has not been considered in detail.

Vagrancy remained important to a later date in Scotland than in England. This was partly due to the poverty of much of society before the later eighteenth century. A substantial proportion of the urban and rural population lived on, or close to, the poverty line and it only took slight additional misfortunes to set them on the roads as vagrants.[18] The lack of strict settlement laws comparable to England from the later seventeenth century and the availability of at least some charity from kirk sessions as well as from individuals may have encouraged vagrancy in Scotland.[19] In addition, the continuation of major subsistence crises in the Lowlands until the end of the seventeenth century, and in the Highlands throughout the eighteenth century, caused periodic surges of vagrancy.[20] The importance of women as an element in the vagrant population has been demonstrated for England,[21] but the distinctive experiences of female vagrants in Scotland have received little attention.

These three types of movement do not encompass every aspect of female mobility in early modern Scotland but they were clearly among the most important aspects. The sections that follow attempt to evaluate their scale and importance as well as exploring their characteristic features.

MIGRATION TO THE TOWNS: THE EXAMPLE OF EIGHTEENTH-CENTURY EDINBURGH

Migration to larger towns and cities has been seen as one of the most important dynamic elements in the economy and society of early modern Europe but most previous work on this topic has utilised sources which are heavily biased towards men, despite the recognition that women were a major element among urban migrants.[22] However, the format of some Scottish urban marriage registers allows the study of the migration of women into some of the major towns before, as well as at, marriage. As urban marriage registers have not hitherto been used in this way some introductory comments about their content will be useful.

Where a marriage register records a woman as living in a particular town when her banns were proclaimed and her father as living elsewhere, then a migratory move between her original home and the town had probably been made, in most cases before, rather than at, marriage. With irregular marriages, which became increasingly common in Scotland during the later eighteenth century,[23] the period of residence in the town prior to marriage may sometimes have been brief. In most instances, however, the move is likely to have been made well before marriage for the purposes of employment.

Although registers rarely differentiate between first and subsequent marriages it can be assumed that a substantial proportion of the women involved were fairly young and that many of them had moved to the town to enter domestic service. Such data provide a female counterpart to apprenticeship migration which has frequently been studied in the past.[24] Indeed, because marriage registers generally record the parish rather than the place of origin of women it is possible, for example, to identify the origins of a higher proportion of female migrants to Edinburgh during the eighteenth century than for apprentices moving to the city.[25] As with virtually all sources relating to migration in early modern times one cannot assume that a single move between home and town had always been made or that, in this case, a father's parish of residence was necessarily always that of his daughter's birth. Nevertheless, given the abundant evidence that most mobility within the countryside took place over limited distances,[26] in a high proportion of cases this is likely to have been a close approximation to the truth. Minor discrepancies of this kind should not prejudice large-scale aggregative analysis of migration patterns.

Where the residence of a woman was recorded in a marriage register as being with her father in a parish outside the town then presumably migration occurred at, rather than before, marriage. In such cases the contact leading to marriage may have arisen in various ways. The groom may originally have come from the bride's place of residence and kept in touch after migrating to the town. Alternatively the bride may have lived in the town for a period of time, met her future marriage partner there and returned home prior to marriage. These two sets of circumstances would tend to produce a pattern of migration similar to that of women moving into a town before marriage. A third possibility is that initial contact between bride and groom was made during regular trips into or out of the town by one of the partners. Contacts of this kind would involve a more local field of interaction between the town and its immediate hinterland corresponding to the 'marriage distances' of previous studies. Without supplementary evidence it is impossible to distinguish between these and other possible sets of circumstances. However, the influence of purely local marriage contacts should tend to reduce the average distance migrated by women at marriage compared with those migrating before marriage. The same should apply to situations where women resident in a town married partners living in parishes elsewhere. In such cases one would expect that the woman concerned would normally have migrated out of the town at marriage, and that contact with their partners before marriage had been produced by similar sets of links to women moving into a town at marriage.

It is not feasible to attempt here even a brief discussion of patterns of female migration into all of Scotland's larger towns at this period. A review of female migration into Edinburgh will, however, illustrate many of the general patterns and problems involved in studying female urban in-migration. The importance of migration to capital cities during the early modern period, particularly its demographic and modernising effects on society as a whole, has often been stressed though again attention has concentrated on male migrants.[27] Although female migration to Edinburgh exhibited features which may have differed in degree from movements into smaller Scottish towns, the use of Edinburgh as a case study does allow comparison with work on migration to capitals and provincial centres elsewhere. In considering the movements of women into other Scottish towns it should, however, be noted that the quality of urban marriage registers is often much poorer than in the ideal situation described above. Those for the city of Glasgow, for instance, do not even record the origins of brides, far less any details of their fathers' occupation and residence, until 1756.[28] Fortunately the marriage registers for the royal burgh of Edinburgh are sufficienctly full to allow a detailed analysis of the movement of women into the city throughout the eighteenth century though not, unfortunately, for the seventeenth.[29] The registers give, for most brides, the name, occupation and domicile of their fathers and also indicate the place of residence of the bride if this was different. This provides a data base of over 30,000 migrants.

TABLE i

MIGRATION OF WOMEN TO EDINBURGH IN THE EIGHTEENTH CENTURY

	Women migrating to Edinburgh before marriage	Women migrating to Edinburgh at marriage	Women migrating from Edinburgh at marriage	Men migrating to Edinburgh
1701–10	54.9 km	41.8 km	49.1 km	77.8 km
1711–20	64.7	38.8	32.9	62.0
1721–30	60.0	46.4	40.7	71.8
1731–40	61.4	41.9	40.6	86.2
1741–50	68.3	40.8	38.2	75.9
1751–60	67.7	42.9	47.2	95.6
1761–70	66.2	47.5	44.2	97.4
1771–80	67.7	56.5	50.3	82.1
1781–90	77.8	48.0	46.0	100.4
1791–1800	62.9	61.2	56.5	74.0

Table 1 shows the mean distances migrated by various categories of women moving to and from Edinburgh. As measurement of the distances between Edinburgh and the thousands of places of origin would have been extremely time consuming the distances have been calculated using an average figure for each county of origin. This figure was obtained by measuring the nearest and furthest point of each county from Edinburgh and taking the mean value. This technique has been used in previous studies of apprenticeship migration to Edinburgh and London.[30] There was a clear difference in the average distances migrated by women before marriage and at marriage, the latter moving over shorter distances, supporting the idea that many marriages in this group were generated by everyday contacts between the inhabitants of the city and its immediate hinterland. The mean distances for all groups are surprisingly high, even in the early eighteenth century. Women moving to Edinburgh before marriage, many of them probably as domestic servants, tended to come from further afield than apprentices. In addition, there was a widening of the migration field during the eighteenth century despite the rapid growth of other Scottish cities. This contrasts with the contraction which has been noted for apprentices migrating to Edinburgh[31] and the trend was only really reversed during the last decade of the century. Overall the pattern corresponds more closely to migration to London during the later sixteenth and early seventeenth centuries that at a later date when the growing industrial towns began to reduce migration to the capital from northern England.[32] The implication is that there was a substantial time-lag in the development of Scottish migration fields and that the truly national pattern of migration to Edinburgh was only starting to become curtailed at the end of the eighteenth century.

Table 2 shows the changing pattern of migration of women to Edinburgh before marriage by region. There was clearly a local hinterland, including the Lothians, Fife and the Borders, from which a high and fairly stable proportion of migrants were drawn throughout the century. The North East and Tayside both provided a growing percentage of migrants on the middle of the century with a subsequent drop. The proportion of migrants drawn from the western

TABLE 2

MIGRATION OF WOMEN TO EDINBURGH BEFORE MARRIAGE BY REGION
(per cent per decade)

	1701 –10	1711 –20	1721 –30	1731 –40	1741 –50	1751 –60	1761 –70	1771 –80	1781 –90	1791 –1800
Lothians	37.7	35.0	37.7	38.3	33.7	35.0	36.7	37.1	33.6	38.1
Borders	10.6	9.0	8.2	8.9	8.1	6.5	7.5	6.8	6.8	8.2
Fife	18.7	14.8	15.1	18.5	16.3	14.5	15.5	15.5	17.1	19.8
Tayside	6.8	11.5	9.8	10.0	13.2	13.7	14.2	14.4	11.5	6.7
North East	4.9	5.0	5.6	6.4	7.2	8.2	5.2	4.9	2.8	3.0
South West	3.4	3.0	2.5	2.0	2.4	3.4	2.7	2.4	1.7	2.4
West/Central	12.5	14.5	15.8	9.6	10.2	9.0	8.2	7.3	9.3	10.6
Highlands	1.2	2.4	3.4	3.3	5.8	5.8	5.9	7.0	11.6	7.3
N. Isles	0.9	1.6	0.3	1.2	1.0	1.5	1.5	0.6	1.0	0.6
Northumber- land	0.4	0.2	1.1	0.5	0.6	1.0	1.2	1.3	1.6	1.5
London	0.0	0.0	0.3	0.7	0.4	0.4	0.7	0.7	1.2	1.1
England	0.4	0.4	1.5	1.7	1.5	2.2	2.5	4.0	4.6	4.1

Lowlands fell significantly over time. Given that the population of this region was increasing rapidly in the later eighteenth century, this represents a substantial relative decline. The growth of Glasgow, as well as the development of other industrial centres in this region, must have provided an increasing pool of local opportunities which diverted potential migrants away from Edinburgh.

The most remarkable feature of Table 2, however, is the steady increase in the proportion of the migrants drawn from Highland counties from a mere 1.2 per cent in the first decade of the eighteenth century to 11.6 per cent in 1780–99. At a general level this reflects the growing integration of the Highlands with the rest of Scotland, particularly after the 1745 Rebellion.[33] The Highlands may have been a source of cheap domestic labour for the capital. However, it must also be remembered that Edinburgh was an important assembly point for Highland girls who came to help with the Lothian harvest.[34] Many of these girls may have met and married local men.

Another notable feature of Table 2 is the increasing proportion of women originating from south of the Border. The percentage of women moving from England increased by over eleven times between the first decade of the century and the 1780s, a rate of growth comparable with that of Highland migrants. Growing contact with England in the decades following the Union must have been an underlying influence with notable increases in the 1720s and 1770s. The two most significant origins are Northumberland—many Scots were employed as keelmen on the Tyne[35]—and London. Many of the women moving to Edinburgh may have been the daughters of expatriate Scots.

This tabular presentation is a relatively simple form of analysis. It only gives a general impression of the effects of increasing distance on the flow of female migrants to Edinburgh and it does not indicate whether levels of migration from any area were high or low in relation to their populations. Previous studies would lead one to expect that the migration of women to

Edinburgh was related positively to the populations of the areas of origin and negatively to increasing distance from the capital.[36] A more refined form of analysis is the technique of log-linear modelling using Poisson regression analysis. The statistical basis of this technique and its interpretation have been described by the authors in previous study of apprenticeship migration to Edinburgh and need not be repeated here.[37] It should, however, be emphasised that the technique makes it possible to relate the numbers of migrants from any source area—in this instance a county—to the population of that source area and its distance from the destination, providing a set of predicted values which would occur if the relationship between migrants on one hand and population and distance on the other was a perfect one. Differences from these predicted values, or 'residuals', highlight areas from which levels of migration were unusually high or low.

Poisson regression analysis of women migrating to Edinburgh was carried out for three decades; 1701–10, 1751–60 and 1791–1800. For the last two of these periods Webster's census of 1755 and the first official census of 1801 provided population data.[38] For 1701–10 the only near-contemporary population data are those which can be derived from the hearth and poll tax records of the 1690s.[39] Both these sources are incomplete in their geographical coverage, and population estimates calculated from them are liable to considerable error. For this reason it was decided to relate migrants during the period 1701–10 to the 1755 population data which at least have the merit of complete coverage and reasonable accuracy. It has been suggested that Scotland's total population in 1755 was little different from that of the early 1690s[40] and differences in population distribution between the two periods were probably not sufficiently great to invalidate the exercise.

Figure 1 shows the pattern of residuals by county for the three periods. In 1701–10 it is clear that virtually all the Highland counties were providing fewer migrants than their distance from Edinburgh and their populations would have led one to expect. This is hardly surprising considering the extent of the divide in Scottish society between Highland and Lowland at this time. Much of eastern Scotland from Shetland to Roxburghshire supplied the numbers of migrants predicted or substantially more. This was a feature of apprenticeship migration to Edinburgh at this period,[41] emphasising perhaps the importance of trading contacts between Edinburgh and other east-coast areas, particularly by sea, in generating the information flows which led to migration.[42] There were also higher than predicted levels of migration from some counties in central, western and south-western Scotland. Negative residuals for Dunbarton, Renfrew and Lanarkshire suggest the effects of competition from Glasgow but also indicate that the city's pull was still fairly localised. The negative residual for Fife may reflect the competing influence of Perth and Dundee as well as those of the many smaller burghs within the county.

By the mid eighteenth century this pattern was beginning to change. Most noticeable is the decline in levels of migration from Ayrshire and some Border counties, as was the case with apprentices.[43] Edinburgh's migration field for women within southern Scotland was contracting markedly. On the other

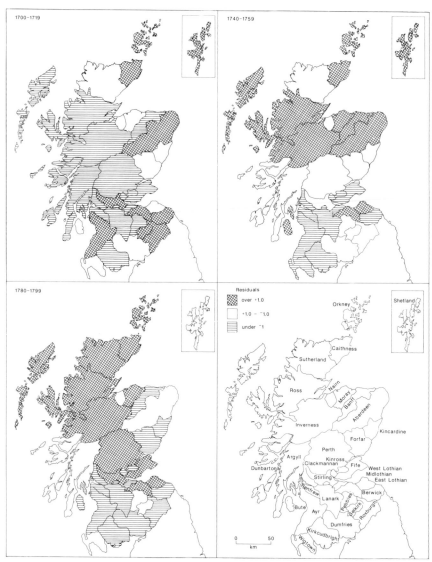

FIGURE 1   Poisson regression analysis of migration of women to Edinburgh
before marriage.

hand this was more than counterbalanced by a growing flow of women to Edinburgh from the north. Increased contact with the Highlands is reflected in the positive residuals for Inverness and Ross while Argyll and Perthshire, strongly negative in the early eighteenth century, were starting to move towards a more positive balance.

By the end of the eighteenth century the pattern of movement of women to Edinburgh was markedly different from the first cross-section. A core area surrounding the Firth of Forth still supplied more migrants than predicted but for almost all of the remainder of southern Scotland levels of migration were lower than expected. In west-central Scotland this is likely to reflect the pull not only of Glasgow but also many other rapidly-growing urban centres such as Greenock, Kilmarnock and Paisley. In the south east the attraction of Tyneside may lie behind the negative residuals for the Border counties. In a similar way the growth of Dundee and the expansion of textile manufacture in its hinterland may explain the low levels of female migration to Edinburgh from Forfarshire and Kincardineshire. On the other hand virtually the whole of the Highlands and Northern Scotland from Perthshire to Caithness and the Northern Isles were providing more migrants than their population levels and distance from Edinburgh would have led one to expect. Even Argyllshire, which lay within the orbit of Glasgow, did not record a markedly negative figure.

This study of female migration to Edinburgh has demonstrated parallels with work on migration (generally male) into other early modern cities but also some very distinctive features. The mean distances migrated by women moving to Edinburgh before marriage were surprisingly high. The increase in mean migration distances during the eighteenth century contrasts markedly with the experience of London during the same period, as well as with the pattern of apprenticeship migration to Edinburgh.[44] When the pattern of female migration to Edinburgh is analysed in more detail it can be seen that the increase in mean distances travelled is explicable in terms of the changing origins of the migrants. A decline in the proportions of women drawn from west-central and southern Scotland was more than balanced by an increase in those drawn from the Highlands and Northern Scotland. This caused the average migration distance to increase despite a marked contraction of the city's migration field over much of the Lowlands in the face of increasing competition from other rapidly-growing towns. This contraction has clear parallels with England[45] but south of the Border there was no counterpart to the Highlands as an area which had generated few long-distance migrants in the past but which now produced an ever-increasing stream. In some respects Ireland may have performed for England a comparable function.

Although the pattern of female migration before marriage to Edinburgh differed from that of apprentices it should be noted that apprentices were becoming an increasingly unrepresentative group.[46] The data on the migration of men to Edinburgh presented in Table 1, drawn from a much wider range of social strata than apprentices, clearly follow the same pattern as for women but with a tendency for men to migrate over greater average distances, a feature of movement to towns first emphasised by Ravenstein.[47] By contrast the pattern of migration of women into and out of the city at marriage showed less variation during the century, emphasising the stable nature of everyday contacts within the local hinterland of Edinburgh.

Some features of female migration to Edinburgh operated in other, smaller towns. Migration to the manufacturing centre of Kilmarnock during the mid eighteenth century showed the same contrast between a local marriage-migration field and a wider hinterland from which unmarried girls were recruited, both migration fields being scaled down to the levels appropriate for a much smaller centre.[48] Further work on Scottish marriage registers may make it possible to establish more clearly the contrasts in migration patterns between towns of different sizes and functions. Were there, for example, differences in patterns of movement into the new manufacturing centres like Glasgow, Paisley and Hamilton on one hand and the old-established regional service centres like Aberdeen, Dumfries, and Inverness on the other? The extent to which the migration fields of the major towns grew or contracted according to their economic fortunes, the existence of definite migration streams linking smaller centres with particular rural areas, and the rise of migration from the Highlands into other Scottish towns would all repay further study.

We have already seen how important female domestic servants were in Edinburgh and other large Scottish towns. However, large numbers of young women were also employed in the countryside as farm servants and it is to the mobility of this group that attention will now be turned.

FEMALE SERVANTS

Research on population mobility in England has emphasised that the movement of male and female servants between households at the end of short contracts was probably the biggest single component in local population movements within the countryside.[49] Scottish rural society was also characterised by the almost universal presence of farm and domestic service and, unlike England where servants in husbandry declined in numbers during the eighteenth century, the system was maintained in Scotland with comparatively little change.[50]

Houston's study of population mobility in Scotland in the seventeenth and eighteenth centuries, based on the analysis of testimonials, has suggested that the frequent movement of servants over relatively short distances was also one of the most important elements in geographical mobility, with female servants tending to migrate at least as often as male ones.[51] Women formed more than 50 per cent of the migrants in most of the parishes studied. Houston suggested that this reflected a greater demand for female than male servants in a mixed farming economy. The poll tax records for the 1690s show, however, that the percentage of female migrants is even higher than the ratio of male to female servants would lead one to expect. Houston was also able to demonstrate not only that single women moved more frequently than single men but that in many parishes the average distances moved by women were greater than for men. This applied both to rural parishes like Dalmeny, Glencorse and Livingston and urban ones like Haddington and Prestonpans. Although migration at marriage, and vagrancy, may have contributed to the high levels of turnover of the women in Houston's study there is little doubt that much of it was due to the movement of female servants beween contracts.

Work as a farm or domestic servant for a period of years during adolescence and young adulthood would have been the normal experience for most women in Scottish rural society during the seventeenth and early eighteenth centuries. This is shown by the ubiquity of female servants in tenant house-holds, and their frequent appearance in cottar households, in the poll tax lists of the 1690s.[52] The limited numbers of daughters of tenants and cottars who were listed as still living with their families at the age of 16 and above shows that it was normal for the daughters of tenants and cottars to leave home by this age and go into service. It was, however, more common for the daughters of tenants to stay at home than those of cottars. Among tenant families in the 1690s sons tended to stay at home in greater numbers than daughters in some regions. In 20 parishes in the Lothians the number of sons over 16 in tenant families exceeded the number of daughters.[53] This may have been because it would have been more advantageous for a tenant to keep a son at home on his holding than a daughter. To replace a son with a male farm servant would have cost twice as much in fees as to replace a daughter with a female servant.

The contrast between the experience of girls from tenant and cottar house-holds probably grew during the eighteenth century. As the tenants of the increasingly large farms in many parts of the Lowlands became more pros-perous there was less need for them to send their daughters into service and female servants became increasingly drawn from among the households of labourers and cottagers.[54] By the end of the eighteenth century it was only in areas where tenanted holdings remained relatively small, like Aberdeenshire, that tenants' daughters continued to go into service in large numbers.

In Aberdeenshire and particularly in Renfrewshire in the late seventeenth century the tendency to keep sons at home rather than daughters was less marked than in the Lothians. In Renfrewshire, with a more pastorally-oriented economy, the work of daughters in the dairy may have made them a greater asset while, with smaller areas of arable land, the need for sons as ploughmen may have been reduced. With cottar families in the Lothians the imbalance worked in the opposite direction. In 15 out of the 20 parishes there were more daughters of cottars at home than sons. The need to keep a son to do heavy labouring may have been less on a cottar holding than a tenant's one as the ploughing was usually done for the cottar by the tenant while a daughter may have been able to contribute proportionally more to the family income by spinning and other work. Nevertheless, despite these differences it is evident that most children from tenant and cottar families did go into service.

Given that in the seventeenth century so few daughters in their teens stayed at home, service was almost inevitable because of the impossibility of young, unmarried girls setting up house on their own. This was frowned upon by the Church for moral reasons; young people were considered to require the supervision of their elders, whether parents or master and mistress, and could not be trusted on their own. These views were echoed by secular authorities although their reasons were in many cases as much economic as moral. They did not want young able-bodied people opting out of the labour force. For example, the burgh council of Edinburgh legislated to prevent young women from leaving service and setting up shops.[55] In this case the reason was less a desire to control women morally as to prevent them from competing economically with burgesses. Moreover, given that the wages for women were usually much lower than for men, it was economically difficult for young women to live on their own. As custom, a desire for independence and sheer necessity forced so many of them to leave home in their teens, and economic and moral pressures prevented them from living alone, service was the principal option. Only towards the end of the eighteenth century did the situation start to change. Church discipline became less stern, or at least less enforceable, in the rapidly-growing towns where population turnover was so great that it was hard for kirk sessions to keep track of individuals entering or leaving the community in the way that had been possible a century earlier. The income which could be derived from industrial activities like spinning yarn, working in the bleachfields or embroidering muslins had risen substantially.[56] These two influences made it possible for young girls to set up house on their own, though the ministers who contributed to the Old Statistical Account still frowned on it.[57]

In the late seventeenth century female servants formed some 9 to 10 per cent of the pollable population (over the age of 16) in many rural parishes in lowland Aberdeenshire or 18 to 20 per cent of the pollable women.[58] In the Lothians and Renfrewshire there was greater variations. In some upland pastoral parishes south of Edinburgh, like Heriot and Stow, female servants could make up 13 per cent or 14 per cent of the pollable population.[59] The higher figures in these areas may relate to the greater need for female servants for dairy work and the reduced need for male farm servants in parishes where the amount of arable land was limited. In many lowland, arable-oriented parishes in the Lothians the proportion of female servants was similar to the 9 to 10 per cent of Aberdeenshire but in Dalmeny it rose as high as 15 per cent.[60] In parishes like this the reason for the high figures may have been linked to the preponderance of relatively large holdings employing less cottar labour and more servants, both male and female. In Renfrewshire the proportion of female servants in the pollable population varied from about 8 to 12 per cent.[61] There were relatively fewer female servants in parishes like Eaglesham and the landward area of Paisley where textile manufacture was important.[62] In areas like these more girls may have remained at home to spin yarn rather than go into service. In Renfrewshire there were fewer male farm servants in relation to female ones, probably because the economy was more geared towards pastoral farming with less need for ploughmen and more for dairymaids, and perhaps too because weaving provided alternative employment to agriculture.

Differences like these between parishes within the same region show that there was a good deal of local variation in the demand for female servants. This related to differences in the rural economy, to contrasts in farm structures between different estates making different demands on cottar and servant labour, and on the presence or absence of alternative sources of employment like textile manufacture. Such differences in themselves may have increased mobility among female servants in search of opportunities. Nevertheless, the purely local character of the movement of women into farm service is suggested by a comparison for parishes covered by the poll tax of the proportions of the pollable population made up of farm servants, and of daughters of tenants and cottars who were over 16 yet still living at home. Wherever the percentage of female farm servants was high that for daughters at home was correspondingly low and vice versa. In the landward part of Renfrew parish, for example, 14 per cent of the population were servants and only 4 per cent daughters at home whereas in Kilellan parish the corresponding proportions were 10 per cent and 9 per cent.[63] Similar patterns occurred in the Lothians and Aberdeenshire.[64] The closeness of this adjustment between servants and non-servants in the same age group suggests that most servants' posts were filled locally.

In the late seventeenth century female farm servants made up smaller proportions of the pollable population in areas like upland Aberdeenshire and Orkney.[65] Their importance in the Highlands is less clear. Servants did occur in the Western Isles[66] in the seventeenth century, and it is clear from the Old Statistical Account that in the late eighteenth century farm servants, both male and female, were an important element in the labour force from Highland parishes as widely scattered as Fortingall, Lismore and Appin, and Tongue.[67] Nevertheless, it is not certain whether the institution of service, with hiring fairs, fixed-term contracts and high levels of turnover, was as well developed in the Highlands as in the Lowlands. If this was the case one might speculate whether in parts of the Highlands, if female servants formed a smaller proportion of the population, girls tended to marry at a younger age on average than in Lowland areas where service was more common. The tendency for early marriage in the Highlands in the eighteenth century, or even earlier, has been noted,[68] as has the possibility that this area had a different demographic regime from the Lowlands with a more steady build up of population during the seventeenth and eighteenth centuries.[69] Differences in the extent to which young girls went into service may provide one mechanism to explain such contrasts.

In the Lowlands too differences in the importance of service for young girls may hint at demographic variations. For the 1690s poll tax lists, if the proportion of younger women who were unmarried is calculated by adding the percentages of farm servants and daughters over 16 still resident at home, it is clear that in Renfrewshire a greater percentage of women were unmarried in many parishes than in the Lothians. This may possibly relate to the greater potential contribution which single women in the western Lowlands were able to make to the economy of small tenanted holdings by dairy work and yarn spinning. Such variations also hint, obliquely, at regional differences in the extent of female mobility both before and after marriage.

A further element encouraging mobility among female servants was wage differentials. Although female servants generally received only about half the fees of male servants[70] the poll tax returns show that in the late seventeenth century there was nevertheless a marked gradation in their fees relating partly to age, but also probably to the kind of work which they did. The fees of female servants on farms in the Lothians ranged from as little as £5 to £6 Scots per annum to as much as £18 though relatively few earned more than £12.[71] The difference was probably linked to age and to differences in the level of skill and responsibility. Female servants working in the households of landed proprietors might earn more than farm servants; fees of £20 to £30 are recorded for some servants in such households in the Lothians though the women receiving them may have been older than most female farm servants. There are also some indications of differences in the going rate for female farm servants between parishes. In the upland pastoral parish of Stow, for instance, the median fee was £11 Scots per year while in lowland parishes in the Lothians it was £12.[72] The difference is not marked and it is not clear whether it was linked to variations in the age structure of servants, the kinds of work undertaken, or competition from Edinburgh driving up wages in the surrounding rural parishes. Nevertheless, whether related to age, experience or locality such variations are likely to have encouraged mobility within a comparatively limited area as girls moved from farm to farm and parish to parish in search of better positions. The poll tax data suggest that average wages for female servants were lower in Aberdeenshire and Renfrewshire than in the Lothians but the degree of difference was relatively small and is unlikely to have generated long-distance mobility.[73]

Contrasts in wage levels for female servants may have led to local mobility during the seventeenth century but probably not to much long-distance movement. By the end of the eighteenth cenury the situation was different. There was a marked national gradient in servants' fees and rates paid for female day labour between the north-west Highlands and the Lowlands where farmers faced increasing competition for their labour force from industry. The Old Statistical Account provides a good deal of information on the wages of female servants but it is not always clear whether the figures quoted for individual parishes are average or maximum rates. As a result many contrasts in wages between neighbouring parishes may be more apparent than real. The regional trends are, however, fairly clear. Farmers close to the developing manufacturing areas, such as those in Renfrewshire and north Lanarkshire, had to pay more than those in purely agricultural areas of the Lowlands like Galloway, the Borders and the Merse in order to attract suitable girls. Wages in many Renfrewshire parishes seem to have been at least 25 per cent higher than in other parts of southern Scotland.[74] In the Highlands, however, the wages of female servants were far lower—a third or even a quarter of what a girl might have earned in most Lowland farming areas.[75] The differential between north and south prompted long-distance migration from the Highlands to farm service in the Lowlands. The recruitment of servants from the far north may have helped Lowland farmers in areas where local girls were increasingly moving out of farming and into industry. For some Highland parishes the Old Statistical Account gives the numbers of male and female servants and invariably the latter are far more numerous. This suggests that long-distance migration to Lowland farm service was more characteristic of men than women. It may have been that in a pastoral economy with comparatively little arable land it was easier to dispense with the services of young men, leaving young women at home to undertake herding and dairy work. Girls may have been more attracted by temporary migration to the south during the summer and autumn to work in the Lowland harvest than by longer-term farm service.

Female servants were usually slightly less numerous than male ones in the countryside but they greatly outnumbered them in the towns.[76] In the 1690s they made up 19 per cent of the pollable population in Edinburgh, 23 per cent in Aberdeen and 18 per cent in Perth.[77] The proportion of female domestic servants in towns was directly related to their size, occupational structure and wealth. In baronial burghs where merchant and professional groups were poorly represented and there was a concentration of less wealthy tradesmen the proportion of female servants could be less than in rural areas: in Dalkeith for example it was 8 per cent and in Musselburgh 7 per cent.[78] The larger towns were an obvious magnet for female servants. Wages were not necessarily any greater than in the countryside. At the end of the seventeenth century the median wage for female servants in the Tolbooth Kirk parish of Edinburgh, £12, was comparable with that in surrounding rural parishes.[79] In Aberdeen the median wage of £10 was comparable with that of nearby rural parishes like Belhelvie but greater than those for more distant parishes. In Edinburgh the wage structure for servant women was, however, more diversified. There may have been more very young girls performing domestic duties than in rural areas. Girls of 12 to 14 earned between £4 and £6 Scots per year while some servants, who were only given bed and board with no additional fees at all, may have been even younger. At the other end of the scale fees of over £20 were more common than in the countryside. Domestic service in a large town may also have been seen as more attractive and less hard than farm work.

On the basis of the poll tax data for Edinburgh and Aberdeen it can be estimated that the four largest Scottish towns would, in the 1690s, have employed some 12,000 female servants. This suggests that around one Scottish girl in ten between the ages of 15 and 24 would, at any time, have been working as a servant in one of the four main burghs.[80] This emphasises the scale of the influx of girls from the countryside and also suggests that women may have accounted for a greater share of the flow of migrants to the large towns than men. A substantial proportion of the women migrating to Edinburgh before marriage, discussed above, must have been moving to the city to work as domestic servants but neither they nor their migration patterns can be isolated. Presumably girls moving to the larger towns for this purpose moved, on average, over much greater distances than those who worked as rural farm servants. If this was so then how were they recruited and how did they hear of the opportunities? Personal contacts between the families which they joined and their home areas is the likely answer, probably due to linkages established by previous migrants to the towns, male and female.

Given that service was a temporary status a substantial proportion of the girls who moved to such posts in the larger towns must have returned to their home areas in smaller burghs and the countryside before, or at, marriage. It is unlikely that they all remained in the major urban centres at marriage given the surplus of females in such towns and of males in the countryside. This emphasises another of Ravenstein's maxims, that every migratory flow has a compensating counter flow.[81] Given the importance of female migration to the towns and its temporary nature in a great many cases it may be suggested that the return flow of women to the countryside after a period in service would have been important not only in bringing money into rural areas but also in spreading urban fashions and values. The spread of new trends such as tea-drinking, which was common in rural areas by the end of the eighteenth century, and the demand for higher-quality manufactured goods may be examples of how new ideas and attitudes which originated in the towns were diffused to rural areas by this two-way flow of young women.

For many young women who worked as domestic and farm servants marriage, the raising of a family, and a bare sufficiency or possibly rather better as the wives of cottars, tenants or artisans awaited them once they had finished their period in service. However, misfortunes such as widowhood, marriage to an improvident partner, or sheer bad luck could easily drive such a woman below the poverty line and, possibly, on to the roads as vagrants. The next section considers the degree to which women contributed to the vagrant population which was a feature of Scottish society throughout the early modern period, and examines some of their characteristics and the events which set them on the move.

POVERTY AND VAGRANCY

Many sets of circumstances might reduce women to poverty. Widowhood, spinsterhood, old age, physical or mental infirmity or unexpected pregnancy might push women to the margins of society and over the threshold of poverty. It is harder to determine the factors which forced women to leave their homes and take to the roads. Certainly relief from the parish poor fund would not usually have been enough to maintain them at home without charity from relatives and neighbours. The kirk sessions who administered parish poor funds, provided regular relief infrequently and for only a limited number of people, and expected their handouts to be supplemented by assistance from other sources.[82] Perhaps it was only when these sources failed that women took to begging and became mobile.

Women tend to figure more frequently than men among parish poor lists and probably formed a substantial majority of the poor.[83] In Dirleton parish, East Lothian, for instance, women accounted for up to three-quarters of the people on the regular poor list during the 1670s.[84] Presumably the women who were listed were single or widowed while at least some of the men to whom payments were made would have been married so that the proportion of women supported by the Dirleton poor fund was probably even higher.

There were probably more old women in most rural communities than old men; women in Scottish rural society undertook their share of hard physical labour but they did not have to do the heaviest jobs; accidents or early death due to occupational hazards may have resulted in male life expectancy being significantly lower that that for women. However, the dominance of women over men in the regular poor lists of Lowland rural parishes also suggests that it was easier for men to obtain casual employment to keep them off the poor list and also that such communities tended to make an effort to maintain poor women at home while impoverished men were more likely to turn to vagrancy. Nevertheless, women did figure among the vagrant population. The importance of female vagrancy and some of its characteristics can be determined from the detailed study of payments made by particular kirk sessions.

In Monikie parish, Forfarshire, between 1660 and 1710 27 per cent of the payments made to individual vagrants went to women, the proportion being comparable with that for English vagrants studied by Beier and Slack.[85] Eighteen per cent of them were described as crippled, dumb or blind. More surprisingly, 20 per cent had once possessed some social status; they were most commonly described as 'distressed gentlewomen' but others were widows of ministers and in one instance a minister's daughter. Very few were described as travelling with children but this may merely have been because the session clerk did not bother to record this. One or two women were on the road because their homes had been destroyed by fire. The origins of the vagrants were rarely given but one woman at least had originated from Edinburgh and another blind woman from Orkney. The fact that such cases were specified may show that they were unusual but it does indicate that at least some female vagrants travelled over considerable distances.

For Dirleton in East Lothian between 1666 and 1690 a similar picture emerges.[86] Women formed a minority, but nevertheless a significant one, among the vagrant population. Female vagrants made up 29 per cent of those whose sex was recorded. Four per cent of them were stated to be travelling with their husbands, 3 per cent with a man who was not their husband and a further 5 per cent with both husbands and children. Twelve per cent of the women were travelling alone with their children; instances of women with up to seven are recorded. These figures are likely to underestimate the proportion of women travelling as part of a family. An unknown number of the men who received payments may have been accompanied by their wives. It does suggest, however, that vagrancy was less a group or family activity than an individual affair. Three out of every four women recorded were travelling alone.

Four per cent of all the women recorded as travelling on their own were described as 'sick', 2 per cent blind and 6 per cent as crippled in various ways while 3 per cent were described as being senile or mentally defective. These figures cannot be considered as representing the total proportion of such women among female vagrants as the recording of such details was sporadic and haphazard but it indicates that infirmity of various kinds was an important element in driving women on to the roads, even when mobility itself was difficult as in the case of the lame woman transported in a barrow who received relief in 1684 and again in 1687.

Surprisingly, only 4 per cent of the payments to women described the recipients as widows but the session clerk may not always have bothered to enter such details. The Dirleton records chronicle the harsh side of vagrancy with expenditure for graves and winding sheets to female beggars found dead in the parish, and for the burial of the children of vagrant women. Eleven per cent of the payments went to women who were described as distressed gentlewomen or the widows of gentlemen and professional men such as ministers. Such women generally received larger payments than ordinary vagrants. This may have been partly because their hard luck stories were not only established by testimonials but, given that testimonials could be forged, by common knowledge and repute. In one or two instances the women were known personally to the minister or elders. One minister's widow had come from as far as Northumberland and another, a 'distempered gentlewomen', was also described as being English. Possibly casual relief was more generous north of the Border. A third of the payments went to women who were specifically travelling with a testificate. Many of these may have been women travelling in search of work and requiring only temporary assistance rather than full-time vagrants.

The Dirleton session seems to have been fair even to women for whose misfortunes they clearly did not have much sympathy. The case of Christian Walker in 1680 is an illustration. While begging in the parish she gave birth to a child whose father, she claimed, lived in Oldhamstocks. On investigation this was found to be false and it was discovered that two or three years previously she had been brought before the session at Cockburnspath for fornication, being imprisoned and subsequently banished from there. The Dirleton session gave her 33 shillings for her maintenance 'lest the child should perish'.

Levels of vagrancy for both men and women fell over most of the Lowlands during the eighteenth century. The cessation of major subsistence crises, the more adequate provision of poor relief, and greater control over vagrancy at a parish level all combined to achieve this. Vagrancy was not, however, eliminated. The Old Statistical Account indicates that it was still a problem in many areas. Among the regions which stand out in this respect is the South West, where an influx of Irish beggars of both sexes, sometimes moving as families, was reported from many parishes.[87] Sporadic parishes throughout the Lowlands reported that none of their own parishioners begged from door to door but that the community was troubled—'infested' was the popular term—by vagrants from other areas.[88] The origins of these vagrants were rarely specified but it is clear that many were from the Highlands. The rise of temporary migration from the Highlands to the Lowlands for agricultural and other work must have contributed to this. Men and women on the move, particularly those on their way south at the start of the summer season, are likely to have begged either from choice or necessity. However, Mitchison's work on poor relief has shown that payments to paupers in many parishes in the Northern Highlands were minimal and entirely non-existent.[89] Rising population, limited opportunities for employment, and lack of money to build up parish poor funds led to begging from door to door being widespread and acceptable within the Highlands where the old tradition of hospitality made people, no matter how poorly off themselves, reluctant to deny anyone alms or a night's lodging.[90]

Inevitably, given the greater wealth in the south, this vagrancy tended to spill over into adjacent Lowland areas. Many parishes in Angus appear to have been badly affected and there was a natural tendency for the poor to drift towards the larger towns.[91] Patterns of vagrancy should not be over-simplified though. In the parish of Fortingall in Highland Perthshire the minister complained that many of the people begging for, and sometimes extorting, alms came from Lowland towns rather than surrounding rural parishes.[92]

CONCLUSION

This essay has demonstrated something of the scale and diverse nature of female mobility in seventeenth- and eighteenth-century Scotland. It has concentrated on three facets of mobility which were present in Scotland throughout this period. Urban in-migration became increasingly important during the eighteenth century and the significance of the contribution of female migrants has been demonstrated here. The movement of women servants continued to be a major element in mobility within the countryside. As with England, the movement of servants from farm to farm together with change of residence at marriage, were probably two of the most important components of the geographical mobility of women. As the eighteenth century progressed new elements, such as the rise of long-distance movement of servant girls from the Highlands, appeared. Female vagrancy in the seventeenth century has probably been underestimated and it was still a feature of Scotland at the end of the eighteenth century, though it had probably diminished in scale from earlier times.

Space has not permitted a discussion of one specialised aspect of female mobility, migration at marriage. Marriage generally involved a change of residence for a woman and marriage distances have been used as a measure of more general social interaction.[93] Recent work on East Lothian marriage registers has suggested that there was an overall increase in marriage distances in both urban and rural parishes between the seventeenth and the late eighteenth century which may have been linked to increases in the general mobility of the population.[94] Other elements of female mobility which increased during the period under study, especially in the later eighteenth century, were the movement of Highland girls to help with the Lowland harvest,[95] and the growing movement of women from purely agricultural areas into the manufacturing districts, a feature brought out again and again in the Old Statistical Account written in the 1790s.

In seventeenth- and eighteenth-century Scotland women were highly and increasingly mobile within an economy and society which was offering them increasing opportunities for work outside the traditional agricultural and domestic setting, opportunities which frequently involved movement, whether on a temporary or more permanent basis, within a limited local area or over long distances. This essay has brought out some of the distinctive features of female mobility and emphasised the importance of recognising gender differences within the more general field of migration studies. However, we are still a long way from understanding the social, economic amnd cultural influences which lay behind many of the patterns of mobility which the sources for this period reveal.

NOTES

1   For example, see: L A Tilly and J W Scott, *Women, work and family* (London 1978), O Hufton, 'Women in history: early-modern England', *Past and Present* 101 (1983), pp 125–41.

2   R A Houston, 'Women in the economy and society of Scotland 1500–1800' in R A Houston and I D Whyte (eds) *Scottish society 1500–1800* (Cambridge forthcoming). R K Marshall, *Virgins and viragos* (London 1983).

3   J Patten, 'Rural-urban migration in pre-industrial England'. Oxford University School of Geography Research papers No. 6. J Patten, 'Movement of labour into three pre-industrial East Anglian towns', *Jnl Hist Geog* 2 (1976), p 114.

4   P Clark, 'The migrant in Kentish towns 1580–1640' in P Clark and P Slack (eds) *Crisis and order in English towns 1500–1700* (London 1972). D Souden, 'Migrants and the population structure of later seventeenth century provincial cities and towns' in P Clark (ed), *The transformation of English provincial towns* (London 1984), p 137.

5   D Grigg, 'E G Ravenstein and the "laws of migration",' *Jnl Hist Geog* 3 (1977), pp 41–54.

6   A Kussmaul, *Servants in husbandry in early modern England.* (Cambridge 1981). Clark, 'The migrant in Kentish towns' in Clark and Slack. P Slack 'Vagrants and vagrancy in England 1598–1664'. *Econ Hist Rev* 27 (1974).

7   For example: B A Holderness, 'Personal mobility in some rural parishes of Yorkshire 1777–1822' *Yorks Arch Jnl* 42 (1970) 444–54. P E Ogden, 'Migration, marriage and the collapse of traditional peasant society in France', in P White and R Woods (eds) *The geographical impact of migration* (London 1980), pp 152–79.

8   Souden 'Migrants and the population structure', in Clark, *Transformation of English provincial towns*, pp 151–2.

9   I D Whyte, 'Population mobility', in Houston and Whyte (eds), *Scottish society 1500–1800*. R A Houston, 'Geographical mobility in Scotland 1652–1811' *Jnl Hist Geog* 11 (1985), pp 379–94.

10 I D Whyte, 'Mobility and marriage in East Lothian in the seventeenth and eighteenth centuries' *Trans East Lothian Antiq Soc* 19 (1987), pp 17–30.

11 W Howatson, 'The Scottish hairst and seasonal labour 1600–1870', *Scot Stud* 22 (1982), pp 13–26.

12 J de Vries, *European urbanization 1500–1800*, (London 1984), pp 199–249.

13 E A Wrigley, 'Parasite or stimulus: the town in the pre-industrial economy', in E A Wrigley and P Abrams (eds) *Towns in Societies* (Cambridge 1978), pp 299–309.

14 de Vries, *European urbanisation*, p 39.

15 I D Whyte, 'Scottish urbanization in the early modern period: a preliminary survey', *Scot Econ and Soc Hist*. Forthcoming.

16 Kussmaul, *Servants in husbandry*.

17 T M Devine (ed), *Farm servants and farm labour in Lowland Scotland 1770–1914* (Edinburgh 1984).

18 R A Houston and I D Whyte, 'Scottish society in perspective', in Houston and Whyte (eds) *Scottish society 1500–1800*.

19 K Wrightson, *English society 1580–1680* (London 1982), pp 43, 166.

20 M Flinn (ed), *Scottish population history* (Cambridge 1977), pp 164–86, 233–7.

21 Slack, 'Vagrants and vagrancy', *Econ Hist Rev* 27 (1974), p 364.

22 Souden, 'Migrants and the population structure', in Clark, *Transformation of English provincial towns*, pp 151–2. O Hufton, *The poor of eighteenth-century France* (London 1974), pp 26–31.

23   Flinn, *Scottish population history*, p 273.
24   Patten, 'Movement of labour'; J Wareing, 'Changes in the geographical distribution of recruitment of apprentices to the London companies 1486–1750', *Jnl Hist Geog* 6 (1980), pp 241–50.
25   A A Lovett, I D Whyte & K A Whyte, 'Poisson regression analysis and migration fields: the example of the apprenticeship records of Edinburgh in the seventeenth and eighteenth centuries', *Trans Inst Brit Geog*, New series 10 (1985), pp 317–32.
26   Houston, 'Geographical mobility'.
27   Patten, Rural-urban migration. J Patten, *English towns 1500–1700* (Folkstone 1978).
28   Scottish Record Office (henceforth SRO) OPR 644.
29   Register of marriages of the city of Edinburgh 1701–1750, 1751–1800. Scottish Record Society, Edinburgh.
30   Lovett, Whyte and Whyte, 'Poisson regression'. Wareing, 'Recruitment of apprentices.
31   Lovett, Whyte and Whyte, 'Poisson regression', p 319
32   Wareing, 'Recruitment of apprentices'.
33   A J Youngson, *After the Forty Five*, (Edinburgh 1973).
34   Howatson, 'The Scottish hairst', *Scot Stud* 22 (1982), pp 13–26.
35   R A Houston, 'Aspects of society in Scotland and North Eastern England c1550–c1750: social structure, literacy and geographical mobility'. Unpublished PhD thesis, Cambridge University 1981, p 379.
36   Wareing, 'Recruitment of apprentices'. Patten, 'Movement of labour'.
37   Lovett, Whyte and Whyte, 'Poisson regression'.
38   G Kyd, *Scottish population statistics*, (Edinburgh 1952). British parliamentary papers. Comparative account of the population of Great Britain in the years 1801, 1811, 1821 and 1831. (Shannon 1968).
39   The details of these are discussed in Flinn, *Scottish population history*, pp 187–200.
40   Ibid p 241.
41   Lovett, Whyte and Whyte, 'Poisson regression'.
42   I D Whyte, 'Early-modern Scotland: continuity and change', In G Whittington and I D Whyte (eds) *An Historical Geography of Scotland*, (London 1983) pp 132–3.
43   Lovett, Whyte and Whyte, 'Poisson regression'.
44   Ibid pp 318–19.
45   Wareing, 'Recruitment of apprentices'.
46   T M Devine, 'The merchant class in the larger Scottish towns in the later seventeenth and early eighteenth centuries, in G Gordon and B Dicks (eds) *Scottish Urban History* (Aberdeen 1983), pp 95–6.
47   Grigg, 'Ravenstein and the "laws of migration"'.
48   SRO OPR, p 597.
49   Kussmaul, *Servants in husbandry*.
50   Devine, *Farm servants*.
51   Houston, 'Geographical mobility'.
52   The poll tax lists for Aberdeenshire and Renfrewshire have been published. J Stuart, *List of pollable persons within the shire of Aberdeen 1696*, Spalding Club, (2 vols Aberdeen 1844). D Semple, *Renfrewshire Poll Tax returns* (Paisley 1864).
53   SRO E70 series. Manuscript poll tax lists for the Lothians.

54 Sir John Sinclair (ed), *Statistical Account of Scotland*, (henceforth OSA), (Edinburgh 1791) vol II p 65.
55 M Wood (ed), *Extracts from the records of the burgh of Edinburgh*, (Edinburgh 1940) vol II pp 27, 40.
56 OSA I 378, II 168, VII 3381, IX 370.
57 Ibid, I 378.
58 Stuart, *List of pollable persons.*
59 SRO E70/8/7 Heriot, E70/8/17 Stow.
60 Ibid E70/13/5 Dalmeny.
61 Semple, *Renfrewshire poll tax returns.*
62 Ibid.
63 Ibid.
64 Stuart *List of pollable persons*. Semple, *Renfrewshire poll tax returns*. SRO E70/8.
65 Flinn, *Scottish population history*, pp 194–5.
66 F J Shaw, *The northern and western islands of Scotland: their economy and society in the seventeenth century*, (Edinburgh 1981), pp 77, 184, 191–2.
67 OSA I 495, II 453, III 529.
68 Flinn, *Scottish population history*, p 279.
69 Houston and Whyte, 'Scottish society in perspective', in Houston and Whyte, *Scottish society 1500–1800.*
70 R A Houston, 'Women in the economy and society of Scotland 1500–1800', in Houston and Whyte, *Scottish society 1500–1800.*
71 SRO E70/8.
72 SRO E70/8/17.
73 Stuart, *List of pollable persons*. Semple, *Renfrewshire poll tax returns.*
74 OSA II 121, II 175, III 536.
75 OSA III 29, 397, 529.
76 Flinn, *Scottish population history*, p 194. I D Whyte, 'The occupational structure of Scottish burghs in the late seventeenth century, in M Lynch (ed), *The early-modern Scottish town*, (London 1987), pp 224–5.
77 Whyte, 'Occupational structure', in Lynch (ed), *Early modern Scottish town.*
78 Ibid.
79 M Wood (ed), *Edinburgh poll tax returns for 1694*, Scottish Record Society, (Edinburgh 1951).
80 This assumes that the age/sex distribution of the population was approximately comparable to that of contemporary England. D Souden, 'Pre-industrial English local migration fields'. Unpublished PhD thesis, Cambridge University, 1981, p 9.
81 Grigg, 'Ravenstein and the "laws of migration"'.
82 R Mitchison, 'The making of the old Scottish poor law', *Past & Present* 63 (1974), pp 58–93.
83 Flinn, *Scottish population history*, p 191.
84 SRO OPR Dirleton.
85 Slack, 'Vagrants and vagrancy', *Econ Hist Rev* 27 (1974). L Beier, 'Vagrants and the social order in Elizabethan England', *Past and Present* 64 (1974), p 7. The data for Monikie parish are discussed more fully in I D Whyte and K A Whyte, 'Geographical mobility in a seventeenth-century Scottish rural community', *Local Pop Stud* 32 (1984), pp 45–53.
86 SRO OPR 705.
87 OSA I 175, 198, III 139, 222, 321.
88 OSA III 229, 232, 475.

89   R Mitchison, 'North and South: The development of the gulf in poor law prac-
     tice', in Houston and Whyte, *Scottish society 1500–1800.*
90   OSA II 455.
91   OSA II 207.
92   OSA II 455.
93   P J Perry, 'Working-class isolation and mobility in rural Dorset 1837–1936',
     Trans Inst Brit Geog 46 (1969), pp 121–41. P E Ogden, 'Migration, marriage and
     the collapse of traditional peasant society in France', in P White and R Woods
     (eds), *The geographical impact of migration* (London 1980), pp 152–79. J Millard,
     'A new approach to the study of marriage horizons', *Local Pop Stud* 28 (1982),
     pp 10–31.
94   Whyte, 'Marriage and mobility'.
95   Howatson, 'The Scottish hairst'.

A New Role for a Lost Cause

Lowland Romanticisation of the Jacobite Highlander

Leah Leneman

The relationship between Highlander and Lowlander was never an easy one. In the early eighteenth century they spoke different languages, and their respective cultures and ethos differed greatly. To Lowlanders the way of life of most Highlanders seemed an offence against the Calvinist work ethic. A modern historian, echoing the views of Lowlanders two or three centuries earlier, has written that 'primitive agriculture requires little exertion, for it involves not much more than sowing the seed in the springtime and reaping the crop in the autumn, along with the largely passive task of herding animals. Coupled with this, the Highlanders were used to war and preparation for war, activities which may entail brief spells of great effort but which are certainly not synonymous with a life of steady toil.'[1] There seemed little or no point of contact. Yet by the early nineteenth century, the appurtenances connected with the Highlands (whether genuine or spurious)—tartan, bag-pipes, the kilt—had already become the symbols of Scotland they have remained to this day. An important change in attitudes took place in the second half of the eighteenth century, and this change is an integral part of the history of Scotland, for perceptions are no less important than facts in the national consciousness. The connection between the Jacobite movement and that change forms the subject of this paper.

It would be untrue to assert that Highlanders and Lowlanders had no dealings with one another. There was certainly trade—especially in cattle—between them, and towns close to the Highland line (as well as the capital city of Edinburgh) had many Highlanders living in them. Yet they still remained culturally distinct. Even near the end of the eighteenth century, the Old Statistical Account provides examples of parishes bordering the Highlands, where the English-speakers and Gaelic-speakers lived in separate communities, with virtually no exchanges between them. (It is worth pointing out, however, that records of an estate spanning the Highland line made no particular distinction between tenants of Lowland and Highland parts of the estate.)[2]

In earlier centuries, the primary ways in which Lowlanders regarded High-landers could best be described as contempt and derision, tinged with a measure of fear. The satiric tradition of the comic Gael dates back at least to the late middle ages—examples can be found in the poetry of Dunbar—and a short poem dating from about 1560 was entitled 'How the first helandman of God was maid of Ane horse turd in argylle as is said'.[3] The Highlander was held to be feckless and thievish, while his costume, the belted plaid,[4] was an object of ridicule. As one author has put it, to Lowland writers the Gael was 'a caricature figure discussed in that special tone of defensive mirth reserved for strange and possibly dangerous animals'.[5]

As few Lowlanders ventured beyond the Highland line before 1745, it is almost impossible to locate prosaic—as opposed to poetical—descriptions of Highlanders in the earlier period.[6] This makes a work written at the time of the 1715 rising, *An Historical View of the Highlanders . . . Set forth in a View of the Rebellion in Scotland*, particularly valuable. The chief aim of the pamphlet was to demonstrate how little the rising was to be feared, and therefore it can hardly be called unbiased, and, being published in Ireland, is arguably presenting a different angle from a Lowland Scottish one. Nevertheless, the view it set forth was often echoed after the Forty-Five and therefore deserves attention.

> These Mountains are inhabited by certain people, who tho' called *Scots*, are more properly *Irish*, and who as they really have their Original, so they claim their Affinity to the *Irish*, by retaining the Habit and Language of the Ancient *Irish*, many of 'em for several Scores of Miles being able to speak or understand no other Language.
>
> The Manners of these People are rude and barbarous, and tho' subject to the *British* Government, yet the Common people know no Laws or Government but the absolute Will of their Chief. They are divided into *Clans* or *Families*, of which the eldest Branch always preserves the Authority, and is called their *Chief*, and by his Primogeniture demands such a Homage that all the collateral Lines or Branches of the Family are subject to him by a kind of Natural Law: Under these Chiefs are the several Gentlemen of the Name, who have again under them their Tenants and Vassals; the first are their absolute Slaves, and being scarce sensible of any other Law, or any other *Government*, the Laird or Landlord commands them and their Substance on all Occasions, either for Civil Service or Military; and when they will not stir upon the King's Call, or the beating Drums for Voluntiers, yet on the Call of the Laird, tho' but with a Whistle or a Sounding-Horn, they will come together arm'd in a Moment, ready for any Mischief that the Laird shall command them to do, whether to Kill, Burn, Rob, Ravish, or whatever else comes to hand.[7]

Although the 1715 rising commanded enough support in the country to have posed a very real threat, it was so ineptly managed that no great stir was caused.[8] A number of participants were transported to the Colonies, but the nobility were, on the whole, treated very leniently. An earlier abortive Jacobite attempt, in 1708, had had the indirect effect of establishing the Society in Scotland for the Propagation of Christian Knowledge, which began setting up charity schools in Highland parishes.[9] The aim was to educate Highland children in English and in proper Revolution and presbyterian principles, thereby turning them into loyal Hanoverian subjects. This idea of 'civilising' the Highlands by turning the people into model subjects also surfaces strongly after the Forty-Five.

However, while this 'political' view of the Highlands, as one might perhaps term it, was held by members of the governing classes, a new 'poetical' view was gaining ground in popular literature. About the time of the Revolution 'The Bonny Highland Laddie' first appeared as an amatory symbol, a symbol which became increasingly prominent with successive Highland rebellions. To quote an author on the subject of Jacobite song, 'The Bonny Highland Laddie is an erotic figure, inhabiting the idealised world of the Scottish pastoral; nonetheless, he owes his popularity and, perhaps, his existence to the Jacobite movement.'[10]

The culmination of the Jacobite movement was, of course, the Forty-Five and the repercussions of that event were enormous and far-reaching. This time there was no question of treating the rebels leniently and leaving the Highlands alone in hopes that if educated properly the people would behave themselves as loyal subjects of King George. Measures were taken to ensure that the Highlands would never again pose a threat. All of the statutes—the Disarming Act, the Disclothing Act (which prohibited Highlanders wearing their distinctive dress and caused much bitterness by being applied to the clans who had fought on the Hanoverian side as well) and, most radical of all, the abolition of heritable jurisdictions, which did away with the summary powers of justice which the Highland chiefs had possessed—were aimed at this end. The Highland Line was no longer uncrossable save at an individual's peril, for the Highlands were opened up—to the improvers, the 'civilisers', the speculators, and the curious.

There were also repercussions of a rather different nature in Lowland Scotland. For in 1745 it rapidly became clear that as far as the English were concerned all Scots were 'rebels'. Those Lowlanders who considered themselves North Britons found themselves lumped together with the wild tartan-clad Gaels beheld en route to Derby and back, and this was a shock indeed. The sense of uncertainty and unease which existed after the Union about who the Scots actually *were* once Scotland was no longer an independent nation became truly traumatic in 1745, when Lowland Scots in London went in fear of their persons if they opened their mouths to reveal their origins. Thus, during that year came the realisation that however superior they themselves might feel to their Highland compatriots, to South Britons (except, of course, that such an animal never existed, since the English remained English, whatever the Scots chose to call themselves), Lowlanders were tarred with the same Jacobite brush.

The main thing that happened after Culloden in the Lowlands was the tremendous surge of attention directed towards the Highlands. Before 1745 it was perhaps not too difficult for an urban Lowlander to forget the High-landers even existed; after 1745 it must have been well nigh impossible.

As for the events and characters of the rising, the fascination which these held for the public at large is evidenced by the flood of 'histories' of the rebellion which rolled off the presses in the immediate aftermath of the rising, and the extensive coverage afforded it by the *Scots Magazine*. It began in July 1746 when the writer of a letter asked for the reform of 'those miserable wretches who have been the rod of God's anger to chastise us for our sins; I mean the banditti that harbour in most of the Highlands of Scotland, that nursery of rapine and violence, where rebellion is always hatching, and brooding her cursed offspring'. This view of the Highlands in the aftermath of a major rebellion is not very surprising, but he went on not to condemn the 'miserable wretches' but to propose a subscription be opened for their reformation. Once enough capital was raised it would be up to the king and parliament to instigate legislation for its most effective use: '. . . by making these people industrious, and enabling them to get their own living honestly, we shall prevent them (either thro' want or idleness) from coveting, or forcibly taking, other people's property; and by employing them better, secure them from being the easy tools and dupes of that power, who has ever been endeavouring to make slaves of them and us'. This notion of the common people as slaves who could be redeemed and rendered respectable citizens if only they were removed from the sway of their chiefs can be found as a constantly recurring theme in this period.[11] The writer himself in a later page enjoined compassion on the 'poor ignorant men, whose whole way of life rendered them incapable of enjoying the benefit, and insensible of the blessing of a mild and gracious government, and so more liable to be drawn into the snare by the subtle insinuations of their chiefs'.

Others cried for vengeance against all the rebels, and this in turn provoked letters calling for pity (the heading which the *Scots Magazine* gave to the whole debate was 'Of lenity and severity to the rebels'). The dignity and courage with which the Jacobite peers met their deaths at the hands of the executioner was admired (many who did not agree with their treasonous views did not hesitate to call them martyrs, a description bitterly contested by others); as for the common people, they were 'misguided' and should be set on the proper path of virtue rather than mercilessly destroyed. Once again writers thought Highlanders could be turned into North Britons. As one such correspondent expressed it, 'The name of *Highlanders*, by this means, would in another century scarcely exist; and yet the number of families in *Great Britain* would not be diminished.'[12]

While the political élite were considering and implementing new policies for the Highlands, the general public were devouring pamphlets describing the events of the rising and the behaviour of the participants. And there is no doubt that the youth and charm of the pretender/prince gave the story an even greater fascination than it would otherwise have had.

Histories of the rising began to roll off the presses as early as 1746. The attitudes of their writers varied. Andrew Henderson's *History of the Rebellion MDCCXLV and MDCCXLVI with the Manifestos of the Pretender and his Son*[13] was uncompromisingly Hanoverian in sentiment, displaying no sympathy whatsoever for Charles or his supporters, and even attempting to excuse Cumberland's soldiers' atrocities after Culloden. More typical was the romantic history entitled *Young Juba or the History of the Young Chevalier*, which was written by the Prince's valet, Michele Vezzosi, translated from the

Italian, and published in London in 1748. In his preface the author remarked of the Prince, 'It must be allow'd on all Hands, even by his Enemies, that he has a martial Spirit, an elevated Genius, and has dar'd Things not unworthy the greatest hero.'[14] The author also gave full credit to Hanoverian actions and sentiments where appropriate, and this balanced view characterised many of the histories of the rising. As far as most Lowlanders were concerned, after Culloden the Jacobite cause was well and truly lost, and therefore loyal subjects of King George saw no harm in praising the courage of the Prince and his followers even while deploring their misguided sentiments. Works by those who had not given up hope of an eventual Jacobite victory were not likely to be published in this period.[15]

Particularly fascinating to the public were stories of the Prince's escape amongst the gallant and loyal Highlanders—which even had a heroine in the person of Flora MacDonald. The most popular and frequently reprinted work describing the escape was *Ascanius or the Young Adventurer, containing a particular account of all that happened to a certain person during his wanderings in the North, from his memorable defeat in April 1746 to his final escape on the 19th of September in the same year*. This anonymous pamphlet was dated 1746 and must have been published towards the end of that year, with the ascription that it was 'translated from a MS. handed about at the Court of Versailles'. The first edition was printed in London, and apart from many other London editions, there were others published in Edinburgh, Glasgow, Cupar, Aberdeen, etc, as well as versions in French, Spanish and Italian. The many editions were by no means identical, the later ones containing many alterations and additions, some highly fanciful.[16]

Another pamphlet, written by Dr John Burton, and drawing heavily on material from *Ascanius*, was published in 1747 under the title *A genuine and true Journal of the most miraculous escape of the young Chevalier by an Englishman, partly written in London and partly in Scotland*. Also published in 1747 was a pamphlet entitled *Alexis or the Young Adventurer, a Novel*, which was written in mock-heroic style, giving classical names to all the places and people concerned in the Prince's escape after Culloden.[17]

To move away from prose, it must be said that Jacobite poetry before the Forty-Five bore little resemblance to the 'sentimental' poetry which people later came to associate with the movement. Much of it was broad satire and invective, directed against enemies of the cause,[18] with references which only those in the know would appreciate. These poems were not so much about Jacobite sentiments or personalities as *against* Hanoverian ones. Naturally, at the time of the risings a battle of note would be commemorated in verse. But as a literary art form, such works hardly seem to merit the vast amount of attention paid to them at a later date. Indeed, Robert Chambers—at the very time when the glorification of Jacobite song was at its height—perspicaciously remarked that 'Jacobite song is in reality an excrescence from the body of Scottish song, not a part of its body corporate. By far the greater part of these political canticles are merely parodies and imitations of other songs; for the Jacobites, like the Puritan clergy of the two preceding centuries, had the sagacity to form their compositions on the frame-work and foundation-stone of songs which were favourites with the public.'[19]

It is also worth noting that Lowland Jacobite poetry, unlike most (though by no means all) Gaelic poetry was part of a written, not an oral, tradition; it has been likened in style, content, production and dissemination to the popular broadside ballad.[20]

Although the period immediately following the Forty-Five was one of intense poetical creativity in the Highlands (see below pp 119–20), where Culloden was viewed by keen Jacobites as a major setback rather than a final defeat, such poetry was not generated in the Lowlands. Yet Lowland interest in the Highlands continued, as did the need to find a way of mentally assimilating the area and people into the Scottish national consciousness. It was *Fingal*, the alleged epic 'translated' by James Macpherson and received with rapture by the Edinburgh literati when first published in 1761, which offered them the means to do this. I have written about Ossian at length elsewhere[21] and so will only summarise some of the main points here.

For his 'epic', James Macpherson refashioned poems which had existed in the Highlands and in Ireland for centuries, about the blind old harper Oisein and his tales of the hero, Finn, which he said dated from the 3rd century AD. The strong belief in primitivism—the idea that earlier societies possessed virtues which more 'civilised' societies had lost—which was such a keynote of Enlightenment thinking made the honourable and chivalrous characters presented by Macpherson very credible. We have already seen the desire which many Lowland Scots had felt to 'civilise' the Highlands, and the very fact that even in the eighteenth century the Highlands were seen as not fully civilised meant that the primitivist label could be attached not just to the Ossianic heroes of the past but also to present day Highlanders, who were, after all, the direct descendants of those ancient heroes. This idealisation of the Highlander to fit the primitivist ideal is beautifully summed up in the following passage.

> The importance and necessity, in a country thus enervated by luxury, thus lost in frivolous pursuits and vain speculations, to cherish in whatsoever remote obscurity they exist, a hardy manly Race, inured to Suffering, fearless of Danger, and careless of Poverty, to invigorate Society by their Spirit, to defend it by their Courage, and to adorn it with those virtues that bloom in the shade, but are ready to wither away in the sunshine of prosperity.[22]

The tale of the 'prince in the heather'—when for all those months the humble Highlanders, who could have earned a huge reward for turning him in, sheltered and aided Charles—obviously dovetailed perfectly into this new image.

Ossian also provided a new way of looking at Highland scenery, for with the new concept of the 'sublime' in nature, views could be admired not for their charm and beauty but for their awesomeness and grandeur. Another aspect of Ossian worth noting which will surface again in connection with later Jacobite poetry is the melancholy elegiac tone which Macpherson adopted throughout and which ever after was associated in people's minds with 'Celtic' poetry, though nothing could be further from the authentic Gaelic tradition.[23]

Fingal almost immediately became the Scottish 'national epic' and gave Lowland literati the means they had been seeking to assimilate mentally the Highlands as an admirable part of the Scottish nation. Scepticism and derision from certain English quarters—most notably Samuel Johnson—merely served to draw Lowland Scots closer together in defence.[24] Ironically, it was during this period of anti-Scottish feeling in England, due to the unpopularity of the Bute ministry, that the caricature Scot *in a kilt* first appeared.

Attention on the Highlands in the 1760s and 1770s was focused chiefly on Ossian, and not much appeared on Jacobite subjects, although a collection of Jacobite songs, *The True Loyalist*,[25] was published in 1779, without causing any great stir.

Interest was, however, still alive in the story of the Prince and his wanderings, as is evidenced by James Boswell's lengthy (and rather tedious) description of it—gleaned from Mrs MacDonald while actually staying in the house of Flora MacDonald on Skye—which he recounted in his Journal.[26] The morning after their first night there he found a slip of paper on which Dr Johnson had written the words, 'Quantum cedat virtutibus aurum' (what a great amount gives way before the virtues). In the first edition of the Journal Boswell admitted he did not understand what was meant by the words, but in a later edition he added the following footnote: 'an ingenious friend has observed to me, that Dr Johnson had probably been thinking on the reward which was offered by government for the apprehension of the grandson of King James II and he meant by these words to express his admiration of the Highlanders, whose fidelity and attachment had resisted the golden temptation that had been held out to them'.

The individual in the 1780s who had the most potent effect on the future preservation of the Jacobite movement as a vehicle for poetry and for nationalist sentiment was Robert Burns. There was a family tradition that the poet's grandfather had been 'out' in 1715, though Burns' complex feelings about Jacobitism have been seen as connected with many facets of his nature, including his egalitarianism: rebellion was perceived as a great leveller, uniting landowner and tenant in a common cause.[27] His many Jacobite songs raised the medium to a new level of artistic importance, and by presenting the Jacobite risings as a context for emotions and aspirations which were not political in any party sense, 'he made it possible for Jacobitism to shed its sectarian connotations and take its part in a national inheritance'.[28]

In the period after Burns' death, other collections of popular poetry, including Jacobite songs, were made, the most respected being that of Joseph Ritson, whose *Scottish Songs* was published in 1794. But the most important figure in the development of Jacobite song between Burns and Hogg was arguably Allan Cunningham, who deliberately forged songs to suit the tastes of the time.

This began in 1809, when Cunningham was introduced to an Englishman, R H Cromek, who was planning to publish a collection of Scottish songs. When Cunningham produced samples of his own poetry they were received with scant interest, but when he produced samples of verse 'collected' from the Galloway region, Cromek was enthusiastic. The collection was published as *Remains of Nithsdale and Galloway Song* and was very well received. The general public did not suspect a cheat, and though Scott, Hogg, and other members of the Edinburgh literati guessed that Cunningham himself had written the bulk of the songs, there was no general exposé at the time. On 29 December 1810 the poet wrote to his brother, James, asking for more detailed criticisms.

> Choose out all your favourites, and write fully about the songs of the two rebellions. Now, you must mind it, that these songs and ballads being written for imposing on the country as the reliques of other years, I was obliged to have recourse to occasional coarseness, and severity, and negligence, which would make them appear as fair specimens of the ancient song and ballad.[29]

In reality, most of the songs were far from being coarse or 'negligent'; they were pervaded with the fashionable melancholy and helped to form the nineteenth-century view of Jacobite poetry. A verse from 'The Lovely Lass of Inverness' is quoted below as illustration.

> O weep, O weep, ye Scottish dames,
>   Weep till ye blin' a mither's ee;
> Nae reeking ha' in fifty miles,
>   But naked corses sad to see.
> O spring is blythesome to the year,
>   Trees sprout, flowers spring, and birds sing hie;
> But oh! what spring can raise them up,
>   That lie on dread Colloden-lee?[30]

The first quarter of the nineteenth century was, without question, the heyday of Jacobite writing. Various reasons may be adduced for this. It was the height of the Romantic era, and the idealisation of the Highlander and Highland scenery reached its apogee. Christopher Smout has noted in connection with William Gilpin's writings on the sublime in nature that, 'whereas the Highlander for Dr Johnson was an object of the genuine interest one human being might have in another, for Gilpin and most after him he was a decoration, imagined to be harmoniously in tune with the remainder of the scene, but not a real person one could talk to. This outlook develops in the nineteenth century into an attitude of reverence for the imagined "romance" of the Jacobite and clannish past'.[31] An apt illustration of this last point is provided by the following lines from Anne Grant of Laggan's poem, *The Highlanders*.

> Where ancient *Chieftains* rul'd those green retreats,
> And faithful *Clans* delighted to obey
> The kind behests of patriarchal sway.[32]

The transformation in the popular Scottish consciousness of Highland chiefs from the brutal oppressors of a slavish people they had been pictured as in 1746 to paternalist protectors of a grateful peasantry is a radical one. It was doubtless due, to some extent at least, to the realisation that for the most part the rapacious landlords who had replaced the old Highland chiefs were even less desirable; reports in the popular press about the Highland Clearances helped to engender sympathy for the hapless victims. The very fact that the Jacobite movement as a political force had long since come to an end, and that, far from being a threat to national security, Highlanders were being forced out of their lands and emigrating by the thousands, obviously made it easier to invest them with a roseate glow.[33]

The changed political climate in the era of the French Revolution was another reason why Jacobite writing could flourish in this period for, as Donaldson has written, 'the spectre of outright Republicanism rendered the traditional opposition of Hanoverian and Stuart obsolete at a stroke'.[34] In this new climate of opinion books like John Home's *History of the Rebellion* could safely be published. However, Sir Walter Scott castigated Home for ending the book with Culloden instead of dealing with the cruelties perpetrated after victory had been achieved. He believed this was because, having dedicated the book to King George III, Home was reluctant to condemn the actions of the monarch's ancestor.[35] Colonel David Stewart of Garth related the following with regard to this work:

> Mr Home, for some years, spent part of every summer, ostensibly for the benefit of his health and for amusement, but actually in collecting materials for his history. The respectability of his character, and the suavity of his manners, procured him everywhere a good reception. But his visits were principally made to Jacobite families, to whom the secret history of those times was familiar. They told him all they knew with the most unreserved confidence; and nothing could exceed their disappointment when the history appeared, and proved to be a dry detail of facts universally known, while the rich store of authentic and interesting anecdotes, illustrative of the history to the times, and of the peculiar features of the Highland character, with which they had furnished him, had been neglected or concealed, from an absurd dread of giving offence to the Royal Family by a disclosure of the cruelties wantonly practised, or by relating circumstances creditable to the feelings of the unfortunate sufferers.

He went on:

> Now, it is very well known with what generous sympathy the late King viewed the sacrifice to mistaken loyalty, and the countenance and protection which he afforded to such individuals as lived to see him on the throne, and which he extended to their descendants. It is equally well known that there is not one individual of his family that would not listen with deep interest to the details of chivalrous loyalty, of honourable sacrifices, and of sufferings sustained with patience and fortitude by those who are long since gone to their account, and who are no more objects of dislike or hostility to them than Hector or King Priam.[36]

The mention of Stewart of Garth brings up another reason for the enormous popularity of Highlanders in this period: the importance of the Highland Regiments in the Napoleonic Wars. Their heroism was undeniable, and with a historian like Colonel Stewart to record their exploits it is not surprising that they should have captured the public imagination to such an extent. The Colonel combined a very real appreciation of Highland culture with an ability to romanticise and idealise. He was far from unique in this—writers like Anne Grant of Laggan and Patrick Graham (minister of Aberfoyle and a keen advocate of Ossian) revealed both an understanding of the mentality of the Highlanders amongst whom they lived and a tendency to idealise them into romantic stereotypes.

This same mixture also manifested itself very strongly in the most influential writer of them all, Sir Walter Scott, whose first novel, *Waverley*, had as its subject the Forty-Five. Unlike Scott's poems about Highlanders, *The Lady of the Lake* and *The Lord of the Isles*, which were quintessentially romantic, the novel had at its core a conflict between two very different visions, one of the heart and one of the head. The 'heart' yearned after the past—and Gaeldom—with nostalgia, while the 'head' admired modernity and inno-vation. The tension between these two opposing instincts provides much of the fascination in Scott's best work and is fully evident in his first novel.

Scott had been strongly influenced in his youth by the Jacobite Stewart of Invernahyle, and it has been said that a good deal of *Waverley* was actually written while the author was staying at Invernahyle. There is no doubt that Scott felt a deep and lifelong admiration for the heroic aspects of Gaelic society.[37] In *Waverley*, when the family bard chants Gaelic verse to the clan, lamenting the dead, exhorting, entreating and animating the living, Scott vividly described how the ardour of the poet communicated itself to his audience: 'Their wild and sunburnt countenances assumed a fiercer and more animated expression; all bent forward towards the reciter, and some laid their hands on their swords. Then the song ceased, there was a deep pause, while the aroused feelings of the poet and of the hearers gradually subsided into their usual channel.'[38]

For readers, much of the fascination of the book lay in the realisation that the events and customs described by Scott had all been so recent. Francis Jeffrey was very much aware of this in his review of the novel, when he wrote of 'the surprise that is excited by discovering, that in our own country, and almost in our own age, manners and characters existed, and were conspicuous, which we had been accustomed to consider as belonging to remote antiquity, or extravagant romance'.[39]

The contrast is brought out very strongly in a scene where the hero, Edward, having been caught up in the Forty-Five by the fervour of supporters of the Jacobite cause, is amidst the Highland army when he suddenly comes face to face with the troop he himself had formerly commanded. He hears the familiar trumpets and kettle-drums and the command given in English. 'It was at this instant, that looking around him, he saw the wild dress and appearance of his Highland associates, heard their whispers in an uncouth and unknown language, looked upon his own dress, so unlike that which he had worn from his infancy, and wished to awake from what seemed at the moment a dream, strange, horrible, and unnatural.'[40] There is certainly nothing 'romantic' about the depiction of this scene, and it epitomises one half of Scott's dual vision, the side which was fascinated by this alien culture, and anxious to understand it more fully, while remaining himself very much of his own age and ethos.

The intriguing thing, however, is that however clearly one can see Scott's rationality ultimately prevailing over his romanticism, somehow at the end of the book it is the romanticism and not the rationality which stays with the reader. And thus—after *Waverley*—Jacobites were forever to be romantic Highlanders.[41]

Stewart of Garth attempted to explain the reasons why the Highlanders had striven to restore 'their ancient line of sovereigns'. He ascribed it partly to the degree of freedom he said they had enjoyed under the Stuart kings, and also to the loyalty of clans for their chiefs, and chiefs for one to whom many were said to be related by blood or marriage.[42] He continued in a *Waverley*-like vein,

> During the progress of this unfortunate rebellion, the moral character of the great mass of the Highlanders engaged in it was placed in a favourable point of view. The noblemen and gentlemen too, who took a lead in the cause, were generally actuated by pure, although mistaken motives of loyalty and principle . . . Into these principles and feelings, the mass of the clansmen entered with a warmth and zeal unmixed with, or unsullied by, motives of self-interest or aggrandizement; for whatever their superiors might expect, they could look for nothing but that satisfaction and self-approbation which accompany the consciousness of supporting the oppressed. They were therefore misguided, rather than criminal, and to their honour it ought to be remembered, that though engaged in a formidable civil war, which roused the strongest passions of human nature, and though unaccustomed to regular discipline, or military control, though they were in a manner let loose on their countrymen, and frequently flushed with victory, and elated with hopes of ultimate success, they committed comparatively few acts of wanton plunder, or gratuitous violence.[43]

The author of an anonymous pamphlet commenting on various aspects of the *Sketches* observed that 'it has of late years been too much the fashion to involve, in one indiscriminate charge of Jacobitism, the whole inhabitants of the Highlands'. He thought this proceeded 'partly from persons whose ancestors had embarked in the Rebellions of the last century, and who wish to lessen their demerit, by increasing as much as possible the number of their accomplices; and from others, who, in a mistaken spirit of chivalry, think they are doing honour to the Highlanders at large by including them all in these insurrections'. He went on to provide evidence of just how small a proportion of the rebel army were genuine Highlanders.[44] His point was very valid, but went unheeded for, as a result of *Waverley*, Jacobites had by now become virtually synonymous in most minds with Highlanders.

Aside from the many works of prose about the Jacobite cause which appeared in the first quarter of the nineteenth century, it was also the key era of Jacobite poetry, the most important collection being Hogg's *Jacobite Relics*.[45] But Hogg was no romantic. His *Relics* included numerous examples of genuine early eighteenth-century Jacobite verse—'a heterogeneous mishmash of squibs and lampoons'.[46] He also inserted some of his own compositions, pastiches of the real thing, and was delighted when a reviewer pointed to one of them as an example of the authentic note.[47] The Highland Society and Colonel Stewart of Garth, who had commissioned the work, were dismayed at what they got. By this time, not only was Jacobite song expected to conform to certain standards of gentility and 'refinement', but collectors of such songs were meant to 'purify' any which failed to meet those standards. Hogg may have been unprincipled enough to fake the odd song himself, but he presented his early material with all the raw vigour of its natural state.

For a truly 'genteel' collection of Jacobite song contemporaries could turn to Carolina Oliphant, Lady Nairne. Lady Nairne was brought up in a fiercely Jacobite family, so to that extent the sentiments she expressed were genuine enough, but she was only born in 1766 and so did not live through an era in which Jacobite hopes had any reality. She composed her own songs, and many, like 'Will ye no come back again?', were filled with nostalgia, recreating an eternally youthful Prince Charles to be endlessly yearned after, although the direct line of the Stewarts was by now extinct. Another short poem, 'The Lass of Livingstane', shows the melancholy strain predominating.

> OH! wha will dry the dreeping tear,
>   She sheds her lane, she sheds her lane?
> Or wha the bonnie lassie will cheer
>   Of Livingstane, of Livingstane?
> The croun was half on Charlie's head,
>   Ae gladsome day, ae gladsome day;
> The lads that shouted joy to him
>   Are in the clay, are in the clay.
>
> Her waddin' goun was wyl'd and won,
>   It ne'er was on, it ne'er was on;
> Culloden field, his lowly bed,
>   She thought upon, she thought upon.
> The bloom has faded frae her cheek
>   In youthfu' prime, in youthfu' prime;
> And sorrow's with'ring hand has done
>   The deed o' time, the deed o' time.[48]

This melancholy strain appears in a different form in the preface to another collection of Jacobite song of this era, the *Jacobite Minstrelsy*. The anonymous author attempted to explain the enormous popularity of Jacobite song in various ways: 'Nothing can exceed the force and variety of their humour, the keenness of their wit, the vigour of their invective, the buoyancy of their hope, and not unfrequently the pathos of their despair.' He admitted that much of the appeal of Jacobite song was 'owing to the *cause* which it sung'— not, of course, that anyone admired the actual principles of the Jacobites, 'for these, it is well known, warred alike against common sense and the natural liberty of mankind'; what was admirable was 'the devoted constancy and heroic valour displayed by the partizans of the House of Stuart, and a melancholy sympathy for the misfortunes that pursued them'. In the last words lie the crux of the appeal, for, as the author went on to say, 'it is chiefly in contemplating the reverses of the Jacobites, and especially the grand catastrophe that followed their short lived triumphs in 1745, that we find our sympathies most powerfully awakened on their behalf . . . to this feeling of compassion for the wretched, must we ascribe that general prepossession which still exists for every thing connected with the Jacobite cause and Jacobite times'.[49]

Of course, as has been indicated, there were other, more complex, reasons for the great popularity of all things Jacobite at this time. One which Hogg certainly felt, and which he shared with many of his contemporaries, was a kind of political nostalgia that harked back to pre-Union days when Scotland was a separate nation. As Colonel Stewart put it, 'there are few Scotchmen, even of the present day, whose hearts are not warmed by the songs which celebrate their independence, under their ancient race of kings'.[50]

This vision of the defunct Stewart line embodying an independent Scotland may derive from the period of the Union debates, but it reached its zenith in the early nineteenth century after the line was defunct. As suggested earlier, the trauma of the Forty-Five revealed to Lowland Scots how fundamentally inferior the English considered them. In the decades that followed, the Scots began to emphasise the *differences* between themselves and the English. While a Stewart claimant still lived, *Ossian* provided the focal point for such aspirations, but by the end of the eighteenth century the Jacobite story was equally important. And, just as the Highland origins of the Ossianic 'epics' were crucial, so too did the Highland connections with the Jacobite cause become central, because the Highlanders really *were* different. As Willa Muir put it, 'Highland dress, Highland music, Highland temperament were all sufficiently unlike the English to make part of a nucleus for the crystallising of this new separateness.'[51]

A final question must be where Gaelic Jacobite poetry fits into the Lowland tradition, and the answer must be that it does not.[52] A good representative collection of the Gaelic corpus—with English translations—can be found in John Lorne Campbell's *Highland Songs of the Forty Five*.[53] Some similarities may be found with the early eighteenth-century Lowland poetry of invective, for there was plenty of that kind of thing in the Gaelic songs. But poetry played a far more significant role in eighteenth-century Gaelic society than it did in the Lowlands. Poets were spokesmen for the populace, not only recording events but also expressing views about the meaning and nature of those events.[54]

Many conventions of Gaelic poetry, such as the panegyric, were used in connection with the Stewarts as 'rightful rulers'. James and Charles were praised not only for their moral qualities but also for their physical strength, good looks, and—most important—nobility of birth. Even the weather was said to be propitious when Prince Charles came over to Scotland. After Culloden there was another Gaelic poetical tradition that came to the fore, that of the elegy. At the same time the poets had to come to terms with what had happened and try to understand the cause; sorcery and witchcraft featured in a number of songs. For those who refused to accept Culloden as a final defeat there was more poetry of exhortation to be composed as a means of rallying the faithful. In 1788, when Prince Charles died in Rome, William Ross, a poet born in 1762, composed a song in which he claimed that he had always believed that one day Charles would return, 'but the tryst has forsaken me until Doomsday'. Professor Gillies writes, 'Ross genuinely wants to make contact with the spirit of 1745 but his poetic sincerity results in an elegy which is manifestly of a different era.' Nor did the Gaelic poetical tradition altogether avoid the early nineteenth-century romanticisation of the Jacobite cause.[55]

Lowlanders may not have known anything about the Gaelic tradition, but it was their idealisation of Highland virtues and their appropriation of Highland accoutrements such as bagpipes, kilts and tartans—not to mention the Stewart line of kings—which helped to create a new Scottish identity.[56] The lost cause of Jacobitism was an important element in Lowland incorporation of the Highlands in their consciousness of what it meant to be a Scot.[57]

NOTES

1   A J Youngson, *After the Forty-Five* (Edinburgh 1973), p 36. Anyone attempting subsistence farming in the Highlands would certainly query the 'little effort' which Youngson considers to be necessary, and in earlier centuries there were also many services which had to be performed for the landowner.

2   See Leah Leneman, *Living in Atholl 1685–1785* (Edinburgh 1986). Kirk session records for Highland parishes do not reveal social mores radically different from Lowland parishes. See Rosalind Mitchison and Leah Leneman, *Illegitimacy and Society in Early Modern Scotland* (forthcoming).

3   Willa Muir, *Living with Ballads* (London 1963), p 216.

4   The kilt was a later invention. For a contemporary description of the belted plaid see *An Historical Account* (Note 7 below), pp 20–21.

5   W Donaldson, 'The Jacobite Song in 18th and Early 19th Century Scotland'. Unpublished PhD thesis, Aberdeen, 1974, p 276. See also W Donaldson, *The Jacobite Song. Political Myth and National Identity* (Aberdeen, 1988).

6   The marvellous classic, Edward Burt's *Letters from the Highlands*, was written in the 1720s and provides a very vivid picture of an Englishman's first-hand experience of the Highlands, but it was not published until the late eighteenth century, and was therefore unread in the period in question.

7   *An Historical Account of the Highlanders . . . Set forth in A View of the Rebellion in Scotland* (Dublin 1715), pp 12–13. The anonymous author went on to say, 'It was earnestly wished that the Liberty of these People might have been obtained by the late *Union*; but that Treaty had so many other enemies, and had such Difficulties in its bringing to pass, that had not the *Northern Nobility* been assured beforehand that their Patriarchal Tyranny should be reserv'd to them, they had never been brought to acquiesce in the proceedings in *Parliament*.'

8   See Christopher Sinclair-Stevenson, *Inglorious Rebellion* (St Albans 1973), and Bruce Lenman, *The Jacobite Risings in Britain 1689–1746* (London 1980).

9   See M G Jones, *The Charity School Movement* (Cambridge 1938).

10 Donaldson, 'Jacobite Song', p 285. See also Muir, *Ballads*, pp 219–21.

11 Dr Nicholas Phillipson has pointed out to me that the term slave is being used in the classic republican sense, revolving around the distinction between notions of personal dependence and the independence which is only possible when a man's life is conducted according to the principles of civil liberty under the rule of law.

12 *Scots Magazine*, vol 8 (1746), pp 313–4, 475.

13 Andrew Henderson *History of the Rebellion MDCCXLV and MDCCXLVI with the Manifestos of the Pretender and his Son* (London 1753).

14 *Young Juba* (London 1748), p xi.

15 Bishop Forbes' contemporary compilation, *The Lyon in Mourning*, which provided source material for so many later historians, was not actually published until 1895.

16 I owe the information in this paragraph to the Introduction to the 'Istoria di sua Altezza Reale' in Henrietta Tayler (ed), *A Jacobite Miscellany—Eight Original Papers on the Rising of 1745–1746* (Roxburgh Club 1948), pp 71–3. She goes into considerably more detail than I have done.

17 Ibid, pp 73–5.

18 'The overwhelming preoccupation is with people, commonly lying, betraying and murdering—disfigured by every deformity of person and moral nature that malice could invent or rumour ventilate. The world of Scottish Jacobite song in the first half of the 18th century is peopled by grotesques moving in a thick and

mazy atmosphere of slander, innuendo and calumny'. Donaldson, 'Jacobite Song', pp 36–7.

19   Robert Chambers, *The Scottish Song* (Edinburgh 1829), vol 1, p lix.

20   Donaldson, 'Jacobite Song', p 21.

21   'The Creation of the Highland Image in Lowland Scotland 1745–1831' (unpublished MA dissertation, Edinburgh 1979); 'Ossian and the Enlightenment', *Scotia* xi (1987), pp 13–29; 'The Effects of Ossian in Lowland Scotland' in J J Carter and J H Pittock (eds), *Aberdeen and the Enlightenment* (Aberdeen 1987).

22   Anne Grant of Laggan, *The Highlanders and Other Poems*, 3rd ed (Edinburgh 1810), pp 73–4.

23   See M Chapman, *The Gaelic Vision in Scottish Culture* (London & Montreal 1978) and P Sims-Williams, 'The Visionary Celt: The Construction of an Ethnic Preoccupation', in *Cambridge Medieval Celtic Studies* No 11 (Summer 1986), pp 71–96. The elegy certainly played a prominent role in the Gaelic poetical tradition but bore no relation to the mushy sentimental style of Macpherson and his successors.

24   In the early nineteenth century John Sinclair wrote, 'It will hardly be credited in these days, but in the year 1762, when the poem of Fingal was published, there existed in many, both in England and Scotland, a great spirit of hostility to every thing connected with the Gaelic language, and those by whom it was spoken, on account of the zeal with which the Highlanders, in the year 1745, had supported the claims of the house of Stuart. Hence many were induced to decry the beauties of Ossian, because they were brought to light by those who were considered as attached to an exiled and obnoxious house.' *Introduction to the Gaelic version of Ossian, translated into Latin* (London 1807), vol 1, p xi, fn. I think that is absolute nonsense. The strong anti-Scottish sentiment during, and after, the Bute ministry is undeniable, but there is no evidence to support his contention of anti-Gaelic prejudice because of supposed Jacobite sentiments at that date.

25   *The True Loyalist; or Chevalier's Favourite: Being a Collection of Elegant Songs, never before printed. Also, several other Loyal Compositions, wrote by Eminent Hands* (np, 1779).

26   James Boswell, *The Journal of a Tour to the Hebrides* (London 1956—text of 3rd edition of 1786), pp 152–68. In a footnote Boswell explained how he had decided what to call 'the grandson of the unfortunate King James the Second': 'I do not call him *the Prince of Wales*, or *the Prince*, because I am quite satisfied that the right which the *House of Stuart* had to the throne is extinguished. I do not call him the *Pretender*, because it appears to me as an insult to one who is still alive, and, I suppose, thinks very differently. It may be a parliamentary expression; but it is not a gentlemanly expression. I *know*, and I exult in having it in my power to tell, that THE ONLY PERSON in the world who is intitled to be offended at this delicacy, "thinks and feels as I do;" and has liberality of mind and generosity of sentiment enough to approve of my tenderness for what even *has been* Blood Royal, That he is a *prince* by *courtesy*, cannot be denied; because his mother was the daughter of Sobieski, king of Poland. I shall, therefore, *on that account alone*, distinguish him by the name of *Prince Charles Edward*.'

27   Donaldson, 'Jacobite Song', pp 314–22.

28   Ibid, pp 365–6. Donaldson also noted that Burns conferred an authority on the theme of exile 'which was to secure it a new prominence not merely in Jacobite songs, but in Scottish poetry as a whole for several generations to come'.

29   Quoted in D Hogg, *The Life of Allan Cunningham* (London 1875), p 87.

30 *Poems and Songs by Allan Cunningham* (London 1847), p 32.
31 Christopher Smout, 'Tours in the Scottish Highlands from the eighteenth to the twentieth centuries', *Northern Scotland* V (1983), p 105.
32 Grant, *Highlanders*, p 32.
33 Donaldson believes that songs deploring the defeat at Culloden became an indirect commentary on the Clearances ('Jacobite Song', 463). He produces no evidence, and I do not think I agree with him, but it is an interesting idea.
34 Ibid, p 423.
35 Sir Walter Scott, *Critical and Miscellaneous Essays* Vol II, p 298 (originally appeared in *Quarterly Review* June 1827).
36 David Stewart of Garth, *Sketches of the Highlanders* (Edinburgh 1822). His explanation was that two or three years before the History was published, Home's carriage overturned, 'on which occasion he received a severe contusion to the head, which had such an effect upon his nerves, that both his memory and judgment were very considerably affected ever after'.
37 See L M McIntyre, 'Sir Walter Scott and the Highlands'. Unpublished PhD thesis, Glasgow 1976.
38 Sir Walter Scott, *Waverley* (Everyman edition), p 181.
39 *Edinburgh Review*, November 1814 in J O Hayden (ed), *Scott The Critical Heritage*, p 81.
40 *Waverley*, p 331.
41 At least one contemporary who was familiar with Highland life—Elizabeth Grant of Rothiemurchus—did not like the book at all. And she considered that the idea given of the Highlands to be 'utterly at variance with truth'. *Memoirs of a Highland Lady*, 2nd edn (London 1911), p 326.
42 Stewart of Garth, *Sketches*, pp 96–7.
43 Ibid, pp 106–7.
44 Anon, *Remarks on Colonel Stewart's Sketches of the Highlanders* (Edinburgh 1823), pp 8–9.
45 James Hogg, *The Jacobite Relics of Scotland* vols 1 & 2 (Edinburgh & London, 1819 & 1821).
46 Donaldson, 'Jacobite Song', p 470.
47 L Simpson, *James Hogg, A Critical Study* (Edinburgh & London 1962), p 54.
48 C Rogers (ed), *Life and Songs of the Baroness Nairne* (Edinburgh 1905), p 211.
49 *Jacobite Minstrelsy* (Glasgow 1829), pp iv–vii.
50 Stewart of Garth, *Sketches*, p 97.
51 Muir, *Ballads*, p 222.
52 Hogg seems to attribute Jacobite song as such to Highlanders, which is nonsense, but he did incorporate some Gaelic material in the *Relics*. However, as he admitted, he himself versified the English prose translations he received from Highlanders, and whether they would have been recognised by anyone familiar with the originals is a moot point.
53 J L Campbell, *Highland Songs of the Forty Five* (Edinburgh 1933, reissued 1984).
54 I am very grateful to Professor William Gillies for letting me see his unpublished paper, 'Gaelic Songs of the Forty Five', which goes into the subject in some depth. My own remarks in this section are largely based on it.
55 E.g. Patrick Turner's own contribution to his collection of Gaelic poetry published in Edinburgh in 1813 (mentioned by Gillies).
56 I do not mean to imply that the romantic view of the Highlander was the only view to prevail in Lowland Scotland. There were the improvers, there were collectors of Gaelic poetry, there were the genuinely interested (who could by

then read Edward Burt's *Letters from the Highlands*)—and there were also plenty who still despised the Highlanders as much as their ancestors had done.

57 I would like to thank William Gillies, Owen Dudley Edwards, and Nicholas Phillipson for their helpful comments on an earlier draft of this paper. (In view of his long association with Rosalind Mitchison, Dr Phillipson asked me to express his regret at being unable to contribute an essay to this volume.)

The Processes of Agricultural Change in the North-East, 1790–1870

Malcolm Gray

A long-held view of agricultural reform in Scotland has been that, largely in the eighteenth century, a powerful landlord class, aided at best by a few enterprising tenants, imposed a modern agricultural system, new both in layout of farms and in modes of operation. A recent forthright statement of this view comes from I H Adams. 'The evidence appears overwhelming', he writes, 'that Scotland experienced an Agricultural Revolution, masterminded by a small, highly motivated group of people . . . The landlords made their lands into efficient income machines, the successful farmers enjoyed a substantial living, and the rest began the long trek either to the town or to the New World.'[1] In a very limited sense this is true. Certain minimum steps had to be taken by landlords before much change was possible on their estates. A strengthening will to change on the part of the lairds was a necessary cause of radical agricultural reform; but it was far from being a sufficient cause. Scotland, in fact, remained, through all the changes wrought by the improvers, a land of many thousands of tenants. Virtually all of them had to adapt as individuals looking at their resources in land and money. Adaptation might come, it is true, in the form of imitation, but the imitation was more often of fellow tenants than of lairds. 'Tenants are more apt to copy from one another, than from gentlemen.'[2] And it was only by tenants investing much money and effort in building, in land improvement and in stocking of farms that the reform process was completed. The effort of will and ingenuity demanded from the multitude of tenants was just as essential as the autocratic planning of land.

The roles of tenants and of landlords were in part determined by a legally defined distribution of powers and to that extent there was likely to be a similarity in the experience of different areas all under the law of Scotland. But many aspects of the push to change agriculture had to be the subject of negotiation between parties whose relative economic strength might vary greatly from one area to the other. Much depended, too, on the scale of investment appropriate to the locality and on timing in relation to changing economic climates. Thus great differences emerge in the balance of the efforts exerted by landlords on the one hand and by tenants on the other.

This paper is concerned with the North-East, defined as comprising the counties of Kincardine, Aberdeen and Banff. It is an area of diverse geographical aspect. Across the projecting, sea-girt corner lies an almost uninterrupted stretch of arable land, as extensive as any in Scotland. Beyond this, towards the interior of the country, the land rises and becomes rougher so that farm-land is in more broken formations, interweaving with hill, moor and forest, till finally, at more than 1,000 feet above sea-level, arable land vanishes from the scene on the eastern slopes of the highest mountain range in Britain. Inevitably, farming has always varied with the nature of the land and the climate, particularly in the balance of crop and stock and in the type of animal suitable for rearing. Yet, in the eighteenth century, in their social composition and in the basic manner of dividing the land, farming communities—known as ferm-touns—were essentially similar throughout the region. And, while the timing of change might vary, the new farms which emerged in the later eighteenth and early nineteenth centuries, still described as ferm-touns, were of a type. Farming in severalty became general and, with the survival of only one common grazing within the area, crofting as known in the western Highlands and Islands had virtually no place.

At the end of the eighteenth century, a distinguishing feature of the region was the amount of potential arable land still awaiting development. Farms were small and tenants numerous; while there were virtually no owner-occupiers, there were numbers of small estates, poor not only because of small size but also because of low productivity; and a very few estates were large enough to give big aggregate rents whatever the state of productivity.[3] There were also some very special features of the time contributing to the area's individual experience of change.

A DELAYED TRANSFORMATION

One peculiarity was the late start to general improvement. By the 1790s many parts of central and southern Scotland contained wide areas of firmly established modern agriculture with holdings separated and under individual control, with intensive rotations covering the land and with a tightly disciplined force of full-time workers on each farm. But in the North-East such arrangements were exceptional rather than typical. True, new farming practices had spread northwards so that coastal parishes of Kincardine and, less solidly, of Aberdeen and Banff, had firm arrays of farms in modern style. In these, two-horse ploughs, each with one man in charge, would be used in the preparation of the land for rotations that obeyed the newly-drawn rules of improved farming. But inland parishes—much more numerous and extensive—presented a different face. Here, large improved farms, compact and subdivided into squared fields, covered to their full extent by crops in regular rotation, were rare enclaves in the countryside.[4]

Many of the farms of the interior were still held jointly and even those held by a single tenant—as they might long have been—were laid out in irregular fields much broken up by bog, stone and winding paths. The division of the land between infield and outfield was still the common form although the retention of the terms did not always mean that old systems of cropping were retained. Common grazings and the communal regulation of pasture were still accepted practice. Joint tenancy did not necessarily mean that every tenant's lands lay intermixed with those of his fellows for there is little mention of full runrig practice. The common arrangement seems to have been that of a central settlement in which several tenants and their dependants would live jumbled in proximity; from such a centre, control was exercised over holdings clearly separated from each other although they did not necessarily, or even probably, lie in compact blocks.

To the mind of an improver the methods of husbandry pursued over these irregular fields were disastrously archaic. Farmers were dabbling with new crops but only in casual and limited fashion. Turnips were widely grown but in amounts which show clearly that they had no part in organised rotations. The acreage in sown grass was greater but betrayed little sign of systematic use. There was still often to be seen the unremitting sequence of cereal after cereal, oats and bere, without the relief of fallow or of nitrogenous crop, such as had been common even in the older infield practice of the south of Scotland. Limited sowings of new crops had been injected into some infield areas but not so as to secure systematic rotation. The outfields, too, might be slightly diversified to escape from the old sequence of oats, year upon year, but, as long as there was any semblance of outfield working, a large proportion of cultivable land was held in unimproved rough state in a form of pastoral protection that had been outdated when sowing of grasses on improved land became possible.

One of the clearest signs of a laggard husbandry was the use of ploughs of an older type. Even when improved by addition of iron plates they required large teams, in the North-East consisting usually of oxen. A variety of ploughs of new type, more economical of animal power, were being extensively put to use in other parts of Scotland but their adoption in the North-East was slow.[5] It was a form of improvement easily identified and many of the parish correspondents of the *Old Statistical Account* set themselves to count old and new. It was rarely that the new ploughs were anything but a tiny minority.

The matter of ploughing was a key not only to the state of husbandry but also to the form of society within the ferm-touns. It can truly be said that the shape and work conditions of the labour force on a nineteenth-century farm were dictated by the need to keep the plough and its team of two expensively-fed horses continuously employed. The ploughman had to be a well-trained specialist and a full-time employee, and other full-time employees had to be engaged to work to rhythms set by the daily working capacity of the horse. In the older scheme it was otherwise. Ploughing was mainly concentrated within the spring season and the whole rhythm of agriculture was one of seasonal bursts of high activity alternating with periods when tasks of other types were pursued. Farmers depended on labour from various sources: services done by sub-tenants—inevitably seasonal—day labour for wages, and a certain amount of help from the full-time employee, a servant, usually unmarried, engaged for periods of six months at a time. One component of this labour force, the sub-tenant or cottar who had to give limited labour services, depended on the sub-division of the main tenancies to accommodate him. The use of such labour was obnoxious to improvers not only because it was untrained and ill-disciplined but also because it caused the splitting of good farm-land into tiny holdings which could not be brought into an all-embracing crop scheme. Thus in the latter part of the eighteenth century even in the North-East there were moves to clear the land of sub-tenants and of cottars providing only occasional services. But in the 1790s this drive was far from complete. Numbers of sub-tenants and cottars were still to be found, their conditions of work unchanged.[6]

By the 1840s the face of the north-east countryside was transformed. Scarcely one of well over a hundred parish reports in the *New Statistical Account* fails to give some evidence of the magnitude of the change. The erasure of the old forms of husbandry that had been so evident in the 1790s had been rapid and complete. The last traces of intermixed holdings were gone. Farms were now completely separate one from the other, within bounds as far as possible squared off. Common grazings and communally used outfields were now embodied in farms each under separate and individual control. The term outfield might still be used but it no longer described a particular system of husbandry; it usually meant just rather poor land. Ferm-touns consisting of tenants' and sub-tenants' dwellings and their associated buildings had been broken up so that each farm unit consisted of the tenant's dwelling house, the steading, and housing for workers—no more.

Crop rotations fell into similar patterns from one farm to the next, from one parish to the next. Almost everywhere turnips and sown grasses were a major element. Two-horse ploughs each with one man in charge were used for most of the work on the land, and one-horse carts provided an economical and efficient mode of transport from one part of a farm to another, or perhaps on the public highway. Threshing machines were standard equipment on farms of more than 50 acres and the scythe was the common instrument of harvest. The substantial turnip acreage and the improved grass-land provided ample feed for the main stock, cattle reared for beef, although the market for fat cattle was only beginning to extend much beyond the needs of the local towns. These generalisations are subject, of course, to many local differences of detail, but such deviations do not cloud the picture of an agriculture effective up to the point demanded by improvers.

Another feature of the countryside was the number of new buildings to be seen. The splitting of the old ferm-touns implied root and branch rehousing. The new farm-houses were for the most part modest in scale because the change in the size of the typical farm had been far from dramatic. But structurally they were of a superior sort to the cottages they replaced, with lime and stone walls. Slates, however, had only begun to replace straw thatch or tiles.

The period between the first two *Statistical Accounts* had undoubtedly been a period of climactic change yet the 1840s provide only a reference point in a process that was far from complete. Indisputably north-east farming in the 1840s had a modern basis in farm layout and followed modern practices in cropping. Yet change had not stopped there and the efforts at improving the potential of the countryside were to continue with, if anything, growing intensity over the next twenty or thirty years. In particular, the enclosing of fields, which at mid-century had been very incomplete, went ahead, hastened ultimately by the availability of cheap wire and the innovation of barbed wire. Much improved land was added around existing farms and substantial increases of acreage were achieved. Much land was also being brought into cultivation by crofters who had been set on empty hillsides and moors, a process which had started in the later eighteenth century. Crofters held their land directly of the proprietor and, unlike the cottars and sub-tenants of old, did not owe any services. Their holdings were, in fact, miniature reproductions of the greater farms, with similar forms of production on a miniscule scale. They were self-contained to the extent that they had no access to common grazings. In building too, there was great activity. Farmhouses were replaced or built to higher standards. Steadily, slated roofs replaced thatch or tiles. Altogether the third quarter of the nineteenth century saw farming capital being created at undiminished pace.[7]

The physical re-positioning of buildings was the visible sign of deep social change, the shift into modern forms of organisation. Typically, the farm community was now reduced to the essential components of effective organisation for working the land—the farmer, or employer, and the staff of full-time employees essential to an efficient husbandry. Fee'd servants whether male or female, now accounted for most of the farm population and sub-tenants or cottars with tiny portions of land and only limited duties to the main tenant had disappeared from within the bounds of the highly organised unit. Small holdings, however, had not disappeared. Indeed in the shape of crofts they had multiplied in numbers—crofts which in their self-containment created the same sort of social separation of one unit from the next as did the farms.[8]

THE WIDER ENVIRONMENT

Such swift and radical changes, extending far into the nineteenth century, demanded greater effort and a stong will to change among both landlords and tenants but also certain factors outside the control of either group helped the process along.

The timing of the North-East's period of accelerating change was an important factor in the agrarian outcome in relation to development in other parts of Scotland. The position of a laggard area in a country where change had for decades been the norm meant, paradoxically, that the forward thrust, once started, could be exceptionally fast. In particular the long process of finding crops and methods suitable to the area was considerably shortened. Long experiment had been needed before the new crops—the roots and sown grass—could be knowledgeably combined in rotations that would meet the fundamental aims of husbandry, a high current yield and the safeguarding or strengthening of the soil in composition and structure. These experiments were made as improvement took a grip on the southern districts. By 1790 several parts of Scotland had evolved and widely applied the rotations and the methods of culture that would suit their particular conditions. A regime of intensive cultivation in Berwickshire combined animal husbandry based on turnips and rotation grasses with cereal cropping. A rotation suited to heavier soils, with heavy cereal cropping and pulse as a relieving crop and a fallow year (when the ground was thoroughly tilled and cleaned) had completely transformed the Carse of Gowrie. In the dairying parts of Ayrshire the Fairlie rotation with its long periods under sown grass supported a traditional system of production in a new way. And there were many subtle variations and adaptations of these very distinct systems in areas such as Fife and parts of Perthshire. None of the tried systems was exactly suited to the climate and soil of the North-East but the basic principles out of which a suitable rotation and regime of cultivation could be devised were known and to hand.[9]

In particular, turnip husbandry had been brought to a high state of effectiveness by innovations started in Berwickshire and Roxburghshire. Turnips had, of course, been grown for many years in Scotland but there was much to be learnt before they became a full rotation crop, interpenetrating other aspects of farm working. The cultivation of the root had proved to be of key importance for two reasons. It was the occasion of a thorough preparation of the soil, a preparation that went on beyond the period of the first annual growth of weeds and which therefore meant a first cleaning, while the sowing in drills allowed further weeding as the crop grew. And secondly, the crop contributed much to the feeding of a stock of animals well in excess of the working beasts that had to be kept. This refinement in raising turnips has generally been attributed to Dawson of Frogden, in Roxburghshire, and was to be the means of integrating turnip cultivation, with all its beneficial aspects, with both cereal and animal production. On the lighter soils which were the domain of turnip husbandry over-cropping had to be avoided and rotation grass often took a major part in the sequence that followed the turnip break. No great modification was needed to move into the methods that were to give power to north-east agriculture.

Just as important as the devising of rotational sequence was the refinement of the instruments of production. Two innovations coming from the South-East stand out. One was in plough design. There had been quite a proliferation through the eighteenth century of subtle variations in the modelling of the different parts of the plough but the new implement that was to prove all-conquering in Scotland was Small's plough. A relatively light but effective implement, it could be drawn by a team of two horses, thus effecting a great saving in the number of animals that had to be kept and fed. By 1790 the opportunity of using this type of plough was being spread by the distribution of plans for local smiths to copy.[10] The threshing machine, too, coming from the same south-eastern area would be adopted speedily enough to be widely in use in the North-East by 1840.

Another factor in the post-1790s surge was a sudden improvement in transport facility, all the more important because of earlier deficiencies. Indeed one main reason for the failure to effect any general improvement in the agriculture of the North-East before almost the end of the eighteenth century had been difficulties of transport. As long as roads were too poorly constructed and maintained to allow much use of wheeled vehicles both the export of produce and the import of needed supplies were bound to remain expensive in the large and well-populated sector of the north-eastern countryside that lies distant from tidewater. Thus lime, regarded as a prime ingredient in any improving regime, was found at only a few spots within the region.[11] Every other part had to depend on a long haul from the ports at which supplies could be landed or from the inland points where lime was to be found.

For most farmers, then, lime was only to be obtained after meeting heavy costs of haulage by horse or pony. Another difficulty lay in the supply of fuel. The area has, of course, no coal reserves and the favoured solution was to work peat where it might be found. Even this could mean labour at a distance and a heavy task of transport to the home. Neither was it a solution pleasing to the agricultural reformer since it could tie up virtually the whole labour force of the farming community at a time of year when the fields of the re-modelled farms required attention. Further, many of the local supplies of peat were wearing out.

Export of farm produce was also difficult, adding an element of cost which could make the price obtained in a main market unremunerative. It is true that the most important generator of farm income was the sale of cattle and that the beasts could be driven on the hoof either to the consumption markets of the region or to the more distant national markets of the central lowlands. Yet, while cattle might appear mobile, there were considerable costs in droving and the sale of lean cattle to the drover could not compare for profit with the fattening of beasts. In this cattle-rearing country the sale of grain even from the remote interior was also important. The difficulties faced by many farmers are indicated in some comments relating to the parish of Alford. A main part of the farmer's trade was in lime and grain, both requiring recourse to Aberdeen markets. Thus, two horses, managed apparently by one carter at a cost of 11s. or 12s., would be sent the twenty-five miles to the city, possibly laden with grain, then return with three bolls of lime; or farmers might use their own cattle for transport to and from a point fifteen miles from Aberdeen; or horses might be sent all the way to the city.[12]

It was clearly, then, of the most substantial importance to improve transport facility for the farmer both as importer and as exporter. That improvement came in substantial measure with the formation of Turnpike Trusts aimed at penetrating all the lowland areas of the region with roads good enough to carry wheeled traffic. These roads would give links with the coast and with Aberdeen to places as much as sixty miles in the interior. There was, of course, a stated cost in using a turnpike road but it was much outweighed by the economies of carrying goods on wheels rather than on horse-back. As in so much else, the North-East was late in joining the Turnpike movement.

It was not till 1795 that the first Turnpike Trust in the area was formed. But thereafter the activity in roadmaking was intense. By 1825 a network had been formed with strands reaching out in all landward directions from Aberdeen to distances of fifty miles and more and with cross-country links to join the main strands. By 1833 a place as remote as Corgarff had been joined to the network.[13]

Another factor was the movement of prices. Any re-organisation of agriculture required substantial investment, and lack of funds may have been one reason why effective change was so long delayed in an area of naturally low productivity which was also handicapped by high costs in getting commodities to market. Landlords and tenants could begin to turn their efforts more effectively to modernisation with the sharp and disproportionate rise in agricultural prices that began in the 1790s. For nearly twenty years thereafter the prosperity brought by high prices reigned through the agricultural community. The impact on different groups was uneven both in time and extent. Where tenants of some substance had leases with some years to run, a sudden sharp rise in prices would bring them more than proportionate gains and they might be in the unusual position of having the means to undertake relatively large investments. Indeed, as we shall see, much of the investment burden was always placed upon tenants. Rents, however, would soon enough overtake, and perhaps more than overtake, the rise in tenants' receipts. While landlords never entirely absolved tenants of their responsibility for a major share in investment, even when rentals were soaring, they might then proceed more by interest-bearing loans with an ultimate obligation of repayment by the tenant.

By the 1790s, then, a conjunction of circumstances beyond the control of either landlord or tenant was beginning to ease the burdens of change. But these could by no means be regarded as sufficient cause of the hectic pace with which modern agriculture was brought into the North-East. A mere glance at the countryside of the 1840s, let alone of the 1870s, is enough to suggest the investment of funds, the effort and the skill of adjustment that had gone into developments. Let the 1842 account of the parish of Clatt which had shown little of the new agriculture in 1792, stand in evidence of the change that had come over so many parishes and estates.

> The abolition of runrig, or intermixed allotments of ground occupied by different tenants; the conversion of crooked and highly raised, into straight and moderately low riggs; the exclusion of surface water from lowlying fields; the efficient draining of marshy ground; the removal of large surface stones, which were alike unseemly in appearance as detrimental to productiveness; the application of lime to reclaimed ground, or to dormant soil, which deep ploughings had brought into contact with manure; the introduction of early seed from the more genial southerly counties; the substitution of an improved breed of horses for the puny and powerless animals, the native breed of the country; the exchange of the cumbrous and wasteful machinery of a twelve oxen plough, for the two horse plough, of a lighter construction; the general prevalence of drill-turnip husbandry; the adoption of the rotation of cropping best adapted for the respective soils; the abolition of servitudes and mill-multures; these, under the auspices of

practical knowledge, and of moderate capital, have conspired in bringing the husbandry of the parish into no distant competition with the boasted agriculture of the finest counties.[14]

Truly, adaptability, toil and money were to be needed from anyone who was to participate in the great agricultural change.

ESTATE PLANNING

Whatever ultimate contribution was required from tenants the first essential step lay with the landlords. They alone could create for the individual tenants the framework of a farm plan—a boundary outline enclosing land of potential quality for personally controlled rotational cropping—which was the necessary basis of the up-to-date farming of the early nineteenth century. In the 1790s, as we have seen, many of the field formations lay as they had done of old. Fields were irregular and sprawling, holdings were broken into fragments of unequal size, uniform sequences of cropping might rule over the wishes of individual tenants, common grazing practices gripped the whole annual routine, the houses and farm buildings would often lie bunched and inconvenient for reaching the land they served. This had to be re-shaped to make a countryside of separated, squared farms, each containing its complement of necessary buildings. Estate planning conceived according to the supposed best principles of individualistic farming was the necessary beginning to the wide adoption of the newest fashions in husbandry.

In one respect the re-planning of Scottish estates to give compact farm units of reasonable scale was simple. Legally there was almost no restriction on how landlords cared to lay out their land. So feeble was tenant right that the intricate network of field systems, of grazing rights, of individual tenant rights to well-defined blocks or strips of land could be swept away on the instant, subject only to some delay while leases ran out. In reality the progress of reform was much more encumbered with difficulty and delay even under the most determined of landlords. For this was a social as much as, or even more than, a legal problem. Tenants had to be found of adequate skill and capital to take up the newly formed farms or existing tenants had to be fitted to new schemes of work and saving. Further, the numerous band of lesser folk—sub-tenants, cottars and servants—had to be absorbed, re-settled or, conceivably, turned off the estate.

Even purely physical planning had its delays and difficulties. The determination of the farm layouts that would allow the most productive use of land—and consequently the greatest rent—was a lengthy business, requiring technical knowledge and fine judgement. The ground must be surveyed and mapped in great detail, the potential as well as the actuality of crop production on the mixture of soils that comprised any farm area had to be determined; even marketing problems must be considered. And overhanging any physical plan was the problem of how suitable tenants, with a sufficiency of capital, were to be found.

Until well into the eighteenth century Scotland had few men trained to meet these problems. Estates did not employ people with the appropriate range of skills; factors, the usual officials, were outsiders, possibly lawyers, concerned with uplifting of rents and administration of the resulting funds. It was well into the last quarter of the century before a cadre of men of established professional skill in surveying and farm management was formed. Only then could landlords begin to plan on a large scale. In fact it was through employment in some of the great houses that experience began to accumulate and the principles of action to be collated and handed on to the trainees of the pioneers. This process of learning and training seems to have been particularly well-defined in the North-East and Adams has put forward the idea of a definite 'school' of the north-east surveyors, forming in the last quarter of the century.[15]

By the 1780s the comprehensive planning of estates seemed to be at least a possibility and much depended on how quickly the experience accumulated under a few of the greater houses could be diffused. The degree of concentration in the ownership of land had a considerable effect on the speed of change. Where estates were few and large there would be only a handful of landlords to convince and each would have the more funds to apply. Where landlords were many the pace was likely to be slower. In this respect the position in the North-East was ambiguous. Property was neither so concentrated as in the Border region and northern Highlands nor so diffused as it was through central Scotland. Timperley's calculations show that just under half the land (as measured by rental values) was in the hands of about 50 great landlords.[16] It should be noticed, however, that the minimum level of rental for an estate to be classed as 'great' was fairly modest. She sets it at £2,000 Scots (as assessed in 1660) which could mean a real rental at the end of the eighteenth century of about £1,500, a tenantry, it might be, of 30 members. Within this class of greater landlords there was a substantial concentration on a very few of their number. A tiny group, scarcely in double figures, controlled a substantial proportion of the tenantry. At the other end of the scale, about half the rental of the region was divided among over 400 minor landlords. From sheer numbers of owners it was unlikely that there would be anything like a concerted move towards estate reform over a considerable sector of the land. Only the rising prices—and adjustments of rents—were likely to create the funds and provide the incentive for widespread reaction among this body of lesser lairds.

Yet the reaction, late as it might be, must surely have been comprehensive and sharp. Not only have we the evidence of a land covered by farms of the neat modern pattern, but also the accounts of the mode of cultivation suggest that years of preparation had gone into working up the new fields. The grand plans must have been firmly imposed some time before 1840. The conclusion must surely be that from the very partial beginnings of land reform in the 1790—beginnings mainly on the great estates—a sweeping but unrecorded planning took place on many lesser estates within the space of the first 20 or 30 years of the nineteenth century.

Re-planning an estate in whole or in part depended on the expiry of leases. The natural sequel, therefore, was the selection of tenants for the re-shaped farms. In this, theories about the best mode of farming, and in particular about optimum size, might play a part. The arguments as articulated seemed to be mainly in favour of the large unit extending to at least 200 arable acres and possibly far beyond. And it was the men who had the skill to manage and the money to stock such units who were likely to have the will and the means to continue with investment. But the smaller farm might be advised on social grounds and the small farmer with a place of his own might well be the most enthusiastic improver. The advocates of the large farm generally won the argument but their ideas might well prove weaker in effect than the pressure of local circumstances. Where were the men of capital and experience to be found? On the whole, they were scarce in the North-East, fewer relative to the land to be filled than in many parts of the south of Scotland.

The North-East even in the seventeenth century had been notably an area of small farms. In the eighteenth century, as elsewhere in Scotland, there was some enlargement as farms of several tenants each were assigned to single control. But the movement was slow and limited and at the end of the century holdings of more than one plough were still a small minority covering only the lesser part of the land. When landlords turned determinedly to improvement they might bring in men from the south to swell the class of substantial farmers. But this left much land to be filled from the ranks of the existing small tenants. The structure of tenancy as it emerged from re-planning can leave little doubt that the new tenants were drawn largely from among the former holders of land; and that most of these held on to their land. Indeed, there seems to be no other possible source for what remained a very numerous body, running into thousands. And to the tenants of full farms must be added, as occupiers of land, roughly equal numbers of crofters each with less than enough land for full independence. It is true that there had been enough concentration—and probably eviction—to enhance the position of the larger-scale farmers. Indeed, by 1875 tenants with between 100 and 300 acres had 59 per cent of the land in their hands. But this left about 40 per cent of the land in the occupation of a mass of smaller people; the one-pair-horse farm was very much the typical unit. The full development of agricultural reform rested firmly on the capacity of such farmers to adapt and invest.[17]

INNOVATION AND INVESTMENT

As indicated earlier, when north-east farmers came to establish the methods and the crops for their new farms there were many examples of successful modern husbandry being practised in other parts of Scotland. The first impulse was to apply a system chosen from elsewhere without alteration. In fact, the peculiarities of the area demanded some degree of local adaptation and innovation. In any case innovation did not stop when the essentials of improved husbandry had been absorbed. A case in point was the adaptation of the mixed husbandry of the South-East to the thinner soils and sterner climate of the North-East. The rotation devised in the South-East which first seemed suitable for imitation in the northerly area, with its existing tradition of cattle-rearing, was that which combined animal feeding on turnips and grass with cereal production, particularly of wheat as a cash crop. But wheat was a precarious crop over much of the north and was scarcely likely to pay with the collapse of wheat prices after 1815. Also the whole of a crop sequence suited to parts of Berwickshire and East Lothian was too severe for much of the North-East. The eventual response was to lengthen the rotation from five to six to seven years, allowing a longer period under grass while oats remained as the main cereal. In the seven-year rotation, two successive crops of oats would be taken in the conviction that the second successive year of oats generally proved better than the first—plainly a case where experience or trial and error won out over a generalised theory.

From the very beginnings of the improving movement landlords had been occupying themselves with the details of farm operation as well as with the strategic planning of their estates. Yet it is clear that tenant initiative was at least as important as landlords' instructions in spreading new ways of working that were to be effective as well as merely fashionable. It is true that where the laird was willing to provide the material means for farming—the buildings, roads, enclosures and drains—an estate might quickly be brought to a general adoption of new methods. But comparatively few landlords went so far. One who did was Barclay of Urie on his Kincardineshire estate and his experience is instructive. He thoroughly improved the lands around his mansion to the extent of 800 acres, and his tenants with, in aggregate, much the same acreage were persuaded and helped to adopt the advised modes of husbandry. But Barclay's influence stopped at the edge of his quite small estate.

> It is to be regretted, that the farmers of the lands of the other proprietors, made no attempt towards improving their farms for a long while after Mr Barclay's tenants commenced their operations, because they had no encouragement given by their landlords. At length, however, some of the most judicious, who were in good circumstances, began to dress and lime a few acres by way of trial, for they wished to proceed by slow and cautious steps. Finding by the crops they produced, that their labour and expense were fully repaid, they made a second and third trial . . . Animated by their example more than by Mr Barclay's, because more on a level with their capacity and circumstances, others were induced to improve their ground. Thus, by degrees, the spirit of improvement is become universal here.[18]

This gives a clue to the essential nature of the improvement process. Very few landlords went as far as Barclay in helping their tenants by investment, although rather more attempted to set an example on the home farm, or by control through leasehold conditions. But this left the great majority of tenants to find their own capital and their own way because both the isolated farm model and the lease were limited in their influence. The model farm was likely to fail because the farming there shown was ill-fitted to the circumstances, in available capital and in extent of land, of the great bulk of the tenantry. The matter of the lease is more complicated.

In the early stages of improvement great store was set on the terms of the medium-term leases that were then favoured to bring about a general improvement of standards. But in fact the lease was a clumsy instrument for imposing even the general principles of good husbandry as understood by landlords, and particularly so when ideas and rotations were in rapid change. For example, the switch from rotations brought from the south, and rigidly applied, to the longer rotations suited to most parts of the North-East often took place within the duration of outstanding leases. 'It is not too much to say that were all the conditions agreed to enforced from beginning to end of a lease, the cultivation of many farms in the parish would come to a stand.'[19] Consequently, while at first leases had stated detailed rules and rigidly defined procedures, eventually, with experience, they merely stated a few very general rules of good husbandry (and even these, as in the matter of not taking two cereal crops in succession, were widely disregarded). For the most part it was tenant initiative, or the imitation of one tenant by another, that spread a modern husbandry suited to the conditions of the particular locality.

The process of finding appropriate crops and methods was intertwined always with the long, laborious and expensive business of fitting the land for the new husbandry. Continuing and heavy investment was very much a necessity for any move into modern husbandry. Some of this—for example, the stocking of the farms—was inevitably done by the tenants, some might be negotiated between landlord and tenant, almost none was uniformly undertaken by the landlord.

Most variable and important were the arrangements for the provision of material facilities such as farm-houses, out-buildings, enclosures and drainage. The improvement of waste land might also be variously undertaken. A few landlords—such as Barclay of Urie, Dingwall of Brucklay, Sir John Forbes of Corse, together with lairds in the parishes of Premnay, Drumblade, Monquitter and Fintray—would provide at least some of the material amenities before the land was let, but the generosity of the provision depended upon the rent to be paid.[20] Such comprehensive and immediate provision was unusual. Generally the contributions of landlord and tenant were divided by rule or the burden of investment was laid wholly on the tenant. The variety of arrangements, found even within a single parish, is illustrated by the following account from Turriff.

> The arrangements between landlord and tenant in regard to houses are not uniform. Some heritors bear the whole expense of the buildings, and others give only the rough timber of the buildings, the tenant executing, at his own expense, all the other parts of the work, receiving an obligation for payment at the end of the lease, according to the valuation at the time. Others allow two years' rent at the termination of the lease if the subject is worth as much. Others, again, charge a percentage on the outlay on necessary buildings; and in some cases no allowance is given for buildings whatever, the tenant accommodating himself as best he can during the lease, who, if he is able to sink his capital altogether, or bear a deferred payment may, perhaps, answer; but if he has not the money at command, it may, and often does, straiten his circumstances, and leave him with nothing to improve or enrichen his farm.[21]

Underlying these variations there seem to have been two basic arrangements. One was for the landlord to advance the money for building in whole or in part and charge interest, in fact an increase in rent; the other for the tenant to meet the expense, with, possibly, the landlord providing the timber in return for the remission of one or perhaps two years' rent at the end of the lease. Such arrangements might also apply to other material additions such as enclosures or drains.

The fairness and expediency of these arrangements was much questioned and it was widely held that improvement was held up because so much of the burden of long-term investment was laid on the tenant. Of Drumblade parish it was said that 'the buildings are of an inferior description, which may be accounted for by the system which prevails, not only in this parish, but in many others in Aberdeenshire, that the burden of erecting houses lies with the occupant, for which outlay he is only allowed a certain sum at the end of his lease . . . the stipulated sum often amounting to a mere trifle compared with the value of the buildings an outgoing tenant has to sacrifice'.[22] The landlord, for his part, might well be hampered by the law of entail which prevented him rising to expenditures which might burden a successor. But whatever the reasons for the insufficiency of the landlord's contribution, the hardship imposed on many tenants and the cramping effect upon improvement of properties are undeniable. The basic problem perhaps was that a tenant was being asked to make an investment which would stand over many years while he would have the benefits for only a relatively short and defined period; the consequent problem of meliorations, the allowance to be given a tenant for improvements he had made but would then come into the hands of the landlord, was long a running sore in the relations of landlord and tenant in the North-East.[23]

Some of the investment inherent in the introduction of a new, and heavily capitalised, system of farming had to proceed without aid from the landlord. It was the tenant who had to prepare the ground for intensive rotations and very often the tenant who converted waste into cultivated land. To switch an irregular and varied land surface such as was found in the old farms to fit the uniform and demanding requirements of squared fields to be cropped in a rotational sequence implied years of hard preparation. The exaggerated ridges had to be ploughed down, a new and orderly pattern of flattened ridges substituted. A peculiarly heavy task in the North-East was the removal of 'sitfast' stones, often of great size, to make way for the lighter ploughs. Multiple ploughings were required to rid the ground of weeds and for years the rotations had to contain a large element of summer fallow. Heavy dosing with lime, an expensive material, was regarded as an essential preliminary. Some land, generally of poor quality, would have to be worked into full cultivation from the roughest condition. None of this could be done within a year or even two. At least ten years was one estimate given for a kindlier land than was to be found in the North-East.[24] It might be undertaken by the labour of the farmer and his normal complement of workers but it still represented investment—labour and cost which did not promise immediate return.

As the land was being prepared, fresh working capital had to be injected. On the whole, the new forms of husbandry had considerable annual expenses originating off the farm and therefore requiring funds. It is true that the theory of improved farming very much stressed the values of self-sufficiency— an aim which tended to economise on the capital required. Farm produce such as hay and turnips should be fed to the animals, so creating the means of fertilising the ground and improving soil structure, rather than be sold for immediate profit. But this self-dependence was always far from complete. Lime nearly always had to be purchased and in the nineteenth century this was followed by the use of other artificial and portable fertilisers; equipment was less and less capable of rough construction on the farm; particularly expensive were items such as threshing mills which became common on farms of more than 50 acres; the heavy work-horses needed for the new ploughs were bought in from the south; and new stock was brought from elsewhere to cross with the native cattle in breeding. Every improved acre required both a heavy initial outlay and a continuing expenditure in stocking and fertilising.

The north-east improving farmer has often been depicted as a man (or woman) condemned to relentless toil in a struggle with an unyielding land. 'The tenants and their families cleared away the stones from the face of the land. They levelled the ground. They drained the mosses. They dug miles of ditches. They surrounded their new fields with drystone dykes. They built a stone house, a barn, and a stable. At the end of nineteen years they had a farm, through the weariness of labour.'[25] Possibly this is the essence of the matter. Certainly it is correct in suggesting that it was the tenant who, in the main, made the farming landscape. But it is less than the full story; if anything, it understates the tenant's achievement, for he (or she) was a man of business as well as a toiler. He managed an intricate cash flow and he made many a decision about investment. Some of the tenants were initiators, finding the methods and crops that would best suit their land and their area. And if they were not initiators they were ready and quick imitators. It is striking that these were the men and women, or their children, who had recently been condemned as hopeless slaves to traditional ways. Truly, 'in the adoption of the most improved systems of culture . . . the farmers have, by a steady spirit of energy and perseverance, converted cold wet soil into "healthy fruitful fields", where nothing but scanty crops of grass and corn grew'.[26]

NOTES

1   I H Adams, 'The agents of agricultural change' in M L Parry and T R Slater (eds), *The Making of the Scottish Landscape* (London 1980), p 173.
2   A Wight, *Present State of Husbandry in Scotland*, 4 vols (Edinburgh 1778–1784), vol II, p 368.
3   L Timperley, 'The pattern of landholding in eighteenth century Scotland' in Parry and Slater, *Scottish Landscape*, pp 140–50.
4   See many of the parish accounts in Sir John Sinclair (ed) *The Statistical Account of Scotland*, New Edition, 20 vols (Wakefield 1973) (OSA), vols XIV, XV, XVI. The extent to which at a slightly earlier stage, the North-East was lagging behind the more southerly parts of Scotland is made clear in Wight, *Present State of Husbandry*. See also J Anderson, *General View of the Agriculture of the County of Aberdeen* (Edinburgh 1794).
5   J E Handley, *The Agricultural Revolution in Scotland* (Glasgow 1963), pp 46–51; A Fenton, *Scottish Country Life* (Edinburgh 1976), pp 38–43.
6   M Gray, 'North-east agriculture and the labour force, 1790–1875' in A A MacLaren (ed), *Social Class in Scotland: Past and Present* (Edinburgh 1976), pp 88–9.
7   The continuing expansion and investment in the third quarter of the nineteenth century is illustrated many times over in A Smith, *A New History of Aberdeenshire*, 2 vols (Aberdeen 1975).
8   M Gray, 'Scottish emigration: the social impact of agrarian change in the rural lowlands, 1775–1875', in *Perspectives in American History*, VII (1973), pp 137–8; Gray, 'North-east agriculture' in MacLaren (ed), *Social Class*, pp 94–6; I Carter, *Farm Life in North-East Scotland, 1840–1914* (Edinburgh 1979), pp 20–32.
9   Gray, 'Scottish emigration' in *Perspectives in American History*, pp 115–23.
10 Handley, *Agricultural Revolution*, pp 49–51; Fenton, *Country Life*, pp 39–42.
11 I Whyte, *Agriculture and Society in Seventeenth Century Scotland* (Edinburgh 1979), p 200.
12 OSA, XIV, 394.
13 Carter, *Farm Life*, p 23.
14 *New Statistical Account of Scotland*, 15 vols (Edinburgh, 1835–45) (NSA), XII, Aberdeenshire, 854.
15 Adams, 'Agents of agricultural change' in Parry and Slater, *Scottish Countryside*, pp 160–73.
16 Timperley, 'Pattern of landholding' in Parry and Slater, *Scottish Countryside*, pp 140–51.
17 Carter, *Farm Life*, pp 26–32; Gray, 'Scottish emigration' in *Perspectives in American History*, pp 137–8; Gray, 'North-east agriculture' in MacLaren (ed), *Social Class*, pp 93–6.
18 OSA, XIV, 117.
19 Smith, *Aberdeenshire*, II, p 1198; Carter, *Farm Life*, p 91.
20 OSA, XIV, 115–7; NSA, XII, Aberdeenshire, 170, 268, 308, 767, 960.
21 Smith, *Aberdeenshire*, p 1316.
22 Smith, *Aberdeenshire*, p 473.
23 Carter, *Farm Life*, pp 70–1, 90–1.
24 OSA, III, 102 (Parish of Coldingham, Berwickshire).
25 J R Allan, *North-East Lowlands of Scotland* (London 1974 edn), p 19.
26 Smith, *Aberdeenshire*, p 1038.

Highland Landowners and the Highland Potato Famine

T M Devine

I

The last great subsistence crisis on the British mainland in modern times occurred in the 1840s and 1850s in northern Scotland. During that period, when the United Kingdom was consolidating its position as the most advanced economy in the world, the inhabitants of the western Highlands and islands were reduced to serious destitution and even threatened with starvation when blight destroyed the potato, their main source of food. Widespread failure of the crop first occurred in 1846 but endured to a greater or lesser extent for almost a decade thereafter in most parts of the crofting region. Not until 1856 did reports finally begin to appear of a general recovery throughout the area. The epic tragedy of the Great Famine in Ireland has caused this regional disaster to be partially overlooked by British historians.[1] The Highland potato famine certainly did not cause the appalling crisis in mortality suffered by the unfortunate population across the Irish Sea, but it was nonetheless an episode of major significance in the history of the Scottish Highlands with fundamental effects on the living standards, emigration patterns and social structure of the region. The concern of this essay, however, is not with the impact of the famine on the Highland people as a whole, but with its effects on the élite of the society, the landowners who were more likely to be hit in their pockets rather than their stomachs by the most devastating Scottish subsistence crisis since the notorious Lean Years of the 1690s.

It is important to begin by stressing that the crisis was both much wider and deeper than a simple crop failure. Poor harvests had been a fact of life in the western Highlands from time immemorial. The loss of oats and bere in years of bad weather always inflicted widespread suffering and usually provoked a wave of emigration. Such was the predictable pattern in 1771–2, 1782–3, 1795–6, 1806–7, 1816–17, 1825 and 1836–7, as well as in a series of other less serious episodes. But the grain crop normally only failed in part and rarely for more than two consecutive seasons. In 1846 and 1847 the potatoes were almost entirely diseased in most areas of the western Highlands and islands, with the exception of parts of Sutherland, and the blight continued to inflict widespread damage for almost a decade after that. The extent of dependency on the crop by the 1840s in this region must also be borne in mind. Many of the subtenant or cottar class, a group which accounted for as much as half of all the inhabitants on some Hebridean estates, eked out an existence almost exclusively on the basis of potato cultivation and some fishing, while even the small tenant or crofter class relied to a considerable extent upon potatoes as a vital element of diet in combination with varying amounts of meal, milk and fish.[2]

But the period of the potato famine was not simply one of biological disaster. Three economic factors intensified the magnitude of the calamity and the impact it was likely to have on the lives of the population and the financial position of the landlord class. First, the potato failure was the climax to the gathering crisis which had beset the crofting economy since the end of the Napoleonic Wars. From the early 1820s through to the 1840s, its fragile supports crumbled as the north-west region was mercilessly exposed both to the postwar recession and the irresistible impact of savage competitive pressures from the urban manufacturing centres of the Lowlands to the south. Kelp production, reckoned to employ between 25,000 and 30,000 people in the Hebrides at its peak, disintegrated to minor proportions; illicit whisky-making for the wider market had all but ceased; military employment, a huge source of regional income during the Napoleonic Wars, dwindled rapidly during the peace which followed; commercial fishing, the great hope for a prosperous economy in the eighteenth century, stagnated in some districts and vanished entirely from others. The famine was then the culmination of three decades of creeping despair, the end not the beginning of an epoch of extended economic agony which not only intensified the burdens on the poor but increasingly exposed the traditional élite of the society as a debilitated and beleaguered class.

Second, during the famine itself, the failure of the potatoes was accompanied by a collapse in the prices of black cattle from 1847. Between that year and 1853 average prices fell by between one-third and one-half. The principal influence here was a change in external market circumstances but demand was also affected by the poor condition of Highland stock being presented at the trysts during the famine years.[3] With their main subsistence crop destroyed in some districts and badly diseased in others, the peasantry was even more likely to depend on income from cattle sales to pay rent and buy meal. But, virtually from the end of the first year of the blight, returns from this vital source contracted.[4] Third, difficulties also soon began to emerge in the labour market for temporary Highland migrants. In 1846 and 1847 there had been a happy coincidence between the needs of the crofting population for jobs in the south and the requirements of the Lowland economy for casual labour. The potato blight struck the western Highlands in the year of the greatest Scottish railway construction boom of the nineteenth century. The demand for navvies together with the effect of railway building on the Lowland economy as a whole stimulated a huge increase in temporary migration which produced a stream of income that did much to compensate for the failure of the potato crop. However, this windfall was short-lived as the boom years were followed by the serious industrial recession of 1848 and 1849 and the labour market for temporary migrants stagnated from then until about 1853.[5]

The potato famine can, therefore, indeed be seen as a disaster of exceptional magnitude. Because of its duration and through the interaction of crop failure and economic crisis it inflicted a quite unprecedented scale of misery. Contemporary observers were stunned into semi-apocalyptic utterances. The Free Church newspaper, the *Witness*, proclaimed that it was a calamity '... unknown in the memory of this generation and of many generations gone by, even in any modern periods of our country's history'. A national day of Fasting and Atonement was proclaimed, '... the hand of God has indeed touched us'.[6] Another commentator drew a close parallel between the trauma suffered by the Highlands in the aftermath of Culloden in 1746 and the even greater calamity which the potato blight would assuredly bring upon the people. For the landlords, the first effect of the disaster was seen in the rapid contraction of rental income from the small tenant class as they desperately switched their meagre resources from payment of rent to the purchase of meal during the bleak months of the autumn, winter and spring of 1846 and early 1847. In the first year of the blight, 25 per cent of all tenants on the Mackenzie of Gairloch estate in Wester Ross (by no means one of the poorest properties in the region) were in arrears; by 1848, the proportion had swollen to 63 per cent.[8] Rental income on Lord Macdonald's Skye estates collapsed by almost two-thirds between 1845 and 1850.[9] On the property of Sir James Riddell in Ardnamurchan, arrears surged from £269 in 1847 to £3,219 five years later and in the three western parishes of Sutherland arrears as a proportion of total small tenant rental climbed from 21 per cent in 1842 to an average of 89 per cent in 1849.[10] These data tend to confirm the accuracy of Sir John McNeill's observation in 1851 that the combined effect of the potato blight and the decline in cattle prices made it virtually impossible for those with rentals of £5 or below, who comprised the majority of the small tenants, both to feed their families and maintain payment of rent at the same time.[11]

But landlords had also to contend with the prospect of a potentially disastrous increase in costs as well as the collapse in small tenant rents. By the early decades of the nineteenth century, many traditional landed families were heavily burdened with hereditary debts which had inexorably grown larger during the recession after the Napoleonic Wars.[12] In some cases, the lion's share of annual income from rents was absorbed in the servicing of interest charges on these accumulated debts. In 1845, for instance, no less than 71 per cent of the gross income of Lord Macdonald's estates in Skye and North Uist was employed in the funding of such payments.[13] The critical factor here was interest rates. In 1848 and 1849 rates moved up during the recession precisely at the same time as the scale of the increase in rent arrears began to become evident. It was reckoned that any rise of half of one per cent in interest rates would further reduce Lord Macdonald's 'free' annual income of £7,000 by a further £560.[14] More seriously it might cause the whole unsteady financial edifice to crumble as creditors became uneasy and sought to secure their assets by having embarrassed estates placed under trusteeship or even by proceeding to drive proprietors into complete bankruptcy.

Such an outcome seemed even more likely when the broad outlines of the government's response to the emergency became apparent. It was clear as early as autumn 1846 that the state was determined that Highland landowners should bear the main responsibility for famine relief. At most, government was only willing to play the role of an enabling agency which would facilitate the measures to be taken by the proprietors. It was not prepared to replace or supersede them. As Charles (later Sir Charles) Trevelyan, Assistant Secretary at the Treasury, and the most influential figure in the management of the government's relief operation, put it: ' . . . it is by no means intended to afford relief in such a way as would relieve the landowners and other persons of property from the obligations they are under to support the destitute poor . . . any assistance contemplated would be rather in the form of giving a proper organisation and direction to the efforts of the proprietors'.[15] This was no idle or paper threat. During the course of the first two years of the famine, those landowners unwilling to fulfil their obligations as defined by the state were warned that they would be charged the full cost of grain should government be finally forced to intervene and send supplies to save the inhabitants of their estates. Particularly recalcitrant proprietors were threatened with public condemnation in Parliament and even with sequestration of their assets to defray the cost of government relief measures on their properties should these be deemed necessary. At the same time, both the Lord Advocate of Scotland and the Chairman of the Board of Supervision of the Scottish Poor Law urged local poor law committees to use their powers of discretion under the 1845 Act to provide 'occasional' relief to the destitute able-bodied population of the Western Highlands.[16] Either by insisting on direct landlord intervention to feed the people or by pressing for an extension of the responsibilities of the poor law authorities, and hence an increase in poor rates, government in 1846 seemed determined to ensure that Highland proprietors would bear the prime responsibility for Highland relief.

The prospects for the landed class now seemed miserable indeed. They were apparently caught in an irresistible and powerful vice between sharply contracting income and the probability of enormous increases in expenditure. In 1846 and early 1847 many petitions from landowners were dispatched to the Lord Advocate's office in Edinburgh and the Treasury in London pleading for assistance as a wave of virtual panic swept across the western Highlands.[17] Given the nature of the crisis, a great transfer of estates precipitated by the insolvency of many proprietors, on a scale akin to that which occurred in the western Lowlands after the dramatic failure of the Ayr Bank in the 1770s, might well have been anticipated.[18] Whether or not this was indeed the eventual outcome will be assessed in the next section of this essay.

II

A search was carried out for the period 1846 to 1860 in the contemporary press,[19] estate papers[20] and petitions and sederunt books of sequestration in the Court of Session[21] in order to determine the extent of financial crisis among Highland proprietors during the potato famine and in the years following it. The exercise was not designed to assess in a comprehensive fashion the range of economic problems caused by the famine but rather to reveal the extent to which these led to 'crisis'. This was a condition which was measured (a) by the number of estates put on the market because of the financial difficulties of the owner, (b) sales of particular sections of estates brought about by the extreme financial circumstances of the owner, and (c) the number of properties which were placed under the formal administration of trustees because of an owner's increasing indebtedness. Entail arrangements sometimes might limit estate sales even when owners were in grave difficulty. However, the greater Highland landowners, whose estates were most often entailed also held property which was unentailed, and the sales of many smaller properties, as the buoyancy of the regional land market between 1810 and 1840 confirms, were not always constricted by such legal arrangements.[22]

The investigation revealed only five cases where acute financial pressure caused estates either to be sold in whole or in part or to come under the administration of trustees in the western Highland and Islands between 1846 and 1856. W F Campbell of Islay and Sir James Riddell of Ardnamurchan were the only two proprietors to become insolvent and only Campbell suffered sequestration of his assets.[23] The estate of Knoydart, the last remaining property of the Macdonnels of Glengarry, was brought to market by the family's trustees in 1855.[24] North Uist, part of the patrimony of Lord Macdonald, whose principal lands were in Skye, was sold in 1856. These estates and those of Norman Macleod of Macleod, also in Skye, had earlier been placed under temporary trusteeship. Parts of these properties were put on the market during the famine period.[25]

Several points about this pattern are worth noting. First, acute financial difficulty was obviously very much the exception rather than the rule among west Highland landowners in this period. There were at least 86 separate estates in the region most seriously affected by the potato blight but in only a very small minority of cases did owners either suffer bankruptcy or concede control of their properties to the authority of trustees.[26] Second, even in the five examples described, the crisis precipitated by the famine was often the immediate cause rather than the fundamental explanation of insolvency. Lord Macdonald, for instance, already had an accumulated debt burden of over £140,000 on the eve of the potato failure and an annual rental income of £7,971.[27] He was clearly teetering on the edge of disaster long before the onset of the subsistence crisis of the 1840s completed his discomfiture. The same could also be said of Walter Campbell of Islay and Norman Macleod of Macleod.[28] There basic problems did not derive from the famine *per se*, but rather from the inability of several hereditary landed families to maintain the rising standards of living associated with their rank in society on the limited rent rolls of Highland estates during the era of economic recession after the Napoleonic Wars.

Third, when examined over the long-run, there seems little especially significant about the scale of land transfers in the western Highlands between 1846 and 1856. In the previous decade, 1836 to 1846 for example, at least eleven large Highland estates were sold by hereditary proprietors to newcomers.[29] The famine, on the evidence presented here, provoked some land sales but not apparently on a sufficient enough scale to radically alter the long-term structure and development of the Highland land market. It is possible, indeed, that in the short-run, the problems experienced by the region's landed class during the famine, may have temporarily reduced external demand for Highland estates.[30] What emerges, however, is an interesting paradox: the resilience and survival of the regional social élite during the greatest single economic and social disaster in the modern history of the Highlands.

III

Many Highland landowners escaped relatively unscathed simply because their properties were located outside the distressed region itself. The most devastating impact of the famine was felt only in the western maritime districts, north of Morvern and Ardnamurchan, and in most of the Inner and Outer Hebrides.[31] The population most affected was about 120,000 or around 40 per cent of the total population of the four Highland counties of Argyll, Inverness, Ross and Sutherland. Relief operations, which took place all over the Highlands in 1846 and early 1847, terminated in the southern, eastern and most parts of the central districts by the end of that year and thereafter were confined to the crofting parishes of the far west. An examination of the rentals of several estates in the eastern and central Highlands reveals little indication of a significant or enduring incease in rent arrears. Indeed, it would be difficult even to discover the existence of a *major* crisis in that region from these data alone.[32] The limited effects of the famine in this area are not difficult to understand.[33] The potato, though important, was not the crucial element in diet that it was in the west. Neither was there the same chronic imbalance of resources and population. A combination of heavy migration to the adjacent Lowlands and the labour-intensive requirements of mixed husbandry, which was important in some parts of the region, helped to preserve a rough equilibrium in most years between demand and supply of labour.[34] In other parishes, the rental income of landlords depended mainly on the operations of big sheep-farmers possessing tenancies of several hundred acres or more rather than impoverished crofters and cottars scraping a living from miniscule areas of land.

In the maritime and insular districts of the western Highlands, however, the landed class was exposed to the worst social consequences of the famine. The evidence suggests that in the short-term, at least, the majority do appear to have tried to assist the people of their estates through the distribution of meal at cost price and the provision of public works. Government relief officers carefully monitored the response of individual landowners during the winter, spring and early summer of 1846–47 and their reports confirm that most proprietors appeared willing, albeit sometimes grudgingly, to assume their responsibilities.[35] The responses of 77 per cent of landowners in the distressed districts are known. Twenty-nine per cent of this group were singled out for praise by government officers for their efforts while only 14 per cent were censured for their negligence. However, government threats to enforce sanctions rapidly reduced the number who were unwilling to provide assistance to a small handful. Charles Trevelyan was warm in his praise: ' . . . the Treasury have been quite delighted with the whole conduct of the Highland proprietors . . . it was a source of positive pleasure to turn from the Irish to the Scotch case. In the former, everything with regard to the proprietors is sickening and disgusting'.[36] He asserted later that ' . . . in Ireland the general disposition of these classes is to do nothing while in Scotland they are disposed to do what is in their power . . . if Skye were in the west of Ireland, the people would be left to starve in helpless idleness'.[37] Such intervention, however, could only be achieved at very considerable and increasing cost. On the Duke of Argyll's Tiree estate, for example, one of the islands which suffered the most extreme levels of destitution, expenditure on 'relief by employment' rose from £8 in 1845 to £1,850 in 1847 and on 'gratuitous relief' from £11 in 1845 to £2,174 in 1847. In the year before the famine, outlay on these forms of relief amounted to less than 4 per cent of total estate expenditure; by 1847, the proportion had climbed to over 74 per cent. The balance of income accruing to the proprietor in 1845 was £2,226. By 1847, on the other hand, the Tiree estate was operating at an annual deficit of £3,173.[38]

Yet, most west Highland landowners did not have to shoulder these burdens for long. From the early months of 1847 the main responsibility for famine relief began to be assumed by the Free Church of Scotland and the Edinburgh and Glasgow Destitution Committees which united in February, 1847 to form the Central Board for the Relief of Highland Destitution.[39] By the end of that year the Board had raised a sum of over a quarter of a million pounds from philanthropic sources at home and abroad. From 1847 to the end of 1850, when its operations came to an end, the bulk of this huge fund was distributed to the needy throughout the stricken region in the form of meal payments for labour. At peak periods of stress, such as the spring of 1849, almost four-fifths of the people of Barra, two-thirds of the population of Skye, one-half of the inhabitants of Wester Ross and one-third of the people of Mull, were in receipt of the Central Board's meagre pittances. But Lowland charity came to the rescue not only of hungry Highlanders; it also supported the position of the Highland landed class as a whole. Several proprietors continued to be active in relief measures after 1847 but the majority left most of the provision for the maintenance of the people to the Central Board and its Edinburgh and Glasgow committees. Above all, it was the charities which saved the landed class from what one contemporary described as 'the bankruptcy of public burdens'. The numbers of 'occasional poor', far from rising sharply and so leading to a huge increase in poor law rates, actually *fell* in the four Highland counties after 1847 to 1851 in the middle of the greatest social crisis in the region in the nineteenth century (see Table 1). There could be no more convincing confirmation of the crucial

TABLE 1
OCCASIONAL POOR, HIGHLAND COUNTIES, 1846–53

County	1846	1847	1848	1849	1850	1851	1852	1853
Inverness	296	1498	746	715	573	2099	2579	637
Argyll	553	932	838	719	716	843	946	602
Ross and C.	169	390	416	383	406	417	1503	464
Sutherland	34	26	39	52	70	120	81	71

Sources: *Parliamentary Papers, Annual Reports of the Board of Supervision for Relief of the Poor in Scotland*, XXVII (1847); XXXIII (1847–8); XXV (1849); XXVI (1850); XXIII (1852); L (1852–3); XXIX (1854); XLV (1854–5).

significance of the Central Board in the provision of minimal welfare services in these years.

Nor was the state entirely indifferent to the threat to the solvency of west Highland property posed by the famine. The government was indeed committed to the orthodoxies of political economy: that an economy thrived best when left to the free play of market forces and that any unnecessary interference with them was bound to do more harm than good. It was also determined to avoid the deep and costly involvement in famine relief which had absorbed its energies in Ireland. On the other hand, there was too much at stake for the tenets of political economy to be followed entirely to the letter. As the senior government official most closely asociated with the problem put it: 'The people *cannot under any circumstances*, be allowed to starve.'[40] There was also recognition of the fact that the policy of relying mainly on individual landlords to provide relief would be inevitably counter-productive if the crisis persisted for very long.[41] Insolvencies would spread and the risk to the people on bankrupt estates would accordingly increase. State aid for the landed class was therefore approved, not in the form of a direct grant, which would have offended the political and economic conventions of the time, but by encouraging proprietors to apply for loans through the existing Drainage Act (9 and 10 Vic. cap. C1 (1846)) which had been passed by Sir Robert Peel's government to assuage opposition from the landed interest after the Repeal of the Corn Laws.[42] Loans were made available at an interest rate of 6.5 per cent per annum and repayment could occur over 22 years. The treasury, which administered the distribution of loans, was instructed to 'strain it (the Drainage Act) to the uttermost' in order to ensure that not only drainage works but fencing, roads and other developments 'subordinate to and connected with a system of drainage' might be approved.[43] In effect, the legislation became a mechanism for channelling state loans to a distressed region of the country which government could not assist directly because of its ideological predilections.

Not surprisingly, therefore, the eventual value of Highland applications for assistance through the Drainage Act was out of all proportion to the value of Highland property relative to that elsewhere in Britain. By the end of March 1847, the landowners in one of the poorest regions in Britain had applied for loans to the value of £488,000 under the Act, a figure which amounted to almost 20 per cent of all applications made in Britain as a whole.[44] As the factor of Lord Macdonald's estate put it: 'It [the Drainage Act] is not, however, altogether adapted to our circumstances but we have like drowning men catching at a straw, been obliged to lay hold of it' .[45] Perhaps more than any other single factor, the huge stream of income which flowed into the western Highlands through the funds released by the Act must have done most to alleviate the misfortunes of the region. The initial application was for a sum more than twice the value of the resources of the Central Board and additional loans were made available from 1850.[46] Many of the loans were used to reduce rent arrears through the wages paid to destitute crofters engaged in draining and trenching work under the Act. The actual payment was usually paid mainly in meal once per week. The residue of the 'wage' went to defray rent arrears and any balance was distributed in cash. In addition, crofts deemed to have been 'improved' by works carried out under the Act were charged the annual government interest rate of 6.5 per cent.[47] Landowners, therefore, sometimes passed on the 'cost' of the loan to their tenants. Some crofters were still paying these charges in the 1880s.[48] In this way, therefore, the Drainage Act not only alleviated the destitution of the poeple but made a powerful contribution to the economic stability of landed property in the distressed districts. The ground officer of one of the biggest estates in Skye noted how rents began to be 'generally well paid' again from 1849–50 and this he attributed mainly to the impact of the loans made available under the Act.[49]

The role of the charities and the influence of government legislation were, therefore, principal factors in allowing a destitute population to be supported without necessarily accelerating the ruin of large numbers of landed families. But these elements mainly explain how the *cost* of maintaining the people through the crisis was met. They do not adequately answer the question why the dramatic contraction in estate *income* from the small tenants did not produce serious financial problems for the landed class in general. The evidence suggests that it did not do so because a large number, and probably the majority of proprietors, by the late 1840s no longer depended on crofting rents as their major source of income. This was due both to the changing social composition of the west Highland landed class and to the new structure of the regional economy which had emerged in the three decades before the famine.

By 1846 the pattern of landownership in the western Highlands had undergone radical change. The hereditary landed families, apart from the two great ducal dynasties of Argyll and Sutherland, only clung on in North Uist, most of Skye, Islay and a few areas on the mainland such as Gairloch, Knoydart and Ardnamurchan. From the early nineteenth century, in a series of great land sales which reached a climax during the potato famine, the old Highland élite was replaced in many districts by a new class who had made their money in trade, industry and the urban professions of banking and law.[50] Typical of the new breed were such men as Octavius Smith, the wealthy London distiller, who in 1845 bought Achranich Estate in Morvern, a parish where between 1813 to 1838 every single property changed hands; James Matheson of the giant East India firm of Jardine, Matheson and Co., the new owner of Lewis, referred to in Disraeli's *Sybil* as '. . . richer than Croesus, one Macdrug, fresh from Canton, with a million in opium in each pocket'; Col. John Gordon, proprietor of Barra, South Uist and Benbecula, dubbed the 'richest com- moner in Scotland' in the obituary written after his death; Francis Clark, a successful lawyer from Stirling, who had acquired the island of Ulva in 1835; James Baillie, a Bristol merchant and banker, who became the proprietor of Glenelg in 1837; Alexander Matheson, another very wealthy East India merchant, whose Ross-shire estate were more extensive by the 1860s than those of such grandees as the Dukes of Argyll and Atholl. In all, an analysis of the ownership of estates in the distressed region indicates that at least 74 per cent changed hands, several more than once, between 1800–40. This was a dramatic and exceptional rate of regional land transfer which was in sharp contrast to the pattern elsewhere in Britain where recent research has identi- fied a decline in estate sales in the first half of the nineteenth century.[51]

The reasons why this should be so are explored in detail elsewhere and need not be examined fully here.[52] They included the fact that much land was now available in the region as the pressures gripping the old Highland élite eventually overwhelmed many families in the post-war economic recession; the advances in steam navigation which rendered access less difficult from the rest of Britain; the new attractions of a Highland estate stimulated by the success of Scott's novels, the romantic appeal of scenic grandeur, Queen Victoria's well-publicised interest in the Highlands and the superb oppor- tunities the region provided for the fashionable sports of hunting, fishing and shooting; the remoteness and solitude of the region which offered successful businessmen the possibilities of escaping occasionally from the pace of life in the cities; the chance also for absentee proprietors to make speculative gains by buying up the possessions of insolvent families, laying the land down to sheep and then later selling at a greatly increased price. For present purposes, however, more important than the reasons for this changing pattern of landownership was its effects on the stability of the landed class during the famine. Quite simply the new men were not dependent on the petty payments of the impoverished crofters of their northern estates. Their income primarily derived from the profits of their manufacturing concerns, trading firms and professional activities. Many were tycoons of massive wealth for whom the provision of famine relief was easily submerged within their other investments in neo-Gothic castles, mansions, steam yachts, hunting lodges and bizarre schemes of agricultural improvement. Sir James Matheson, for example, spent almost £200,000 in famine relief and emigration assistance in Lewis and still had enough change to buy up several more properties in Wester Ross in the early 1850s.[53] Historians have underestimated the scale of this silent revolution in Highland landownership before 1846 and hence have tended to overestimate the vulnerability of the landed class as a whole during the famine after that date.

The changing economic structure of Highland estates was also conducive to the resilience of many proprieors. In all districts of the western Highlands for which we have detailed records the majority of tenants rented land at less

TABLE 2

RENTAL STRUCTURE OF HEBRIDEAN AND WEST HIGHLAND ESTATES

Parish/Estate	Per cent Share of Total Rental paid by Tenants with holdings rented at over £20 per annum. Selected West Highland and Hebridean Districts
Kilfinichen (Mull)	68
Kilmuir (Skye)	54
Snizort (Skye)	71
Portree (Skye)	43
Strath (Skye)	54
Sleat (Skye)	59
North Morar	73
Knoydart	90
Glenelg	87
Glensheil	97
Lochalsh	70
Kintail	77
Lochcarron	58
Applecross	52
Torridon	70
Average	74

Source: *Parliamentary Papers, Report to Board of Supervision by Sir John McNeil*, Appendix A, *passim*.

than £20 per annum.[54] The numerical dominance of the crofting class is therefore not in doubt. What is more open to question is the *proportion* of rental paid by this group, because on that depended the real impact of the famine on landlord income. The available evidence suggests that tenants renting land above £20 per annum were more able to weather the storm and much better equipped to maintain their rent payments than those below them on the economic scale. For instance, on the Gairloch estate in Wester Ross, arrears among the bigger tenants rose marginally from £89 in 1845 to £214 in 1848 out of a total annual rental of £3,000 paid by this group. But this still represented only 12 per cent of total arrears which had accumulated on the estate by that year. Overwhelmingly, it was the smaller men who failed to maintain their rent payments.[55] The flow of rental income therefore crucially depended on the tenant composition of west Highland properties. An estate where the greater value of rents was paid by bigger tenants was self-evidently likely to be less vulnerable during the famine years than one where the bulk of revenue depended on the payments of destitute crofters.

Crofting rentals remained more important in several areas, such as the Ardnamurchan estate, Barra, South Uist, the Coigach section of the Cromartie estate and the Duke of Argyll's lands in Tiree and Mull.[56] But Table 2 demonstrates that in many other districts bigger tenants were now dominant, not numerically, but rather in the value of their contributions to total rental. A typical pattern was that in North Uist. There less than 6 per cent of all tenants paid £20 per annum or more, but they accounted for 76 per cent of the entire rental.[57]

There seems little doubt that the presence of these larger tenants largely reflected the extensive development of sheep-farming in the western Highlands in the decades before the famine. A dual structure clearly existed on some estates. Large pastoral farms coexisted beside congested communities of crofters and cottars who possessed their own small fragments of land. By c. 1846 commercial pastoralism had penetrated virtually all the western Highlands and islands with the exception of Tiree, Barra, Islay and parts of Skye.[58] In the early 1840s, the *New Statistical Account* suggests that at least 85 per cent of parishes in Sutherland, 61 per cent of those in Ross and Cromarty, 60 per cent in Inverness and 35 per cent in Argyll, had experienced large-scale sheep farm development which resulted in the emergence of bigger tenancies and much land comsolidation.[59] It followed also that many estates primarily depended on the prices of wool and mutton for rental income rather than the cattle sales of a multitude of poor crofters. Significantly, as Figure 1 reveals, sheep prices began an almost uninterrupted climb from the mid 1840s from the doldrums of the period after the Napoleonic Wars, a trend which lasted until the later 1860s. The era of the famine was one of considerable difficulty for cattle farmers but it was also the early stages of a phase of buoyant prosperity for sheep farmers. For many Highland estate owners this expanding market was a crucial advantage. It not only insulated them from the worst economic consequences of the potato failure but also stimulated further expansion of large-scale pastoral husbandry during the crisis itself.[60] As the blight persisted, several landowners began to turn the misfortunes of the small tenants and cottars of their properties to their own advantage by enforcing policies designed to increase income by altering the social and economic structure of their estates. In order to understand their strategy and its effect it is necessary in the first instance to outline the problems which had confronted them during the three decades before the crisis of 1846.

IV

The basic issue in Highland history in the first half of the nineteenth century was the imbalance between rising population and the contraction in indigenous employment opportunities which was initially generated by the postwar economic recession and then accelerated by the remorseless advance of commercial pastoralism. The Select Committee on Emigration (Scotland) of 1841 estimated that in the western Highlands and islands there was a surplus of population of 44,600 people or almost 38 per cent of the total inhabitants. The imbalance would have been even more acute if it had not been for the increasing pace of out-migration.[62] But the exodus was still not on a sufficient enough scale in all areas to effectively counterbalance natural increase and the impact of the dramatic decline in the labour-intensive sectors of the economy after 1820. Despite the increasing volume of emigration, only in Sutherland and a few other districts was there *mass* desertion from the land

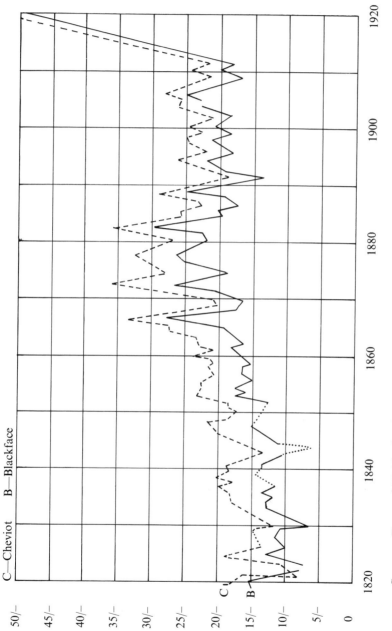

Source: *Trans. of Highland and Agricultural Society*, 1921; *W. Orr, Crofters, Landlords and Deer Forests*, (Edinburgh, 1982), *p.*155.

FIGURE 1   Sheep Prices, Cheviot and Blackface, 1820–1920.

during the postwar crisis. In 1841 around 85,000 more people were living in the crofting region than the total recorded in Webster's census of the 1750s. This represented an increase of about 74 per cent over that period.[63] In addition, there were wide regional disparities in the scale of haemorrhage. Depopulation was mainly confined to the county of Sutherland itself and to a few parishes on the western mainland. Numbers continued to rise in many of the islands of the Inner and Outer Hebrides despite the collapse of profitable kelp manufacture and the stagnation in fishing. Of those parishes which reached their maximum level of population *before* the 1841 census, only 37 per cent were in the islands.

It is vital to this analysis, therefore, to recognise that before 1846, despite dispossession, clearance, economic recession and harvest failure, the grip of the people on the land had not been broken. This was still a peasant society and its members possessed the tenacious attachment to land which is characteristic of all such societies. As Pierre Goubert has remarked: 'No peasant will voluntarily give up his land, be it only half a furrow'.[64] It was to this set of social values that the parish minister of Duirnish in Skye referred when he explained how the people '... feel a blind, and therefore, a very powerful attachment to the rocks and glens amid which they were brought up—an almost invincible aversion to abandon them'.[65] Even grinding poverty, usually tolerated because it was familiar, could not easily or quickly dissolve these attitudes. Heavy emigration was normally confined to periods of great distress such as recurrent harvest failure. But even at such times there was often great reluctance to move. An enquiry into attitudes towards emigration in 1837–8, in the aftermath of the most serious nineteenth century subsistence crisis before the potato famine itself, revealed a very great diversity of response. In 16 of the 45 parishes which provided information, more than one-third of the inhabitants were disposed to accept offers of emigration assistance, in 21 less than a third and in 8 parishes few or none were keen.[66]

Not surprisingly, these attitudes were anathema to the landowners.[67] The continuing rise in the Hebridean population deepened destitution and forced up rent arrears. The people became increasingly vulnerable to the effects of harvest failure in 1816–17, 1825 and 1836–7. At each crisis several proprietors were forced to intervene to prevent starvation on their estates by distributing meal at cost price and adding the outlay to rents which were unlikely ever to be repaid in full. Some also provided employment in road-building and estate improvement for the destitute. Strategies of clearance and assisted emigration were more commonly employed as the social crisis in the western Highlands became more acute. Though these did have an effect in some areas of the region, they did little to solve the underlying problem. On several estates draconian mesaures actually exacerbated social destitution as dispossessed crofters were pushed further down the social scale into the impoverished mass of cottars and semi-landless people. Clearance in itself was just as likely to intensify congestion as cause depopulation since some of those who lost their lands crowded into slum villages or crofting townships in neighbouring districts rather than leave the region altogether for a new life elsewhere. If contemporary opinion is correct, it was often the poorest, those who could not easily raise the cost of passage and resettlement across the Atlantic, who were forced to remain.[68]

In the event only a disaster on the scale of the potato famine could reduce the intractable demographic problems which had harassed the administration of Highland estates since the early decades of the nineteenth century. The famine not only precipitated a huge increase in migration from the region in general but caused the greatest haemorrhage to occur in the Hebrides, which had sustained the fastest rate of actual population growth before 1846. Six of the nine crofting parishes estimated to have lost 20 per cent or more of their inhabitants between 1841 and 1851 were located in the islands.[69] In the following decade, ten of the twelve parishes which lost 20 per cent or more were also in the Hebrides. Over the two decades of the famine, Uig, in Lewis, lost an estimated half of its total population; Jura, almost a third (1841–51); the Small Isles, almost a half (1851–61); Barra, about one-third (1841–51). An examination of the census enumerator books for two representative insular parishes, Kilfinichen in Mull and Barvas in Lewis, shows a loss respectively of 45.5 per cent and 24.4 per cent of all *households* between 1841 and 1851 and a further substantial haemorrhage in the following decade.[70] The overwhelming majority of the 17,000 emigrants assisted either by individual landlords or the Highland and Island Emigration Society during the famine were also from the Inner and Outer Hebrides. 76 per cent of those assisted by landlords and 78 per cent supported by the Society were natives of the islands.[71]

Only a crisis of the severity and duration of the potato famine could have enforced such a radical increase in emigration. The long series of bad years, punctuated only by a few periods of ephemeral improvement, temporarily relaxed the peasant grip on the land. Communities where there had previously been little enthusiasm for emigration were seized with a desperate urge to get away. The Duke of Argyll's Chamberlain in the Ross of Mull and Tiree reported in 1849 that the cottars were '... ready to go in hundreds to Canada if provided with the means'.[72] During the course of the famine his correspondence indicates that many more wished to emigrate than the estate was prepared to assist.[73] Similarly in Skye, the termination of the operations of the Central Board in 1850 and the financial problems experienced by Lord Macdonald and Macleod of Macleod, the two greatest landowners on the islands, induced a mood of desperation in 1851–2 which resulted in a widespread anxiety to emigrate.[74] Only in Lewis did the old hostility to emigration apparently persist and that may have been due to the relief schemes of Sir James Matheson and the resilience of fishing around the coasts. As a result, the island's inhabitants may have suffered less than those elsewhere.[75]

The fundamental influence of the stress of hunger and destitution on the pattern of movement is confirmed by the cycle of emigration. The return of slightly better times, even if they did not last for long, could quickly dissipate the urge to leave. Thus, although 50 families from Edderachillis in Sutherland petitioned for emigration assistance in January 1847, only ten were still willing to go by March. Spring weather and improved prospects at the fishing had led to a change of heart.[76] There was an even more remarkable example of a similar type of response in the Macleod estates in Skye in 1855. Over 1,000 of its destitute inhabitants had sought to emigrate with the help of the Highland and Island Emigration Society. In the event, however, only 237 individuals finally presented themselves for inspection and registration by the Society's officials.[77] The vast majority had changed their minds because of the arrival of a steamer at Dunvegan with a cargo of meal and potatoes sent out for distribution by the Free Church and other sympathisers in the Lowlands.

The Society also found that the demand for emigration assistance fluctuated markedly with sudden changes in economic circumstances. Fifty-three per cent of the 4,910 emigrants it assisted to emigrate to Australia between 1852 and 1857 left in the first year of its operation which was a time of terrible destitution. However, only 13 per cent (628 individuals) emigrated in 1853 because conditions then were much better.[78] The Secretary of the Society explained: '... the disinclination to emigrate is because their condition at home is so far better by the increased demand for labour, the high price of cattle and sheep, the abundance and good quality of their crops, especially of potatoes—and the success of the Herring Fishery on the West Coast'.[79]

But the volume, pace and timing of the exodus was not linked only to prevailing economic circumstances. Those who suffered most from the crops failures and the associated economic crisis were the very same families and individuals who could not normally afford the costs of passage and resettlement from their own resources. In the final analysis, the poor had to rely on landlord assistance, the efforts of such charitable organisations as the Highland Emigration Society and the Central Relief Board and kinsmen already settled abroad, to embark on emigration. The landed class was therefore able to develop a significant influence on the timing, the sequence and, above all, the social composition of the movement. In addition, though the Highland Emigration Society was an independent public charity, landowners were intimately involved in its operations as the Society's officials relied partly on proprietors and their agents in the selection of suitable candidates for assistance.[80] Their association with the Society was consolidated further after the passage of the Emigration Advances Act (14 and 15, Vic. c.91) in 1851 which made available public funds at interest rates of 6.25 per cent per annum to proprietors wishing to assist emigration from their estates. Those landowners who took advantage of these loans mainly sent out the emigrants they supported under the auspices of the Society to Australia. It covered two-thirds of the total cost from its own charitable resources, leaving only the remaining one-third to be contributed by individual proprietors.[81]

Landowners exploited these opportunities with considerable energy. From 1849, in particular, they intensified the pressures which were already fostering emigration by enforcing a series of sanctions designed to accelerate the flight of the very poor. As the Duke of Argyll proclaimed in 1851: 'I wish to send out those whom we would be obliged to feed if they stayed at home—to get rid of that class is *the object*' (underlined in original letter).[82] The measures taken towards this objective included the confiscation of the cattle stocks of those in considerable arrears of rent, a more resolute and thorough-going programme of clearance (especially in the linkage of eviction with schemes of assisted emigration on a much greater scale than ever before), a veto on tenants cutting peat during the summer who were scheduled for emigration assistance and denial or reduction of famine relief except in dire circumstances.[83] The development of coercion is made most apparent in the steep increase in summonses of removal obtained at west Highland sheriff courts in this period. Between 1846 and 1852, a total of 1,052 summonses were issued at Tobermory with over 84 per cent given from 1849 to 1852.[84] The Matheson estate in Lewis obtained no less than 1,180 summonses of removal in the three years after 1849.[85]

At the same time, much discrimination was employed in the selection of those to be given emigration assistance. The policy was framed not in a spirit of paternalistic benevolence but mainly out of a desire to exploit the circumstances of crisis to best economic advantage. In general, the retention of those communities who depended mainly on fishing was favoured while determined efforts were made to enforce the expulsion of those who traditionally relied more on kelp-burning and also, though to a lesser extent, on cattle farming. On several properties, indeed, such as Lewis and the Macdonald estate in Skye, a very close correlation developed between eviction, assisted emigration and removal or thinning of kelping townships. The policy, therefore, was designed above all else to eliminate or reduce the very core of the 'redundant' population. On the other hand, there was also a reluctance to provide emigration assistance for tenants paying rentals above £10 per annum and those with only small arrears of rent. Instead, it was the cottars and the poorer tenants who were more likely to receive aid. Most landowners and their agents sought to increase social differentiation among the population of their estates, to rigorously control subdivision after the famine emigrations had taken place, to drive out the weaker elements and consolidate the position of the stronger and, at the same time, to release even more land for the pursuit of large-scale pastoral husbandry. As a result several Hebridean estates were, in economic terms, in leaner and fitter condition after 1856 than they had been before.[86] The potato famine was certainly painful for some landed families and a disaster for a few others but the majority of proprietors were less at risk. They might regard it in a more sanguine light as a great crisis which eventually provided the opportunity at great social cost to reduce the social and demographic problems which had confronted their predecessors for over a generation.

NOTES

1 Aspects of the Highland famine are examined in James Hunter, *The Making of the Crofting Community* (Edinburgh 1976), ch 5 and M W Flinn (ed), *Scottish Population History from the Seventeenth Century to the 1930s* (Cambridge 1977) The only attempt at a comprehensive analysis is T M Devine, *The Great Highland Famine: Hunger, Emigration and the Scottish Highlands in the Nineteenth Century* (Edinburgh 1988). The research for this paper was conducted as part of a larger project supported by ESRC (Grant no. B00232099). I am grateful for the Council's generous support and the energetic help of my research assistant, Mr W Orr, in the collection of data.

2 Devine, *Highland Famine*, ch 2.

3 These generalisations are based on market reports in the *Inverness Courier* and *John O'Groats Journal*, 1845–1854.

4 Prices were buoyant throughout most of 1846 and only declined sharply the following year. See, *Inverness Courier*, 21 October 1846; *Edinburgh Evening Courant*, 3 October 1846.

5 See Devine *Great Highland Famine*, ch 6 for this paragraph.

6 *Witness*, 21, 25 November 1846.

7 Anon, *Extracts from Letters to the Rev Dr Macleod regarding the Famine and Destitution in the Highlands of Scotland* (Glasgow 1847), p 71.

8 Conon House, Mackenzie of Gairloch MSS, 'Gairloch Rentals, 1846–49'.

9 Scottish Record Office (SRO), Lord Macdonald Papers, GD221/43, 46, 62, 70, 82, 'Macdonald Rentals, 1796–1858'.

10 SRO, Riddell Papers, AF49/6, 'Report of T G Dickson for Trustees, 1852'; National Library of Scotland, Sutherland Estate Papers, Dep. 313/2283–2302, 'Small Tenant Rentals, Eastern and Western Districts'.

11 *Parliamentary Papers, Report to the Board of Supervision by Sir John McNeill on the Western Highlands*, XXVI (1851), IV.

12 M Gray, *The Highland Economy, 1750–1850* (Edinburgh 1957), pp 181–92.

13 SRO, Lord Macdonald Papers, GD221/62, 'General View of the Affairs of the Rt Hon Lord Macdonald, 3 February 1846'.

14 *Parliamentary Papers, Correspondence relating to the measures adopted for the Relief of Distress in Ireland and Scotland*, LIII (1847), Mr Trevelyan to Sir E Coffin, 11 September 1846.

15 Ibid, Trevelyan-Coffin Correspondence, September–December, 1846.

16 SRO, Lord Advocate's Papers, AD58/86, 'Lord Advocate to Mr Tytler, 5 January 1847'.

17 SRO, HD7/26, Miscellaneous correspondence from Highland landowners, 1846–7.

18 This disaster resulted in the transfer of landed property estimated at a value of £750,000. Several of the bank's partners were substantial landowners. See H Hamilton, 'The Failure of the Ayr Bank, 1772' *Econ. Hist. Rev.*, VIII, 2nd series, 1955–6, pp 405–18.

19 These included the files of the *Inverness Advertiser, Inverness Courier, Witness, John O'Groats Journal, Scotsman* and *Glasgow Herald* for the relevant years. Highland properties were regularly advertised in these papers.

20 SRO, Breadalbane Muniments, GD 112; Campbell of Barcaldine MSS., GD 170; Campbell of Jura Papers, GD 64; Clanranald Papers, GD 201; Cromartie Estate Papers, GD 305; Loch Muniments, GD 208; Lord Macdonald Papers, GD 221; Maclaine of Lochbuie Papers, GD 174; Riddell Papers, AF49; Seafield Muniments, GD 248. Inverarary Castle, Argyll Estate Papers. Achnacarry

Castle, Cameron of Lochiel Papers. Conon House, Mackenzie of Gairloch MSS. Dunvegan Castle, Macleod of Macleod Muniments. Islay House, Islay Estate Papers.

21 SRO, CS 277, Sederunt Books in Sequestration; CS 279, Petitions in Sequestration, 1839–56.

22 J Barron, *The Northern Highlands in the Nineteenth Century* (Inverness, 1907), vol. I, *passim*.

23 SRO, CS 277, Sederunt Books in Sequestration, W F Campbell of Islay; SRO, Campbell of Jura Papers, GD 64/1/347/1, 'Report to the Creditors of W F Campbell of Islay'; SRO, Riddell Papers, AF49/6, 'Report of T G Dickson for Trustees, 1852'; *North British Advertiser*, 15 July 1854.

24 Anon., *The State of the Highlands in 1854* (Inverness 1855), pp 21–44.

25 SRO, HD 20/31, 'Report of Committee on the Case of Macleod of Macleod, 5 March 1847'; SRO, GD 221/160/4, 'State of Debts due by Lord Macdonald, November 1849'.

26 The figure is based upon SRO, HD 6/1, 'Map of the Distressed Districts by D W Martin'.

27 SRO, Lord Macdonald Papers, GD 221/62, 'General View of the Affairs of Lord Macdonald, 3 February 1846'.

28 Dunvegan Castle, Macleod of Macleod Muniments, Box 51, 'C E Gibbons to Macleod, 27 December 1833'; I F Grant, *The Macleods: the History of a Clan, 1200–1956* (London 1959), pp 584–5; J Mitchell, *Reminiscences of My Life in the Highlands* (1833, reprinted Newton Abbott, 1971), pp 299–300; SRO, Treasury Correspondence relating to Highland Destitution, HD 6/2, 'Deputy-Commissary Dobree to Sir Edward Coffin, 21 April 1847'.

29 The estates and their purchasers with date of acquisition in brackets were: Kintail, Sir A Matheson (1840, 1844); Aros, Mull, D Nairne (1842); Ulva; F W Clark (1835–6); Raasay, G Rainy (1846); Glenelg, James Baillie (1837); Lewis, James Matheson (1844); Barra, S. Uist, Benbecula, Col J Gordon (1838–45); Torridon, Col McBarnet (1838); Arisaig, Lord Cranstoun (?). The figure of eleven is unlikely to be definitive and should be taken as a minimum number based on land sales reported in the *Inverness Courier*, 1836–46 inclusive. For a more detailed examination of land sales see T M Devine, 'The Emergence of the New Élite in the Western Highlands and Islands, 1790–1860', in T M Devine (ed), *Scottish Society in the Era of Improvement and Enlightenment* (forthcoming, Edinburgh 1989). The references to estate sales during the famine period do not apply to all transactions but are confined to those where other evidence indicates that sales were rendered necessary either through the insolvency of the landowner or through the actions of trustees.

30 For instance, in December 1846, the Marquis of Lorne, heir to the Duke of Argyll, admitted that the 'potato panic' had reduced demand for Highland property (SRO, Loch Muniments, GD 268/45, 'Marquis of Lorne to James Loch, 12 December 1846'). However, this malaise was probably only temporary. In early 1848 Lord Cranstoun sold Arisaig to Mr Mackay of Bighouse without reducing the upset price. The estate of Lynedale in the distressed island of Skye was acquired by Alexander Macdonald of Thornbank, Falkirk at a cost of £9,000 in 1849. This represented an advance of about ten per cent on its 1837 price (*Scotsman*, 29 January 1848, 11 August 1849).

31 See Devine, *Great Highland Famine*, ch 2, for the basis of the generalisations which follow in this paragraph.

32 National Library of Scotland, Sutherland Estate Papers, Dep. 313/2216–22; Conon House, Mackenzie of Gairloch MSS, 'Account of Charge and Discharge,

Conon and Kernsaray estates, 1845–1849'; SRO, Cromartie Papers, GD 305/2/84-121, Strathpeffer and New Tarbet rentals, 1834–1855, SRO, Seafield Muniments, GD 248/408, Urquhart Rental, 1816–1856.

33 There is a useful summary of the main reasons for the varying regional impact of the potato famine in *Reports of the Edinburgh Section of the Central Board for the Relief of Destitution in the Highlands, 1847–50*, (Edinburgh, 1847–50), Second Report by the Committee of Management to the Edinburgh Section for 1850 11.

34 T M Devine, 'Highland Migration to Lowland Scotland, 1760–1860'. *Scottish Historical Review*, LXII (2) (1983), pp 137–49.

35 SRO, Treasury Correspondence relating to Highland Destitution, February– September, 1847, HD 6/2; SRO, Lord Advocate's Papers, AD 58/81, 'Reports on conditions of various estates in the Highlands and Islands, 1846–7'.

36 SRO, Breadalbane Papers, GD 12/14/19, 'Alexander Campbell to Earl of Breadalbane, 23 April 1847'; Trevelyan's opinion was communicated in private correspondence to Campbell who then informed Breadalbane.

37 SRO, Destitution papers, HD 7/46, 'Sir Charles Trevelyan to William Skene, 2 March 1848'.

38 Inveraray Castle, Argyll Estate Papers, Bundle 1522, 'Abstract of Accounts etc. of Tiree, 1843–49'.

39 See Devine, *Great Highland Famine*, ch 5 for detailed references for this paragraph.

40 *Parliamentary Papers, Correspondence relating to the relief of Distress* Mr T-evelyan to Mr Horne, 20 September 1846. The phrase is italicised in the original source.

41 Ibid, Mr Ellice to Chancellor of the Exchequer, 31 August 1846.

42 J B Denton, 'Land Drainage etc. by Loans', *Journal of the Royal Agricultural Society of England*, 4 (11), 1868.

43 *Parliamentary Papers, Correspondence relating to the relief of Distress*, Chancellor of Exchequer to Lord Advocate, 13 October 1846; Sir E Coffin to Mr Trevelyan, 22 October 1846.

44 *Parliamentary Papers, Return of Applications under the Drainage Act*, XXXIV (1847); SRO, Papers relating to the Drainage of Land Act (1847) including returns, HD 7/33. £2 millions were allocated under the original legislation and a further £2 millions were made available by the Treasury from 1850.

45 *Parliamentary Papers, Correspondence relating to the relief of Distress*, Mr McKinnon to Capt Pole, December 1846.

46 See n 44 above.

47 *Parliamentary Papers, report to Board of Supervision by Sir John McNeill*, Appendix A, Evidence of Angus McDonald, 60: evidence of C Macleod, 81; *Witness*, 28 July 1849; *Inverness Courier*, 6 February 1851; Conon House, Mackenzie of Gairloch MSS, Black Deed Box, Bundle 53, 'Report by Mr Inglis on Management, 1854–57'; SRO, Lord Macdonald Papers, GD 221/46, 'Charge/ Discharge, 1850–51'.

48 *Palrliamentary Papers, Report and Evidence of the Commissions of Enquiry into the Condition of the Crofters and Cottars in the Highlands and Islands of Scotland*, 1884, XXXII–XXXVI, 302, Q.5564.

49 *Parliamentary Papers, Report to Board of Supervision by Sir John McNeill*, Appendix A, 60.

50 What follows is based on Devine, 'The Emergence of the New Élite', *passim*.

51 Lawrence Stone and Jeanne C Fautier Stone, *An Open Élite? England 1540–1880* (Oxford 1984), pp 407–21.

52   Devine, 'The Emergence of the New Élite', *passim.*

53   *Parliamentary Papers, Report to Board of Supervision by Sir John McNeill,* Appendix A, Evidence of J M Mackenzie, 93; MS. Diary of J M Mackenzie, Chamberlain of the Lews, 1851. (In private hands. Copy made available courtesy of Ms M Buchanan.)

54   Gray, *Highland Economy,* ch 5.

55   Conon House, Mackenzie of Gairloch MSS, 'Account of Charge and Discharge of the Intromission of Dr J Mackenzie as Factor for the Mackenzie estates, 1846–8'. For a similar pattern on the Sutherland estate see National Library of Scotland, Sutherland Estate Papers, Dep. 313/2207–15, 'Sutherland Rentals'.

56   Inveraray Castle, Argyll Estate Papers, Bundle 1522, 'Abstract of Accounts, Tiree, 1843–50', 'Abstract of Accounts Mull property, 1843–50'; SRO, Cromartie Estate Papers, GD 305/2/84–121, 'Estate rentals'; SRO, Riddell Papers, AF 49/6, 'Report of T G Dickson for Trustees, 1852'; MS. Diary of J M Mackenzie, 1851.

57   SRO, Lord Macdonald Papers, GD 221/43, 'Report by D Shaw, Factor for North Uist, 1839'; GD 221/70, 'North Uist Rentals, 1853–4'.

58   *Reports of Central Board of Management of the Fund Raiser for the Relief of the Destitute Inhabitants of the Highlands* (Edinburgh 1847–50), First Report of Central Relief Board (1847), 2; *Report on Mull, Tiree . . . etc. by a Deputation of the Glasgow Section of the Highland Relief Board* (Glasgow 1849), 8, 10; *Parliamentary Papers, Report to Board of Supervision by Sir John McNeill,* Appendix A, Evidence of Thomas Fraser, 35.

59   These estimates are based on a scrutiny of the parish accounts for the four Highland counties in the *New Statistical Account of Scotland* (Edinburgh 1835–45).

60   Devine, *Great Highland Famine,* ch 12.

61   *Parliamentary Papers, Report from Select Committee on Condition of Highlands and Islands,* 21.

62   Flinn (ed), *Scottish Population History,* pp 327–34, 338–9.

63   The region referred to in these figures is the West Highland survey area as defined by F Fraser Darling in *West Highland Survey* (Oxford 1955), pp 15–17.

64   P Goubert, *The Ancien Régime: French Society 1600–1750,* (London 1973), p 44.

65   *New Statistical Account,* XIV, p 344.

66   A Fullarton and C R Baird, *Remarks on the Evils at Present affecting the Highlands and Islands of Scotland* (Glasgow 1838), p 128.

67   The generalisations in this paragraph are based on a survey of the following material: Public Record Office, London, T1/4201, Correspondence and reports of Robert Grahame to Fox Maule, 6 March–6 May 1837; *Parliamentary Papers, Report from Select Committee on Condition of Highlands and Islands, passim;* SRO, Lord Macdonald Papers, GD 221/122/1,4,11,19; Fullarton and Baird, *Remarks on the . . . Highlands and Islands;* Inveraray Castle, Argyll Estate Papers, Bundle 1529, SRO; Brown MSS, TD80/100/4; National Library of Scotland, Sutherland Estate Papers, Dep. 313/2283–2302; SRO, Riddell Papers, AF49/4, Sunart and Ardnamurchan rentals; SRO, Cromartie Papers, GD 305/2/84–121, Estate Rentals, 1834–1855; Dunvegan Castle, Macleod of Macleod Muniments, 3/107/5, Macleod Rentals, 1800–58.

68   See, for example, SRO, HD 21/35, 'Petition of the Inhabitants of Glenelg (1848)'.

69   For the basis of these estimates see Devine, *Great Highland Famine,* ch 8.

70   General Register Office, Edinburgh, Census Enumerators Books, Kilfinichen (Mull) and Barvas (Lewis), 1841, 1851, 1861.

71   For the Society's figures see SRO, HD 4/5, 'List of Emigrants of the Highland and Island Emigration Society'; for those of individual landlords see Devine, *Great Highland Famine,* Appendix 10.

72 Inveraray Castle, Argyll Estate Papers, Bundle 1535, 'J Campbell to Duke of Argyll, 27 February 1849'.
73 Ibid, Bundle 1805, J Campbell to Duke of Argyll, 17 May 1851.
74 *Report of the Highland Emigration Society* (Edinburgh 1853), 10. Another witness confirmed that 'the people are anxious and willing to get away'. See Dunvegan Castle, Macleod of Macleod Muniments, 659/7/3, 'J D Ferguson to Madam Macleod, 25 June 1852'.
75 MS. Diary of J M Mackenzie, Chamberlain of the Lews, 1851.
76 National Library of Scotland, Sutherland Estate Papers, Dep. 313/1512, 'E McIver to R Horsburgh, 27 March'.
77 SRO, HD 4/4, 'J Chant to H Rollo, 30 April 1855'. See also, Mitchell Library, Glasgow, Letterbook of Sir J McNeill, MS. 21506, 'McNeill to Sir Charles Trevelyan, 23 June and 21 August 1852'.
78 SRO, HD 4/5, 'List of Emigrants of the Highland and Island Emigration Society'.
79 SRO, Letterbooks of the Highland and Island Emigration Society, HD 4/2, 'Sir Charles Trevelyan to Capt W Denison, 4 July 1853'.
80 For the Society see D S Macmillan, 'Sir Charles Trevelyan and the Highland and Island Emigration Society, 1849–59', *Royal Australian Society Journal*, XLIX, (1963) and R A C S Balfour, 'Emigration from the Highlands and Western Isles of Scotland to Australia during the Nineteenth Century'. Unpublished MLitt thesis, Edinburgh University, 1973.
81 *Parliamentary Papers, Seventh Report of Board of Supervision of Scottish Poor Law*, L (1852–3), XII; *Eighth Report* XXIX (1854), IX.
82 Inveraray Castle, Argyll Estate Papers, Bundle 1558, 'Duke of Argyll to ?, 5 May 1851'.
83 Unless otherwise indicated all generalisations until the end of the essay are based on a survey of: MS. Diary of J M Mackenzie, Chamberlain of the Lews, 1851; Inveraray Castle, Bundles 1522–4, 1804, Campbell—Duke of Argyll correspondence, 1848–55; SRO, Riddell Papers, AF 49/6, 'Report of T G Dickson for Trustees (1852); SRO, Campbell of Jura Papers, GD 64/1/347, 'Report to the Creditors of the late W Campbell of Islay'; Mitchell Library, Glasgow, MS. 21506 Letterbook on Highland Emigration of Sir John McNeill; SRO, Lord Advocate's Papers, AD 58/83, 'Threatened Eviction of the tenants of Strathaird, Skye'; SRO, Lord Macdonald Papers, GD 221/122/4, 11, 19', GD 221/123/1; SRO, Lord Advocate's Papers, AD 58/85, 'Evictions of Tenants from the District of Sollas'.
84 SRO, Sheriff Court Processes (Tobermory), SC 59/2/4–14.
85 SRO, Sheriff Court Processes (Stornoway), SC 33/17/26–33.
86 Devine, *Great Highland Famine*, ch 12.

Landlords and Tenants in South-West Scotland in the late Nineteenth Century*

R H Campbell

I

Though the political and economic power of landowners has been greatly eroded in Scotland, it is still possible to muster much opposition to them. Who owns the land is a provocative question, and attempts to answer it are riddled with emotion.[1] Apparent supporters of the way of life of the landowners—the gamekeepers and the water bailiffs—are denigrated in popular discussion, while the poachers are accorded a sympathetic regard, which sits uncomfortably with the present reality of gangs of mobile, urban dwellers poisoning fish in rivers on a large scale for commercial profit. The landowners themselves have encouraged the persistence of this resentment by failing to adopt a way of life more akin to that of the suburban dweller who dominates British society. However down at heel life may be in a crumbling country seat, it is still very different from that of most people in Britain today. The landowners suffer from the exceptional disability, from which most others are free, that the activities of their ancestors are well-recorded and survive to haunt judgements made on their descendants who live in totally different conditions. In an age which insists that the individual should be judged without reference to his origins, the sins of the landowners of the past are visited on their children to the third and fourth and more generations. It is in keeping with this critical evaluation that the examples chosen for detailed evaluation are often from among the more reprehensible. Highland landowners loom large in much discussion; among them the apparently more iniquitous and their henchmen often take the leading place, as with the Sutherlands and Patrick Sellar. It almost seems that to achieve popular recognition a landowner must leave some such notorious legacy. Few attempts are made to offer any explanation, let alone justification, of the actions of those who are criticised so freely. Failure to do so is because the options open to a landowner in difficult circumstances are rarely evaluated either as the landowner saw them himself or, even more reasonably, as some impartial spectator may have regarded them. The assessment is made so often from the standpoint of those who were most likely to suffer from the actions of the landowner and who were therefore most likely to be prejudiced in their assessment in any case.

The experience of the landowner in the years before 1914, especially from about 1870, warrants particular attention: first, because the changes in agricultural prospects and potential were affected as international competition worked to the detriment of landowner and tenant alike; and, second, because the landowner had to face not only adverse economic prospects in world markets but mounting political pressure, which restricted his freedom on his estate and which led by the end of the century to increasing taxation, of which the imposition of death duties was the most conspicuous example.

Though the landowner faced increasing criticism and opposition, he retained a leading position in rural society until 1914 and the beginning of the end of an old social structure became evident only thereafter. In retrospect it is possible to see that the crumbling of the edifice had not gone far, but was sufficient to cause enough apprehension in the early twentieth century to lead in 1906 to the formation from various local associations of the Scottish Land and Property Federation. The Federation could do little more than bring about some useful amelioration of the general move to undermine the position of the landowner. It helped to ensure the removal of the proposal that tenants with rentals of under £50 should be entitled to become proprietors; it helped to gain greater relief from assessment for tax under Schedule A for certain items of expenditure: and it tackled much less successfully the provision which required landowners to take over bound sheep stocks at valuations which were often much higher than any recognised market values.[2]

To generalise about the position of the landowners, and especially about their relations with their tenants, can be misleading because of differences in the size of their holdings and in their location, differences which led, and can still lead, to contrasting experiences. There is a tendency in much discussion to assume that the key to the standing of a landowner is in the amount of land owned. To do so underestimates the extent to which differences in the quality of the land, as much as in its quantity, determines the ability of the landowner to provide services and assistance to his tenants. Variations in the quality of the land and the possession of land with industrial potential led to significant differences in rentals. In 1874 William Forbes of Callendar, with 43,464 acres of generally poor land, mostly in Kirkcudbrightshire, and Edward Stopford-Blair of Penninghame, with 37,268 similar acres in Wigtownshire, moved from ninth and tenth places in the south-west when ranked by acreage to twenty-third and twenty-first places by land values and to twenty-fifth and twenty-eighth places by gross annual value respectively.[3] Whatever his record, a truly major landowner was always a target for criticism and was likely to engender feelings of hostility, as with the Duke of Buccleuch in Dumfriesshire, where he owned 38 per cent of the land. He was exceptional. Generally the south-west was not marked by such domination. Most districts had more than one landowner, sometimes rivals, who could even be played off against each other. In 1874 the ten largest landowners had only 43 per cent of the land in Ayrshire; in Kirkcudbrightshire they had 50 per cent. By contrast, the ten largest in Wigtownshire had 75 per cent of the land and in Dumfriesshire 62 per cent.

The potential for unrest between landlord and tenant was lessened more directly in the south-west for two reasons. First, it was an area where some of the more sensitive issues, which gained most public support, were less evident. It was not an area which could be turned over easily to deer forests when the attractiveness of sheep farming on its remoter hills declined. The Earl of Galloway tried to convert his well-known, but unproductive, and at times unlettable, sheep farm of Buchan in the heart of Glen Trool into a deer forest, with so little success that the attempt was given up. (In 1911 a new factor, somewhat ahead of his times, suggested incorporating the land into adjacent farms and improving the house and furnishings simply, when 'it would command a high rent from artists and others for summer and winter months'.[4]) Second, and more important, the south-west's concentration on livestock husbandry, and especially increasingly on dairying, which was such a marked feature of its agricultural development in the later nineteenth century, gave opportunities for economic survival to landlord and tenant alike in difficult years.

Though the landowners of the south-west may not have been so vulnerable to popular criticism as those in other parts of Scotland, they are as representative as others often chosen for detailed examination. Evidence of their acitivities offsets those of others more commonly recognised.

II

A notable feature of the south-west was that much of the dairying in the area was carried on in small family farms. In the early twentieth century over 40 per cent of the holdings had gross annual rentals of from £50 to £300. Ayrshire led with 70 per cent of its holdings in the range; Wigtown had 45 per cent; Kirkcudbright had 42 per cent; Dumfries, which had a higher proportion of lower rented holdings, had only 35 per cent. The small tenants, and some small proprietors, were especially common in north Ayrshire, where many parishes had over two-thirds, and some over 80 per cent, in the £50 to £300 range. It was from these districts, and especially from those farms in the £50 to £150 range of annual rental, which accounted for almost 40 per cent of Ayrshire's holdings, that dairying spread throughout the south-west and further afield in the late nineteenth century.[5] The men from Ayrshire earned a reputation for hard work and stinginess not always appreciated by those they came among. They stamped their characteristics on much of the tenantry of the south-west away from the uplands.[6]

Of many fertile sources of dispute between such tenants and their landlord none engendered more acute differences than the question of the rent which should be paid. On many other contentious matters—the form and financing of improvements, the rotation of crops, the consumption of crops on the farm, and others—it was possible to strive towards some common ground

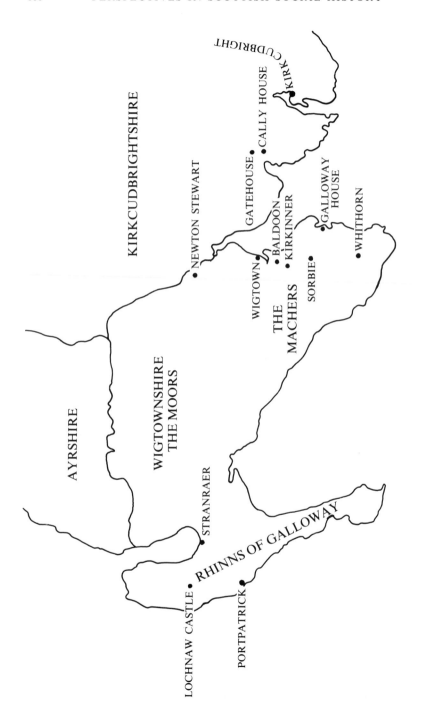

FIGURE 1

through an ultimate complementarity of objectives. It was not possible to do so over the payment of rent. How much it should be became a particularly contentious issue in the later nineteenth century. Few of the small-scale family farmers of the south-west had any notion of how to maintain the records necessary to enable them to strike a balance of profit and loss. Until the coming of the Second World War most kept few financial records.[7] Any which were kept were regarded as of limited relevance to the agricultural or general economic decisions of the farm, and as required only to meet some external, and seemingly irrelevant, demand. What mattered to most practical farmers was their financial liquidity: their own cash resources or the readiness of someone to allow them to borrow. Twice a year the landowner's demand for rent absorbed some of these resources. The payment of rent was more onerous and controversial in the later nineteenth century. It was a fixed charge, fixed in many cases in the years of greater prosperity in the 1860s and even more so in the early 1870s, when many rents had been increased on the conclusion of new leases, and so the real burden rose as prices in general drifted onwards from the mid-1870s until the mid-1890s. The long leases—generally of nineteen years—did not offer a simple escape, such as became more common later with breaks after around five years, or even annual tenancies. When prices rose, as before the 1870s, the tenant stood to gain as the real burden on him fell. The landowner suffered, but his problems were never regarded so sympathetically. To the landowner, the income from his rent was often of as critical importance as it was to his tenant. Much depended on whether it was the landowner's only or major source of income. If it was, then he, like his tenant, was dependent on the cash income from rent to maintain his liquidity, and in most cases was able to borrow only if the rent roll could be kept up. To both the rent was critical: one sought its lowering and the other its increase, a guarantee of trouble in all circumstances.

Over-renting was, of course, an easily accepted explanation of all the difficulties in agriculture at a time when any faulting of landowners was grist to the mill of political criticism in many quarters. Whatever the explanation of hard times most favoured—foreign competition, disease, public burdens, or simply bad weather—a remedy commonly advocated was the need to reduce rents. Avoiding doing so was difficult where farms could not be let, but that was not the case in the south-west where there was no shortage of prospective tenants, and of tenants willing to pay existing or even higher rents.[8] It was possible to allege that many of those who did so had additional resources—the complaint that some people play at farming is not new; that those who offered the high rents which were current were incapable of judging accurately how much they would be able to pay; that—and this was the most convincing explanation to accompany the expansion of dairying from its heartland in Ayrshire throughout the south-west—those who were able to pay the rents did so only by working in conditions approximating to slavery.[9]

From such criticism it was easy to indict the landowners as grasping and as failing to pay attention to the needs of their tenants. Evidence given to the two Royal Commissions[10] which examined the state of agriculture late in the nineteenth century, as well as elsewhere, show that they did help their tenants.

Certainly the defence of the landowners before the Royal Commissions often followed attempts by questioners sympathetic to landowners to elicit favourable answers. In doing so they represent no more than the bias usual to all forms of public questioning.[11] The statements were generally vague and so it is easy to dismiss the help as insignificant. The nature and form of help is given more precisely in estate records. Only through such evidence is it possible to see what the landowner was able to do, which is a more reliable basis on which to judge him than by what someone else thought he should do. The estate records show that the expectations of action by the landowners were often incapable of realisation.

The rentals of three estates[12] covering 18 per cent of the land in Kirkcudbrightshire and almost 13 per cent in Wigtownshire show how rents were reduced. The Galloway rental[13] from almost 80,000 acres in 1874 reached a peak of £34,324 in the year ending 31 December 1878; the Broughton and Cally rental[14] reached its peak of £17,725 in the year ending 31 July 1880, but that year included the rental of an additional property of Rusko for the first time. Excluding its contribution, the remainder, which was almost 46,000 acres in 1874, gave £16,438. On the Lochnaw estate, of under 13,000 acres in 1874, the peak came later, of £10,542 in 1882.[15] By 1900 all had fallen sharply from their respective peaks: the Galloway rental by 24.6 per cent, Broughton and Cally by 13.2 per cent, and Lochnaw by 16.0 per cent. From the slightly different test of the payments made of rent and other miscellaneous dues, such as interest on improvements, a similar pattern emerges. The peak on the Galloway estates of £33,903 in 1878 had fallen by 24.7 per cent to £25,438 in 1900, a fall of almost the same proportion as the rental. On Broughton and Cally the peak receipts of £17,894 in 1882 had fallen by 15.7 per cent to £15,086 in 1900, a slightly greater fall than in the rental alone. On Lochnaw the peak receipts of £11,271 in 1882 had fallen by 21.0 per cent to £8,900 in 1900, again a fall greater than on the rental alone.

What this meant to individual tenants may be illustrated from the rents of six arable farms on the Lochnaw estate, which provided 25 per cent of the total rental in 1870. They show the steady reductions given from the 1880s.[16]

Three had higher rents fixed at Martinmas 1876 on new leases to run to Whitsun 1895:

> Baltier's rent was increased from £246 to £420; it was reduced to
>   £340 (1885); £330 (1888); £300 (1895); £270 (1899); £255 (1905); £265 (1909).
> Cruggelton's rent was increased from £510 to £855; it was reduced to
>   £800 (1883); £700 (1887); £560 (1897); £500 (1903).
> Palmallet's rent was increased from £345 to £560; it was reduced to
>   £530 (1882); £500 (1883); £470 (1886); £420 (1887); £350 (1896); £315 (1903).

Two had new rents fixed on leases for the same duration at Martinmas 1877:

> Cults's rent was increased from £400 to £555; it was reduced to
>   £530 (1884); £480 (1887); £450 (1888); £430 (1889); £400 (1898); £370 (1906).
> Kevans's rent was increased from £305 to £504; it was reduced to

£479 (1881); £454 (1882); £430 (1887); £400 (1888); £329 (1897).

One had its lease renewed at Whitsun 1880 at £250, significantly without an increase in rent; it was reduced to £210 (1897); £185 (1900).

To the tenant a reduction in rent was the most attractive form of help. It was usually permanent and gave the stability desired, though, in a period of falling prices, the reduction needed to provide stability for one year was unlikely to be sufficient to provide the stability needed for the next. To the landlord a formal reduction in rent meant not only a future battle to have the rent increased again when economic conditions improved; a more immediate danger in reducing the rent was that the extent of borrowing was determined by the rent roll and so any reduction in it undermined the possibilities of borrowing, a dangerous procedure when the need to do so was often more pressing than ever.[17]

Help was given in other forms, most directly as various allowances, 'a deduction as a kind of gift out of the rent', as a questioner on the Royal Commission of 1881 phrased it.[18] Practice varied on different estates. Two types of allowances have to be distinguished. The first were those given at the beginning of a lease, and, less frequently, by negotiation subsequently, as concessions to provide for or encourage improvements. At the beginning of a lease the expenditure could often lead to the landlord losing the rent of the first year or two and still find that expenditure on repairs and improvements continued thereafter. At Lochnaw, to take one example among many, three farms were let on new leases in 1894; one had a rent of £200 and it was agreed that £500 would be spent in three years on cottages, the dairy and other buildings; another had a rent of £265 and it was agreed that the dwelling house would be repaired, a new barn built and £500 spent on draining over five years; the third had a rent of £250, and it was agreed that £300 would be spent on draining in the first two years and £80 on draining in the first five.[19] This type of allowance was routine and not linked directly to the fluctuating fortunes of the farmer or landlord, though the extent to which it could be maintained by the landlord depended on the fluctuating resources of the estate. A second type of allowance was aimed more directly at helping the tenant out of a difficult situation. These were the gifts to which the questioner of 1881 referred. On the Galloway estates they were small, often trivial, and given for special reasons especially in the 1870s. Typical examples were reductions in rent of £24 because of land resumed for pheasant rearing and £11 for land taken by the Wigtownshire Railway in 1876, £43 for land taken for a new church at Sorbie and £3 for land resumed for planting in 1879. From 1880, and especially in the late 1890s, allowances were given to tenants for the application of fertilisers, notably bonemeal. Also in 1880 came the first significant allowance of a once-for-all reduction in rent (£76 out of total allowances of £417), which was not compensation for the loss of land. They became substantial in the late 1880s. Of the £1,070 allowed in 1888, the largest sum for one year, £629 was for rent rebates and £477 of the total of £824 allowed in 1889.[20] The procedure on the Broughton and Cally estate differed slightly, though the ultimate effect was similar. Allowances were greater and more regular than on the Galloway properties. They included abatements of rent all over the estate from the mid-1880s to the mid-1890s, usually of small amounts, and were continuous. When the leases fell due for renewal, a new rent was fixed, often at the level of the old rent less the allowances, and then the allowances ceased.[21]

These allowances were often obtained in an informal way through the personal intervention of the landlord. Detailed personal interest was evident on the Galloway estates, where the rent rolls frequently note an allowance made personally by Lord Galloway. The possibility of such personal allowances was most likely where there was a custom, as on the Galloway estates, for the tenantry to have the customary right to approach the landlord personally for concessions if they were unable to reach agreement with the factor. Liberality on the part of the landowner was not amiss when the general economic condition of the estate was prosperous; that it could be continued beyond the bounds dictated by financial prudence was obvious in the Galloway estates in the early years of the twentieth century. The factor had to warn Lord Galloway to be less ready to grant concessions than he might have been otherwise.[22]

Reductions and rebates did not meet the tenants' demands. Their protestations, that they could not pay the rents to which they had agreed on entering into their leases, were translated into a failure to pay them, whatever their resources may have been. The assistant commissioner who reported on the south of Scotland to the Royal Commission in 1881 stated accurately that: 'The fact is that there are a lot of people not paying. You do not know who is paying and who is not, and it is difficult to find out.'[23] The major reason why it was difficult to find out was that the extent of arrears of rent is not easily determined, though in Scotland there was an added difficulty through the convention of paying rent some time after it was due, the custom of back-renting.[24] Arrears increased considerably on the estates examined, particularly on those of Galloway and Lochnaw, reflecting the generally benevolent and less strict way in which they were conducted. On the Galloway estates arrears were £16,408, or 53 per cent of a rent roll of £31,039 in 1886; on Broughton and Cally they were £1,671 or 9 per cent of a rent roll of £17,712 in 1889; on Lochnaw they were £8,914 or 91 per cent of a rent roll of £9,806 in 1894.

Allowing arrears to accumulate was one matter; more permanent aid came through writing them off subsequently. Writing off could follow the bankruptcy of a tenant, but, with the exception of 1893, major bankruptcies were not a cause of doing so on the Galloway estates. In 1893 £1,886 was written off, of which £1,862 was because of three bankruptcies, each case being the balance which remained after composition had taken place. In subsequent years the death of a tenant, evidently with inadequate funds to meet obligations rather than a technical sequestration in bankruptcy, led to arrears being written off, as with £112 in 1895, £380 in 1896, and £246 in 1897. The arrears on the Galloway properties were transformed in the early years of the twentieth century, after an unfortunate gap in the records at the new succession.[25] From the rent ledgers of individual holdings for those years it is possible to see the reductions which were taking place. In 1901 some very large sums were written off for a few tenants: £1,026 on a rental of £103, reduced to £60, leaving £30 to be carried forward. On another farm when the lease ended, £1,940 was written off and £400 carried forward and paid in 1901.

Two detailed examples each from different types of farms on the Galloway and Lochnaw estates show that frequently the writing off of arrears was a retrospective reduction of rent when a new one was fixed. On the Galloway estates[26] the sheep farm of Auchinleck had a rental of £1,005 lasting until 1887. At the end of 1897 the tenant was £503 in arrears. In 1880 the rent became £690, but effectively the reduction was back-dated to Martinmas 1879 by writing off £158 of arrears (one-half of the annual reduction), the balance of £345 being paid. In 1887 the rent went down to £500 but arrears still grew and it was reduced further to £420 in 1896, when £275 of arrears were written off and the balance of £177 was paid. The rent was reduced yet again to £360 in 1900, when the arrears were £30. At the largely arable farm of Baldoon Mains the tenant who followed James Caird in 1862[27] had a rent of £1,020 for the first five years and then one of £1,200 until Martinmas 1881. He was in arrears of £930 at the end of 1874. A new lease was concluded in 1879 to run to Martinmas 1898: for four years at £1,200, then at £1,050. At Whitsun 1883 it was reduced retrospectively to £1,050 from Martinmas 1879 to Martinmas 1882 and to £900 thereafter, leading to the writing off of £525 arrears and leaving £450, which continued to increase. In 1893 the rent was cut yet again to £800, but effectively back-dated for nine years by writing off £900 of arrears.

On the Lochnaw estate,[28] Knocknain's rent of £281.10s. in 1870 was increased to £356 in 1878. When arrears emerged in 1886, the rent was reduced to £350 in the following year but the arrears grew steadily from £30 in 1886 to £480 in 1895. A new lease was then concluded at a rent of £265 and the arrears were written off, representing six years back-dating of the reduction. At Mains of Dhuloch arrears were more endemic. In 1866 at £217 they exceeded the rent of £194, but had been eliminated by 1869. A new rent of £320 was fixed to run from Martinmas 1877 to Whitsun 1897, but by 1880 arrears of £329 had appeared and had increased to £763 in 1883. At Martinmas 1884 the rent was reduced to £250 and arrears of £628 were written off. From 1887 the tenant remained without a lease and arrears of £121 in 1887 had become £530 in 1895 and were eliminated by writing off £380 in the following year, when the rent became £220. No arrears were recorded until £60 in 1903; they were £480 in 1912.

The nature of the difficulties faced by the tenants depended on their agricultural specialisations. The widespread Galloway properties in Kirkcudbrightshire and Wigtownshire show the differences. The sheep farms in the Galloway hills had least trouble. Though there were arrears, they were not endemic. On six of the largest, with a total rent of £3,012 in 1875, there were no arrears. One farm had £452 in 1895 and the rental on all had fallen to £2,345. In 1907 there were no arrears though the rental was then down to £1,921. Even on the arable farms there were marked differences. When cropping was mixed, and opportunities for dairying were greater, arrears were less than on those on the heavy clays of Baldoon where the possibilities of diversification were more limited and where three farms had arrears of £1,778 on a rental of £2,792 in 1875. Though the arrears had been eliminated by 1907, the rental was then only £1,660.[29]

The Cally and Lochnaw estates had arable farms adjacent to each other in the Machers of Wigtownshire on the borders between the parishes of Sorbie and Whithorn. A sharp increase in land under temporary grass in both parishes between 1875 and 1895 was provided, as generally in the south-west, through more land being added to the total being cropped in some form; the acreage under grain fell only slightly, but whereas Sorbie had 324 acres under wheat in 1875 and Whithorn had 248, wheat had been given up by 1895 and oats were virtually the only grain crop grown. Confirmation that the move to more grassland husbandry was to accompany the expansion of dairying comes from the increase in each parish in the numbers of cows/heifers in milk/calf, from 581 in Sorbie in 1875 to 1,044 in 1895 and from 523 to 1,056 in Whithorn, a higher, but still only a small proportion of Wigtownshire's 24,000 in 1895.[30]

Six adjacent farms from each estate in these parishes show that this was a problem area, though the possibility of changing agricultural specialisations prevented the extreme difficulties experienced on the Galloway properties at Baldoon. The six on the Cally estate accounted for ten per cent of its rental in 1870 and Lochnaw's six for 25 per cent of its rental in the same year. Arrears grew and were responsible for a large part of the total on each estate.[31]

	1875		1880		1885		1890		1895		1900	
	£	%	£	%	£	%	£	%	£	%	£	%
Cally	n/a		342	33	349	41	630	44	nil	—	nil	—
			(342)		(289)		(130)					
Lochnaw	nil	—	841	43	707	35	2782	39	3664	43	511	14

(The figures in parentheses show amounts paid since the close of the accounting period but before the accounts were written up.)

The much less serious situation on the Cally properties was not so favourable as the low level of arrears indicates as all six farms were given various allowances from 1886, reaching £343 in 1892, in which year £330 of arrears were also written off on one of the six at the end of a lease. Throughout the south-west many farms were in financial difficulties but few were heavily dependent on the least successful specialisations.

III

The landlords' toleration of tenants who were failing to meet their obligations was confirmed further by their apparent reluctance to sequestrate the assets of their tenants for rent, and by the continuity of tenants. The failure to sequestrate is of more general interest because it has to be linked to the long-standing and vociferously expressed complaints over the landlord's right of hypothec, which culminated in a Royal Commission in 1865.[32]

Hypothec, which gave a landlord a general right over a tenant's moveable property as security for payment of the rent, was resented as much by other creditors as by the tenants because it placed the landlord in the position of a preferred creditor. In practice the right was not as simple or extensive as it was sometimes portrayed: the produce of the land could be hypothecated for the rent of the year of which it was the crop, not for any previous or subsequent years, and livestock on the farms was similarly available to be appropriated for the rent of the current year only until three months after the usual term of payment of the rent.[33] If the landlord did not act speedily his preferred position was lost and in a general sequestration in bankruptcy he did not have a preferred position. Complaints that the landlord had an unfair advantage came from manure and seed merchants who became more numerous and influential from the middle of the nineteenth century. Some easing of their position came in 1867 in an act which also set up a Register of Sequestrations for Rent, but the right was not abolished on new leases of agricultural land of over two acres until 1880.[34]

The incidence of hypothec varied, and generalisations based on the experience of one area only are misleading. Witnesses from the south-west before the Royal Commission and before a House of Lords Select Committee in the 1860s suggested that the problem was of no great importance in the area, least of all in Kirkcudbrightshire and Wigtownshire.[35] The major complainant from the south-west was a grazier in Nithsdale, aggrieved because the Duke of Buccleuch had taken priority over him.[36] To ascertain how many were sequestrated for rent is not easy before 1867. Even later it is necessary to examine the registers of the sheriff courts to find the number of cases: annual returns are of depending actions and some of these continued in form only. The legal processes themselves are not necessarily complete, not only because of recent weeding of processes, but because the return of the sale to the court was generally neglected.[37]

The total number of cases in Wigtownshire from 1867 to 1880 was 438, but not all were for the rent of farms.[38] The two major proprietors in the shire, who between them held 34 per cent of the land and 31 per cent of the land values in 1874, were the Earl of Stair and the Earl of Galloway. Stair had five actions in Wigtown Sheriff Court, but the bulk of his actions against tenants were in Stranraer Sheriff Court:[39] 50 against 33 tenants from 1871 to 1893, though the number of actions faded sharply after 1880. Galloway's actions were all in Wigtown Sheriff Court and numbered 25 from the first in 1870 to the last in 1891, against only ten tenants. The position on the Lochnaw estate was similar: it had 15 actions from 1868 to 1882 against nine tenants, one tenant being responsible for three and being also the subject of a general sequestration in bankruptcy at the time of the last in 1882.

The number of cases alone indicates that sequestration for rent was not used as a general policy but only in special cases against tenants who habitually failed to pay the rent or was a prelude to general sequestration. Sequestration for rent did not lead to a change in a tenant's behaviour, as in the case of one tenant on the Galloway estate. He was sequestrated for rent in 1888 and 1891 to try to recover the rent for four years of £350 each, but the arrears at the end of 1887 were £1,710; at the end of 1891 they had climbed to £1,945. In March 1893 the tenant paid £702 for two years rent and the balance af arrears outstanding, of some £1,419, was written off as he had become bankrupt and the tenancy terminated in 1892. A similar case can be identified on the Lochnaw estate. In this case the tenant was sequestrated for rent three times, the third taking place at the same time as his general sequestration in order to ensure the payment of rent as a preferred creditor at Martinmas 1882 and Whitsunday 1883 of £215 each, though arrears of rent then outstanding of £775 received only £316. A balance of £628 of arrears was written off before the tenant, having purchased much of the stock at a roup in May 1883, carried on. His arrears grew again to £530 in 1895 when £380 was written off and the rest paid.[40]

Only about a dozen of those sequestrated for rent in Wigtown or Stranraer Sheriff Courts from the Stair and Lochnaw estates—split equally between the two—were also sequestrated in bankruptcy. In these cases the debts due to the preferred creditors were only a small proportion of the total. That may have led to greater resentment when they were met from the very limited assets available, but even among the ordinary, non-preferred creditors the landlord was sometimes a substantial creditor because of old arrears of rent. That the landlord gained at the expense of other creditors was less likely than the strict legal position would suggest. Though the landlord may not have gained greatly from his preferred position, it still rankled with the grain and manure merchants who usually initiated actions for sequestration in bankruptcy.[41]

In view of the apparently limited number of sequestrations for rent and the readiness to allow rent arrears to accumulate it is not surprising that tenants continued to hold leases when their tenancies might well have been expected to be brought to an end. Since even they were allowed to stay on, continuity of tenancy among others was only to be expected, even when replacements could be found. The Lochnaw estate provides an example which was also representative of others.[42] The tenancies on the six farms on the estate where reductions in rent were examined in detail were held as follows:

Auldbreck: held by the same family from 1881 to 1912;
Baltier: the tenant in possession in 1864 died in 1885; the same family held
              from 1885 to 1909;
Cruggelton: held by the same family from 1864 to 1876 and by the same tenant
              from 1876 to 1902;
Cults: held by the same family from 1864 to 1912;
Kevans: held by the same tenant from 1867 to 1877 and by the same family
              from 1877 to 1912;
Palmallet: held by the same family from 1864 to 1876 and by another from
              1876 to 1912.

With such continuity, almost with such security, even tenants in arrears do not seem to have placed the need to pay the rent high in their priorities.

Examples may be culled from letters to the factor on the Galloway estate. A law agent, who also tenanted a small unit near Whithorn at a rent of £96 for the first five years and £100 thereafter until Martinmas 1902, and whose arrears mounted from £156 to £222 between the end of March 1890 and 1893, wrote at the end of 1892: 'I am sorry I have not been able to make you a payment but in a little time I hope to be able. I cannot sell anything just now owing to the prohibitory prices or I should have had something for you. I hope you will have patience'.[43] A more pointed approach was adopted by a tenant at Kirkinner, whose arrears were at £984 at the end of March 1899 on a rent of £103. At that time he wrote to provide an explanation and to make a request: 'I am sorry to say that I will not be able to make a large payment at the end of the month owing to missing the sale of my cattle last back end and no prospect of selling them before May Market. I have 4 two year old and 9 stirks which will help to reduce arrears. I am informed you give tiles for drains when the tennant [sic] opens. The drain dries a very wet place in the middle of a field and cannot sow until filled';[44] and, in June 1899 he wrote even more to the point, enclosing a bank draft for £30 and explained the deficiency because 'I expected would have sold the 2 years old Ayrshire cattle and made one payment do for all but you will receive every farthing as when they are sold they are nearly fit for the butcher'.[45]

A series of letters of the early 1890s from the tenant of North Balfern highlights the toleration in what was the most difficult case on the Galloway estate. On 27 June 1891, he wrote, '. . . owing to the unfavourable nature of the feeding trade this year . . . I am constantly deficient in funds from what I expected . . .'; on 10 May 1892, 'I can assure you that I have all along been doing my utmost to get some of the arrears paid up, but last year was a very profitless year and the rent was not made off the farm'; on 8 July 1893, 'I fully agree in all your observations as to my position regarding these arrears, but what could I do? I paid the rent always as long as I could even to the sacrifice of my capital and such a system comes to an end sooner or later'.[46] Though strenuous efforts were made to bring the situation under control payments were intermittent: in 1891, £100 in August and £200 in December; in 1892, £350 in May, £100 in August, £185 in December; in 1893, £100 in February, £250 in May, £50 in August; in 1894, £440 in February, £200 and £300 in August, £100 in December.

Toleration of poor tenants would have been more explicable if it had been in the context of properties which were still yielding good returns and even more so if the landlord had an additional source of income. The estates which allowed such accommodation to the tenants were by no means in such favoured circumstances. A survey of the actions of sequestration for rent from 1867 in the sheriff courts of the south-west seems to indicate two groups of landlords who were most ready to take action. There were a few landowners, generally of substantial means, who did so, notably the Earl of Stair in Stranraer Sheriff Court and the Duke of Portland in Kilmarnock.[47] Their estates were run in a more remote fashion—perhaps that is why there was more resentment at the factors, especially lawyers whom they employed[48]—where the factors had greater say and where, in short, the estates were run much more on professional than on practical lines. The second group which took actions had one contrasting and one comparable feature. The contrasting feature was that it consisted of small proprietors, especially conspicuous in Ayrshire—again Kilmarnock Sheriff Court recorded them incongruously beside those of the Duke of Portland—or of actions on sub-tenancies. The comparable feature was that, though they operated at a vastly different level from Portland or Stair, the properties of those in the second group had to be run on the most economic lines, with no possibility of allowing personal generosity to intrude as to do so would have been the most likely path to rapid bankruptcy for landlord as well as for tenant.

The group of proprietors whose willingness to accommodate the needs of the tenant was most surprisingly those who ran their estates in easy traditional ways and continued to assist their tenants even when their own resources were limited. The key to their ability to assist lay in the extent to which their rents, or more accurately the amounts which were paid, were able to service the debts of the estate. Since a major factor in that readiness was the existence of a large rent roll, the accumulation of arrears rather than the formal reduction of rent, which was reflected in the diminished rent roll, had an obvious short-term attraction to the landlord. It was, however, an attraction which was likely to lead to an increasingly difficult situation for all; it merely postponed the need for radical adjustment on the estate, which could have been mitigated, even avoided, by action earlier. Where the debt was allowed to accumulate, the collapse was eventually one which affected the landlord more adversely than the tenant. It gave the tenant the opportunity to purchase his own farm. The later the opportunity to do so was postponed, the more likely that opportunity was to arise, though it was only after the First World War, and the increasingly unattractive nature of landholding, that such sales became more probable and general.

The evidence of rentals shows that it is possible to underestimate the contribution of the landlords to the alleviation of their tenants' difficulties. Rents were reduced, allowances granted, arrears accumulated, and, when written off, frequently on the expiry of a lease, landlords provided retrospective reductions in rent. It was easy for critics to suggest that the landowners might have granted further concessions, but an examination of the financial burdens on estates shows how illiquid they could be. That experience, at least, some landlords shared with their tenants in full measure.

Three calls on the rentals were well recognised: public burdens, though less onerous than the complaints about them indicated; repairs and improvements, which continued in spite of the difficulties, even if not on a scale adequate to satisfy the insatiable demand of the tenants; and the interest which had to be paid on the debts of the estate. The percentage of the rental required to meet these burdens shows how critically important the interest payments were on the Galloway properties:[49]

Year	Public Burdens %	Repairs & Improvements %	Interest %
1875	12.1	24.2	37.2
1885	13.3	21.2	47.6
1895	12.5	14.3	51.1
1905	17.3	21.1	58.9

Interest charges were high on the Galloway estates and they absorbed an increasing proportion of the rental. The illiquidity of the estate was increased and the need to borrow more was intensified.

When all three items are expressed as percentages of both the rental and of the amount of rent and other related charges received during the year, their onerous burden on the cash flow to the estates becomes clear. The landlords were caught between the twin pressures of falling rentals and the burden of relatively fixed charges, conditions which explain a reluctance to agree to any permanent reduction in rents so long as some expectation could be entertained that the profitability of agriculture would improve sufficiently to enable the rent to be paid. It seemed better by far to let the arrears accumulate. The increasingly illiquid position of the estates was not appreciated by those who demanded more aid from the landowners. It is doubtful if they could have done much more without a radical reorganisation such as came on the Galloway estates. The landlords could cushion the blows of agricultural depression on their tenants, and were expected to do so, often with little thanks for their pains. By doing so some may have jeopardised the long-run survival of their estates.

The crisis came on the Galloway estates in 1907 when a major sale of property, including Galloway House, which had been let to successful businessmen for some years, took place to Sir Malcolm McEachern, an Islay man who had made a fortune in Australia.[50] Even that major sale did not provide stability. Further sales were made on the eve of the war and on an even larger scale in the 1920s of individual farms, often to their tenants. McEachern's purchase itself did not remain intact and was sold off in the early 1930s by his widow and son, again chiefly to the tenants. The day of the owner occupier had arrived, hastened more than hindered by the toleration of the landlords in the depressed years of the later nineteenth century.

NOTES

* I am grateful for permission to use the records of their estates from Mrs E Murray-Usher of Broughton and Cally; Sir Crispin Agnew of Lochnaw, Bt; and the Trustees of the late Earl of Galloway. The study would not have been possible without their co-operation and kindness.

1 See among recent publications: J McEwen, *Who Owns Scotland?* 2nd edn (Edinburgh 1981); Irene Evans and Joy Hendry (eds), *The Land for the People* (Blackford 1985).

2 *Scottish Land and Property Federation: Its objects and what it has achieved.* Scottish Landowners Federation MSS. Scottish Record Office [SRO], GD 325/1/242.

3 The detail of the distribution of landholding in the south-west (Ayrshire, Dumfriesshire, Kirkcudbrightshire and Wigtownshire) is taken from the *Return of Owners of Land.* Part III (Scotland). British Parliamentary Papers [BPP]. 1874. LXXII. The subsequent investigation of the *Return* by John Bateman confirmed its general validity for the south-west of Scotland: 'Kirkcudbrightshire being *facile princeps* in excellence'. John Bateman, *The Great Landowners of Great Britain and Ireland* (4th edn, 1883; reprinted, Leicester 1971), p xi of preface.

4 Factor of Earl of Galloway, 22 September 1911. Letter Book, 1910–1, Galloway MSS. SRO, GD 138/2/30. James Biggar was generally a critic of the landowners but conceded that, on the question of the preservation of game, 'As a rule . . . the farmers of Galloway have little cause of complaint'. James Biggar, *The Agriculture of Kirkcudbrightshire and Wigtownshire.* A tenant, and another critic of the landowners, provided confirmation in evidence to the Royal Commission on Agriculture, 1881–2. BPP. 1881. XVII. Qs. 36, 985–93 (George Cowan).

5 *Return showing the Number of Occupiers of farms (whether owners or tenants) in each County and Parish in Scotland with the Gross Rental according to the Valuation Roll, for the Year ending Whitsunday 1906.* BPP. 1907. LXXIII. 411. The earlier return for 1881 in BPP. 1882. LII. 507 did not give information for the Cunninghame and Kyle districts of Ayrshire.

6 '. . . they are by far too hard working; they work, and work, very hard', Royal Commission on Agricultural Depression, 1894–6. BPP. 1896. XVII. Qs. 47,001 and 47,003 (John Spier).

7 The difficulties of collection information on the profitability of Scottish agriculture even in the late 1920s are evident in the schemes of the Department of Agriculture to do so from 1928. Department of Agriculture and Fisheries, Farm Economics, General Files, 1927–9 and 1929–36. SRO, AF43/407 and 408.

8 John Spier, the assistant commissioner who reported on the south-west of Scotland to the Royal Commission on Agricultural Depression 1894–6 was adamant: 'There is no land idle, and no farm is on the hand of those landowners who wish to get clear of it'. The three witnesses from the south-west agreed on that, if on little else, and the evidence of rent rolls shows practically no farms in hand. BPP. 1896. Qs. 46,765 and 46,777; 51,258 and 51,274; 53,728 and 53,768; 55,334.

9 One of the most perceptive of several commentators on these characteristics was the successful farmer and pioneer of scientific dairying, John Spier of Newton, Cambuslang, who was a native of north Ayrshire. See especially his report to the Royal Commission of 1894–6. BPP. 1895. XVII. See also, A Sturrock, 'Report on the Agriculture of Ayrshire'. *Transactions of the Highland and Agricultural Society of Scotland* (THAS), Fourth series, I (February 1866), pp 89–90 and J Drysdale, 'The Management of a Dairy Farm', *THAS*, Fifth series, XXV (1913), p 58.

10 Royal Commission on Agriculture, 1881–2 and Royal Commission on Agricultural Depression, 1894–6.

11 An example is in the evidence to the Royal Commission of 1881 from Qs. 37,494f, which dealt with the practice of the Commission's chairman, the Duke of Richmond.

12 Broughton and Cally, Lochnaw, and Galloway.

13 States Books, 1861–1915 (except 1901–3), Galloway MSS. SRO, GD 138/2/143–52.

14 Rent rolls, 1861–1900 (except 1865, 1875–7), Murray of Broughton and Cally MSS. SRO, GD 10/1331–59.

15 Factors' Accounts, 1860–1912, Agnew of Lochnaw MSS. SRO, GD 154/414–6.

16 *Ibid.*

17 The reason why lending was possible only on the security of the rents on an entailed estate was stated clearly by Patrick Irvine, a legal authority and landowner himself, '. . . I mean a Scotch Entail; I mean an Entail which can be rendered effectual against the world, by which the heirs of Entail can keep possession of the property so long as they do not disobey the terms of the Entail. The creditors cannot attack that property or estate in any manner or way; they may attack the rents but not the estate'. Evidence to the Select Committee on Scotch Entails. BPP. 1828. VII. 151, p 9. An heir of entail could not grant a heritable security but it was held that he could grant one over his own interest, which enabled the creditor to lift rents in the lifetime of the granter. Such a policy was usually combined with the assignation of life insurance policies. W M Gloag and J M Irvine, *Law of Rights in Security Heritable and Moveable including cautionary obligations* (Edinburgh 1897), p 22.

18 BPP. 1881. XVII, Q. 37,203.

19 Lochnaw Estate Book, 1892–1918, Agnew of Lochnaw MSS. SRO, GD 154/766.

20 States Books, Galloway MSS. SRO, GD 138/2/143–52.

21 Rent Rolls, 1861–1900, Cally MSS. SRO, GD 10/1331–59.

22 Factor to Lord Galloway, 15 July 1907, Letter Book, 1906–7, Galloway MSS. SRO, GD 138/2/24.

23 Royal Commission on Agriculture, 1881–2. BPP. 1881. XVII. Q. 44,203.

24 David Low, *On Landed Property and the Economy of Estates* (London 1844), pp 50–1. The matter was fully discussed in investigations on the landlords' right to hypothec. See below note 32.

25 Some of the gaps can be filled from the General Ledgers, 1823–1912, Galloway MSS. SRO, GD 138/2/74–104.

26 The record of rents and of their payment on individual farms are in the Rent Ledgers from 1818, Galloway MSS. SRO, GD 138/2/104–34.

27 In common with many less illustrious tenants, James Caird had substantial arrears. Rent Ledgers, Galloway MSS. SRO, GD 138/2/104–34.

28 Factors Accounts, 1860–1912, Agnew of Lochnaw MSS. SRO, GD 154/414–6.

29 Rent Ledgers, 1818–1915, Galloway MSS. SRO, GD 138/104–31.

30 Agricultural Census. Parish Summaries, 1st series. SRO. AF 39/32/1.

31 Rent Rolls, Cally MSS. SRO, GD 10/1331–59 and Factors Accounts, Agnew of Lochnaw MSS. SRO, GD 154/414–6.

32 Royal Commission on the Law relating to the Landlords' Right of Hypothec in Scotland in so far as regards agricultural subjects. BPP. 1865. XVII. 413 and Select Committee of the House of Lords on the Law of Hypothec in Scotland. BPP. 1868–9. IX. 305. In contrast to the law of distress in England the landlord could take action for the rent accruing and not only for the rent due, and the right extended to goods sold to a *bona fide* purchaser. On the other hand in

England the landlord was able to take action without a legal process and his right extended to all goods on the premises, even if they were not the tenant's. See Report of Royal Commission, p xi.

33   R Hunter, *Law of Landlord and Tenant* (3rd edn, 1860), ii, pp 363–7; G J Bell, *Principles of the Law of Scotland* (10th edn, 1899), para 1239; Report of Royal Commission on Hypothec, vii.

34   Hypothec Amendment (Scotland) Act, 1867. 30 & 31 Vict. c. 42; Hypothec Abolition (Scotland) Act, 1880. 43 Vict. c. 12.

35   See evidence to the Royal Commission on Hypothec: 115 (James Drennan); 276 (William Sproat); 298 (James McLean).

36   Royal Commission on Hypothec: 284 (James Kennedy).

37   G J Bell, *Commentaries on the Law of Scotland* (7th edn, 1870), ii, p 33.

38   Register of sequestrations for rent, 1867–1909, Wigtown Sheriff Court. SRO, SC 19/15/1.

39   Register of sequestrations for rent, 1871–93, Stranraer Sheriff Court. SRO, SC 18/15/1.

40   Details of the sequestration in bankruptcy of this case is in SRO, CS 318/33/294.

41   Their resentment was clear in the evidence they gave to the Royal Commission on Hypothec in the 1860s. Thomas Biggar of Urr commented (p 118), '. . . the landlord has generally been paid in full, while the manure merchant and other dealers have had to come in for a very small dividend'.

42   Agnew of Lochnaw MSS, Factors Accounts. SRO, GD 154/414–6; Estate Book of Lochnaw, 1869–71. SRO, GD 154/375; Lochnaw Estate Book, 1829–1918. SRO, GD 154/766.

43   Rent Ledger, 1890–5, Galloway MSS. SRO, GD 138/2/125.

44   Rent Ledger, 1895–99, Galloway MSS. SRO, GD 138/2/126.

45   *Ibid.*

46   Rent Ledger, 1890–95, Galloway MSS. SRO, GD 138/2/125.

47   Register of sequestrations for rent, 1871–93, Stranraer Sheriff Court. SRO, SC 18/15/1; Register of sequestrations for rent, 1867–88, Kilmarnock Sheriff Court. SRO, SC 7/10.4.

48   'The great majority of the factors being lawyers study the interests of the land-lords; and they have no practical idea of the improvements wanted on a farm; indeed they have no practical knowledge of the business, but simply look to its producing the rent, and increasing the rent roll'. Royal Commission on Agriculture, 1881–2. BPP. 1881. XVII. Q. 37,339 (George Cowan).

49   States Books, Galloway MSS. SRO, GD 158/2/143, 145, 147, 150.

50   The sale was not made easily. A substantial part of the Galloway estate was offered for sale by public roup in December 1908 at an upset price of £487,000 but there were no bidders. McEachern purchased part in the following year by private bargain.

Index